Remodel!

Without Going
Bonkers or Broke

Remodel!

Without Going Bonkers or Broke

ELIMINATE 3 CRITICAL MISTAKES
AND SAVE THOUSANDS USING THIS
PROVEN STEP-BY-STEP METHOD

Jim Molinelli, PhD
the 'Remodeling Professor'

ISBN 10: 0-692-84868-1
ISBN 13: 978-0-692-84868-5

Praise for

Remodel!

Without Going Bonkers or Broke

"Very, very informative. Well written and easy to understand. I enjoyed reading this book from the first page." Sandra Altizio – New Jersey

"This is the most comprehensive book on the subject that I have ever seen!" Janine Wooten – Realtor & Real Estate Investor - Florida

"I would label Jim Molinelli's book 'a Bible' for anyone considering a remodeling project. Use it as a handy reference." Lilly Brock – Retired Interior Designer & Remodeler - Washington

"A first-rate guide to remodeling your home written as if the author was sitting across from you at your dining room table answering all of your questions." Ted Sugges – New Jersey

"Jim Molinelli is the American Mike Holmes." Lisa Schatz - California

"This was easily the most practical 'how-to' book I've ever read." Adam Drummond – Wagga Wagga, Australia

"Remodel changed everything for me. I now have real confidence where I had serious doubts before." Laura Lynn - Tennessee

"My confidence is sky-high now. I'm so excited about planning my project that I could burst!" Terrica Simmons – Mississippi

"People terrified of being ripped-off by remodelers are going to LOVE this. I know. I was one." Dr. Marlena Corcoran – CEO – NYC

The Reader's Favorite
2017 GOLD MEDAL WINNER

Sometimes...
you still have questions or concerns,
even after reading a book like this.

———•———

Now you can...

Ask the

Remodeling Professor!

Jim offers **1-on-1 video calls** and
gives **clear answers and action steps**
for your specific situation!

Jim is a life-long industry insider and
remodeling expert who is impartial,
and whose only interest is your success!

———•———

SCHEDULE YOUR CALL NOW:
www.JimMolinelli.com/call

CONTENTS

CONTENTS

DEDICATION

This book is dedicated to my awesome wife, Shawn. Your companionship means everything to me. Your confidence in me and your support of this project has aided me from the first day it was conceived. I would not have written this book without your love and encouragement.

I also wrote this book being ever mindful of my two wonderful children, Ann and Tim. May this book become a part of the legacy and remembrance you have of me. Let it also prove that you can achieve amazing things, even when that doesn't seem possible. You can positively impact people's lives in profound ways, making the world—your world—a better place.

Finally, I thank my parents. I would not be who I am without the boundless love you gave me. You led by example, tirelessly showing that living an honest life was a mark of great distinction. You remained strong and prevailed in the face of every adversity. Your passion for learning, your love for your family, and your respect for those around you is an example I will always aspire to.

ACKNOWLEDGEMENTS

I am indebted to those who have helped me become the architect I am today: Bob Forte, George Collict, Herman Litwack, Tom Parker, Jerry Maffei, Ed Romieniec, Raymond Reed, and Bill Keeney. To become a residential architect was the first significant goal of my life.

I also owe significant thanks to those who fueled my love of learning and teaching, including: Mr. Powell, Charles Haas, Paul Rashap, Brenda Karlos, Keith Farber, Chester Budd, Eugene Cerrigone, Larry Degelman, Valerian Miranda, Bill Nash, Ed Hoag and countless others who taught me, and in so doing, showed me how to teach others when I was given the opportunity.

I also thank many of my professional colleagues and mentors, without whom I would not be where I am today: Nunzio De Santis, Brian Dougan, Wayne Gibson, Tim Shields, Richard Campbell, Paul Arnold, and Tom Shaner.

I wish to thank several people who profoundly impacted my growth as a person, enabling me to arrive at this place and time: Dorothy Vinson, Jessica Phelps, Bill & Anne DeNenno, Steve Sann, Paul Flockhart, Michael Bean, Bill Gerwig, Jeff & Maggie Whall, Aaron & Sally Miller, and Cathie Driver.

Thank you to everyone who consulted, advised, discussed, read, edited, reviewed, and in numerous other ways helped me produce this book. I owe you all my thanks. And an extra special thank you to my editor Stacey Kopp and my cover designer Les. The work you both did makes me look great!

This book would never have happened without Chandler Bolt and the dedicated folks at Self-Publishing School, who have earned my deep and sincere gratitude. They helped me achieve my goal of writing and publishing a bestseller. The proof that their method works is in your hands. Thanks to my many friends and co-authors in the SPS author community who also provided amazing encouragement and support to me throughout the process.

For nearly half a century I have received unlimited support and encouragement, been showered with boundless optimism, and benefitted from the contagious enthusiasm of my best friend Mark Clausen. Without him, my life would not have turned out nearly as successfully as it has, nor would it have been half as much fun. The laughter and smile lines etched into my face are his fault.

AUTHOR'S NOTE

On the surface, it's totally logical why I am writing this book and teaching courses to help homeowners master the remodeling process. After all, I am a residential architect and I spent the last twenty-five years in the remodeling industry. So, nobody knows more about educating homeowners about 'how-to' remodel their homes.

But how I became the remodeling expert I am today is the real story. For years I was an excellent residential architect, but I could never get my designs to hit my clients' budgets. I would devise clever solutions to their remodeling problems, but their contractor's prices were always 25 to 50 percent above their stated budget. It was a devastating experience for me, and a crushing one for the clients as well. I watched far too many clients fall in love with the designs, and buy into the dream I had created for a better life at home, only to have that dream destroyed by too-high price tags.

Ultimately, I admitted to myself that my inability to accurately estimate the cost of my designs was a major failing. I realized that I had to remedy that flaw in order to continue to work in residential design. When my time on faculty at Texas A&M ended, I returned to Maryland, where my architecture license had been issued. However, this time I didn't work in an architect's office. I chose instead to design projects for a remodeling contractor who agreed to teach me how to estimate residential remodeling costs. Since then, I've never looked back. I fell in love with design-build remodeling. I found I was finally able to truly help my clients. Fifteen or twenty families a year could now drastically improve their quality of life through my remodeling designs. The reason why? Because I learned how to accurately estimate my designs, and how to design within the budgets of my clients.

Today, I have a tremendous understanding of the architectural side of the remodeling coin, and I am equally familiar with the truths from inside the remodeling world. I've witnessed just about every mistake a homeowner can make when remodeling. And I can help any homeowner to properly prepare for their unique remodeling journey and avoid the common mistakes and pitfalls made by so many others. The process I teach saves homeowners time, energy, countless mistakes, and thousands of dollars.

And that's why this book is in your hands today. I truly loved personally helping fifteen or twenty families each year to remodel their homes and their lives. But now I now help thousands of families achieve remodeling success. The immense gratification of helping so many more families to achieve success and enjoy their remodeling journey is beyond words.

January, 2017

INTRODUCTION

Consider the cost of this book an investment. This small investment will help you save thousands off the full price of your project. It will spare you from 'horror story' results, because you'll avoid the three main remodeling mistakes (a savings easily worth tens of thousands). You will also be spared the headaches and confusing uncertainty that plague those who remodel without the benefit of an insider's advice.

See, I believe that every homeowner should enjoy their remodeling experience, and I'll show you how that can happen with your project. Plus, it is always a great time to fix, alter, or expand your home so that it can serve your needs and truly become your "dream home"!

In fact, this is the very crux of remodeling: keeping a house in shape to serve our needs, perhaps adding-on or changing a home's features as our family grows and our needs change.

Let us begin **your** remodeling adventure...

"HOME"

Home is the nicest word there is.

—Laura Ingalls Wilder

Where we love is home—
home that our feet may leave, but not our hearts.

—Oliver Wendell Holmes

Home is the most popular, and will be the most enduring
of all earthly establishments.

—Channing Pollock

Section 1:
ABOUT REMODELING

Every building must have its own soul.

—LOUIS KAHN

*A man travels the world over in search of what he needs,
and returns home to find it.*

—GEORGE MOORE

CHAPTER 1

The Industry Reputation

The remodeling industry is often perceived by the public in a negative light. So-called horror stories about remodeling appear regularly in print, on television, and even in Hollywood films. For example, perhaps you have seen *Tin Men* with Danny DeVito and Richard Dreyfuss, or *The Money Pit* with Tom Hanks. If so, you understand my point. While darkly humorous and entertaining, these films exploit the very worst of the remodeling industry. I dare say if situations like these happened during your remodeling project, it would be no laughing matter. And the fact is, sometimes these movies aren't too far from the truth.

Remodeling lore and reality *both* contain a cast of characters that have sullied the reputation of the industry through the years: Pushy, know-it-all remodeling salespeople rival the worst found on any used car lot. In some jurisdictions, any "Harry with a Hammer" or "Pickup Truck Pete" can declare himself a craftsman and sell his services. And worse, disreputable remodeling contractors have committed fraud; disappeared, leaving projects incomplete; and used bankruptcy to hide from creditors.

Unfortunately, homeowners lose millions of dollars to these types of unscrupulous practitioners every year. Good folks' projects are compromised in unimaginable ways and fall prey to fraud. As a result, many homeowners see only one way to avoid the problems inherent in the remodeling industry: by refraining from remodeling.

And who can blame them? Horror stories like the ones I told you above breed fear in the minds of the public. In fact, I have worked with dozens of families that have waited ten, fifteen, even twenty or more years before finally pursuing their remodeling projects. Why? All due to their fear that others would take advantage of them. Such fear and uncertainty can paralyze good people.

But let me say this now: You are **not** one of those homeowners. By buying this book, you have chosen a different path. I'll teach you how to fully and carefully prepare to remodel. You will learn about and master the remodeling process. Follow the advice I provide, and you will avoid the common mistakes and pitfalls that have befallen so many others.

One thing to keep in mind as you read through this book is that only a very tiny segment of the industry has earned the reputation I've mentioned. I assure you that there are tens of thousands of fine professional remodeling companies are hoping to work with people just like you. Their common goal is to make a good living while delivering high-quality projects that help homeowners achieve their remodeling goals.

CHAPTER 2

Some Remodeling Facts

The following four facts about the remodeling industry give a very interesting perspective to anyone considering a remodeling project.

Remodeling Spending

The remodeling industry accounts for almost 2 percent[1] of the gross domestic product (GDP) of the United States (GDP = the value of all goods and services produced in the US in a full year). Remodeling spending is comprised of all spending on both residential building maintenance and on residential remodels.

Financial numbers related to the industry come from just a few sources. These include the National Association of Homebuilders, trade partner Houzz.com, and the US Census Bureau. But the most consistent data source for years has been the Joint Center for Housing Studies (JCHS), at Harvard University. JCHS reports that total remodeling spending has been above $280 billion since 2005, with their estimate of total spending for 2016 far surpassing $300 billion.[2]

---

[1] Joint Center for Housing Studies [Marcia Fernald, Ed.] (2015). *Improving America's Housing: Emerging Trends in the Remodeling Market.* Harvard University, Cambridge, MA.

[2] Joint Center for Housing Studies [Kermit Baker, Ed.] (2016). *The Home Improvement Outlook for 2016 and Beyond.* Harvard University, Cambridge, MA.

So Many Houses!

The 2005 American Housing Survey by the US Census Bureau indicates that there are over 124 million dwellings in the US. About 109 million of those homes are regular, occupied housing units; 11.6 million others are vacant; and about 4 million are seasonal.[3]

Aging Gracefully?

The housing stock in the US is aging rapidly. In 1986 the median age of the US home was just twenty-three years old, while in 2011, the median home was thirty-five years old. These figures were published by HUD in their American Housing Survey (AHS) of 2011. This survey also points out that houses in the Northeast are generally older than in other regions of the country. For instance, homes had a median age of fifty-seven years in New York and sixty-one years in Washington, DC.[4]

But Houses Simply Wear Out

How does this effect you? For one thing, no one can put a precise figure on the lifespan of a house. It all depends on its initial construction quality and the quality of its original materials, the performance of regular maintenance, and the climate or weather conditions it has endured.

---

[3] National Association of Home Builders / Bank of America Home Equity [Jackie Jackson, Ed.] (2007). *Study of Life Expectancy of Home Components*. NAHB, Washington, DC.

[4] Josh Miller (2014). *The Age of Housing Stock by State*. Retrieved from: http://eyeonhousing.org/2014/02/the-age-of-the-housing-stock-by-state/

Let's face it, many parts of homes just wear out and need replacing or repairing at regular intervals. By the time a home is twenty-five to thirty years old, it has had many features upgraded or replaced, such as the roof surface, siding, gutters, windows, cooling systems, all appliances, and perhaps the kitchen and bathrooms. In short, remodeling is how we constantly renew the housing supply in the US. It is also how a home can continue to serve the shelter needs of its occupants.

CHAPTER 3

Why We Remodel
(and Why We Don't)

Before you read this chapter, ask yourself the following question: What are your reasons for remodeling?

Having a clear understanding of the motivation for a project helps you become mentally settled during project planning, and it can help you accurately focus on both the scope and the budget of the work.

If I were teaching a live class, I'd ask the questions, "Why do people remodel?" and "What are the reasons that US homeowners spend over $300 billion per year improving our homes?"

The answer is, people typically remodel for one or a combination of the following six reasons.

Emergencies

Regardless of the disaster and the severity of the damage, when something goes wrong and the house is compromised in a serious way, it NEEDS to be fixed, and usually fixed quickly. This is the one type of remodeling project I hope you never face.

Nevertheless, there is an entire segment of the remodeling industry that specializes in mitigation, restoration, and other insurance-driven remodeling and repair. In these circumstances, insurers typically have a team of specialists that can be mobilized immediately to aid with home protection and reclamation.

Because this is urgent work, homeowners typically cannot hire architects and interior designers and work on designs and plans for months before rebuilding or remediation work begins. But this does not mean that you cannot select the tile, the carpet, or the new cabinet style. However, those tasks are not done at a leisurely pace that allows for prolonged deliberation like you might have in a typical remodel.

The good news is that even in expedited circumstances like these, you can still apply the procedures I teach in this book and select the best contractor to help rebuild your home.

Maintenance

Our homes have a finite life span—at least fifty years, and up to seventy-five or more. But long before our homes get that old, parts and pieces of them wear out and need to be replaced. Shingle roofing lasts about twenty years. A water heater or AC unit might go ten to fourteen years before quitting. Kitchens and bathrooms have a fifteen- to twenty-year "life" before becoming old and "dated." Have you seen a kitchen with "harvest gold" or "avocado green" appliances? Or a bathroom with pink or blue tile and matching toilets? If so, you can understand what I mean when I say "dated" rooms.

This type of remodeling falls under home maintenance and is a part of an owner's responsibility for their condos, apartments, and single-family homes. These all need parts and pieces replaced as time passes. For this reason, it is not too surprising that home maintenance spending is the largest portion of the total remodeling spending pie.

In Preparation to Sell

When the time approaches to sell a home and move elsewhere, there are two types of remodeling projects most often performed: repairs (remedial improvements) and cosmetic improvements.

Both of these types of remodeling are logical prior to selling a home. They are also commonly needed, as homeowners tend to put off some repairs or maintenance over time and have to perform those tasks prior to listing a home for sale. If they don't handle these types of issues, it could significantly lower the listing and selling price of the home.

Typically, maintenance projects include things like painting, replacing worn carpet, refinishing hardwood floors, or even sprucing up sidewalks, driveways, and landscaping. Cosmetic, or "curb appeal" projects are also chosen to make the home look fresh and inviting to a new, prospective buyer. New doors and windows, new siding, new roofing, and perhaps some landscaping projects fall into this category.

All these projects are relatively simple, and they generally have low overall costs as far as remodeling projects go. They also positively impact the sale price, and most yield a high return on investment.

By comparison, large remodeling projects typically do not fare as well with regard to significantly increasing a home's value prior to sale. If you choose to perform this type of project in preparation to sell your home, be careful not to personalize it too much. After all, the work you do at this point is for the new buyer! But if you still have that harvest-gold kitchen or pink tile bath with matching toilet, that could negate a swift, top-dollar sale. So occasionally even kitchen and bath remodels can be performed as resale-based remodeling projects.

Generally speaking, though, most professionally performed repairs and cosmetic improvements raise the home's perceived value prior to selling and are a significant bonus for the new buyer if the home is "move-in ready."

When the Need Changes

A significant number of remodeling projects are performed for the simple reason that a family's need has changed.

Adding a new bedroom or a new bathroom are very common projects of this type. A new baby or an in-law joining the family might also necessitate projects that enlarge family rooms or eating areas. Perhaps the passage of time requires the updating of a bathroom or a kitchen. As you can see, *need* is not universal. Each family must assess its own personal need compared to its current conditions, and then choose to either remodel their current home or move to another house that adequately meets their need.

Adding Value

There are two types of value that a home improvement project can deliver. Obviously, remodeling can increase the home's price (the home is simply worth more than it was before the project). However, don't overlook the improved "quality of life" that a well-done remodeling project brings. The fact that many remodeling projects deliver both these values is the reason so many value-type remodeling projects are performed each year.

Keep in mind, though, that large remodeling projects are usually suggested only when a family plans to remain in place for four or more years after the project's completion. In that case, after the project, the first value received is the daily use of the new improved home until it is sold. For example, an additional bathroom reduces congestion and conflict at peak times. A remodeled kitchen makes preparing food easier and more enjoyable, and may also deliver improved serving and eating of food or a better connection to other rooms and areas at the same time. Value-added factors like these are often the prime motivation for choosing to start a remodeling project.

The other type of value relates to the home's worth. Every well-done remodeling project increases the sale price of the improved home. Sometimes that raises the value of the remodeled home above the price of other nearby houses, and sometimes it only returns a home to the price level of other neighboring homes.

For example, consider a home with the infamous harvest-gold kitchen. That forty-year-old kitchen significantly reduces the home's sale price. In this case, a modest kitchen remodel will simply bring that house back on par with other maintained homes in the neighborhood. The same can be true for dated or worn-out bathrooms. (I will discuss this type of value increase in much more detail in the cost versus value section of Chapter 12).

So if you might be moving in the near future, then value-based remodeling and/or resale-based remodeling projects might make sense. You can enjoy the improvements while you remain in the home, and still sell it a few years later at an increased price.

For Pleasure

Sometimes improvements are made "just because we want them."

Does the average home need a home theater? A gourmet kitchen? A spa-like oasis of a master bathroom? Nope. But are those projects wildly popular? Yes.

These types of projects make sense when you love your location but you simply want a change or an upgrade to your living space. When you know you're staying put, you can fix the home exactly the way you want it.

Of course, you still perform routine maintenance or perform projects to improve curb appeal and to add value. But putting the computer-simulated golf driving range in the basement near the wet bar is done simply because you want it. And that's OK!

Why People *Don't* Remodel

Suppose we are back in our classroom and I ask this question: "So why don't people remodel?"

Most likely, you don't know why other people don't remodel. But perhaps you have put off your own project for several years. It's actually quite common. So why have you hesitated until now?

The most common reasons that homeowners delay their projects are their **unfamiliarity** with the remodeling process, and **fear**.

People are unfamiliar with whom to call and why, and what to do or in what order to do it. They also struggle with how to select the right remodeler, and what different projects will actually cost. Their fears can include choosing the wrong remodeler, being overcharged, being ripped-off, and not knowing what they really need.

If any of these reasons sound familiar, you are not alone. But you can rest easy now. Buying this book was your first step down the road to remodeling success. Here, you will learn what you need to know and need to do so that you will be comfortable with the remodeling process from your initial inspirational idea through signing a contract.

CHAPTER 4

Myth Busting

The general public has many incorrect ideas about how things work in the remodeling industry. Many of these erroneous thoughts and beliefs rise to the level of a myth (a widely held but false belief or idea).

In some cases people are misinformed by things they've seen on TV shows. Others got their wrong ideas from things they have heard or read. Regardless of the source, erroneous thinking needs to be corrected as soon as possible.

So join me now in some remodeling myth busting!

As Seen on TV

These days, remodeling is everywhere! People are repairing, adding on, rehabbing, flipping, and DIY-ing on just about every channel on the TV. Which leads to our most widely held and most dangerous myth: it can be done "that cheaply and that fast" for me too, just like I saw on TV.

The truth is, TV has just thirty or sixty minutes to show you the entire remodeling process from the initial idea through completion. So they simply don't show you everything. And they don't tell you everything either. By omitting the facts, they promote the myth. And when it comes to the price of the work and the speed of performing the projects, they often . . . well . . . um . . . they lie—though more by omission than by intentional deception.

In reality, with regard to project costs, the hosts that perform physical labor on TV projects are typically paid by their TV contract, and NOT by the homeowner. Many times, the subcontractors on TV shows do not charge at all, or they deeply discount their fees in exchange for being featured on TV. And very often the manufacturers whose products are prominently featured on the shows donate or drastically reduce the cost of their products. So even if these TV shows total up the "bills," the total can be very misleading, and it's almost always on the low side.

Additionally, when it comes to how swiftly a project gets performed on TV, remember the saying "time is money." If the TV production company has to have a film crew and support staff on a remodeling site for twelve weeks instead of five or six weeks, imagine the significant additional costs. To counteract that, they often line up workers and subs in two or three shifts (around the clock), and in some cases even over weekends, in the effort to reduce TV production time significantly by shortening the project duration. This is a major cost savings for the TV show production company. They also don't include the premium costs for overtime in the final TV show remodeling cost tally. If those fees had to be paid by the homeowner, it would drive the cost of the project ridiculously high and be unaffordable.

Simply put, the entire timing of the work is condensed, and the fee for that is paid by the TV production company. You cannot expect project durations like you see on TV when it comes to a project at your home. Nor can you expect the price to be as low as you've seen on TV, since you (and not a TV production company) need to pay the remodeling team to do the work and supply the products.

Finally, with regard to TV remodeling, they seldom show the entire process. Planning, preliminary design meetings, work by architects, obtaining permits, and the like are simply skipped. During the two minutes of commercials between the decision to buy a particular house and the start of demolition, a minimum of two to three months' work had to take place in real life.

The fact is, they don't show many of the preliminary tasks prior to the start of demo and remodeling simply because it doesn't fit neatly into thirty minutes and it takes away from the face time with the host. Besides, it's a slow and costly process that is not very glamorous. And TV is all about speed and glamor.

The bottom line is this: *in real-life, it takes longer and costs more than the projects you've "seen on TV."*

Pro Tip:

If you want to watch TV and also learn the correct way to remodel, evaluating those you hire, and why it's important to pay the right price to get a qualified professional- -watch any of the shows that feature Mike Holmes. His analysis is usually spot-on in my opinion, and he repairs the shoddy work of others while teaching owners and viewers why he does what he does.

Ratings, Rankings, Lists and More

These days, we hardly buy anything that isn't rated, ranked, or listed. If you have ever used Amazon, Yelp, Consumer Reports, or the Better Business Bureau, you are familiar with the idea of how we use ratings, rankings, and lists to make our purchases.

And for better or worse, there is no shortage of sites that rank, promote or connect you with remodeling companies. The public is invited for free to find or be connected to 'the most reputable contractors' who are 'rigorously vetted'. But all you need to do is ask one question to find out the truth about these sites: "Who profits from this site, and how?"

I'd guess that you might be thinking, "Jim, they're not taking money from the consumer, and companies don't even have to pay to be listed."

But again I ask: "Who profits from the site, and how?"

The answer is, there are three different ways that most of these sites function, which you will discover as I introduce you to the three different types of referral sites you may encounter.

Remodelers Pay to Advertise

Most ranking sites sell preferred listings, ads, and advertorials (editorial ads) to help promote the presence of paying remodelers. By promoting their user demographics, they get remodelers to spend money on campaigns to get noticed and generate leads. That is where the sites' revenue comes from. So, are these sites really pure, unbiased rating sites? No. Do they list all remodelers in a market? No. And honestly, I'm not against these sites existing or profiting. What I *am* against is the public believing that these sites exist to serve them and give them unbiased information.

If money is flowing from a remodeler to a website in exchange for advertising or a greater presence in front of the users of the site, so be it. But it's a money-making venture for both if it works—the remodeler making money from getting many leads on new jobs while paying the website. But it's not free, it's not unbiased, and it's not the way you should find or choose a contractor.

The best-known example of this site type is Houzz.com.

Site Connects You To Remodelers

This website model "serves" the unsuspecting homeowner who is trying to find a reputable local contractor. This type of site has you enter your information into a form (name, address, phone, email, type of project, brief description, budget) and promises to connect you with a number of pre-scanned and approved 'top contractors' who 'specialize in your type of project'. Once again, the truth is easy to see when you ask, "How does the site make money?" If the site asked you to **pay $200** to get several names of home improvement contractors--you'd log off. So instead they sell your information to local contractors who have pre-registered and agreed to pay on a per-lead basis. Sometimes there is even a larger fee if the job gets signed.

Examples of this type include 1-800-Contractor, Contractor Connection, and many more.

Again, I can't begrudge the remodelers for seeking work this way, or the website for selling leads if it can attract enough users to stay in business. But once again, this is **not** a fair, unbiased site that is concerned with the welfare of the remodeling public. It is a business that wants to sell you and your job to a paying company near you.

Rated, Ranked, and Listed

Another prevalent homeowner thought these days is that online sources that let consumers rate or review lists of local, 'pre-screened' providers are a safe and time-saving method to identify an excellent contractor.

What I am talking about here are remodeling-based rating/ranking/listing sites and services like Home Advisor and Angie's List. These are widely thought to be very credible sites for hiring professionals, probably because of their prominent advertising presence on television. But they are no more accurate and unbiased than any other site mentioned. Nor do they consider all local remodeling companies! They only list sites that register on their own (with no or limited screening) or ones that pay to register.

Along those lines – the Better Business Bureau, Chamber of Commerce, Google and Yelp are all thought by consumers to be credible sources for identifying local pros. But no site that ranks or rates remodelers along with restaurants and dog groomers should ever be considered credible. False testimonials are the bane of such sites.

In summary

Using rating, ranking, and listing websites or services to select a remodeling contractor is dangerous. My advice is this: don't ever give away your right to investigate, identify, and choose your own remodeler. When you choose your remodeler, you can be certain that you get a perfect match of their core skill set to your project needs. But using an automated or 'blind' service is no way to 'select' the right remodeler for your project. You have no idea exactly why a given company got referred to you, other than the fact that they paid the website in exchange for your information.

So what is a homeowner to do? In my experience, there is no substitute for carefully looking into each remodeler that you think may be qualified to work on your project, so that you can be certain they are right for you. I will spend a good deal of time later in the book showing exactly how you can identify the right type of remodeler to use (yes, there are types of remodelers). You will also learn how to find companies that are specifically suited to your size project. This is impossible to do on any referral site, listing site, or ranking site.

There simply are no 'easy button' solutions that help you achieve successful remodeling results. Shortcuts are always a very big gamble, and usually a bad one.

Consider this favorite phrase of mine, and use it as your mantra as you start your remodeling journey: Never let anyone else choose your remodeler for you.

Referrals from Friends

Tell anyone that you're planning a remodeling project, and they'll try telling you who to use. Because everyone knows a guy. Or has a company you really must call. And they are wonderful, swift, cheap, and oh so talented too!

But, if someone tells you, "Use my guy," my advice to you is this: just say no.

If you must be polite, I suggest that you smile, nod, thank them for offering to help. Then take their referral and stick the card or phone number in your pocket until you can discard it properly.

Why? Because your project, your needs, and your situation are anything but identical to your friends'. Bottom line: their guy or their company is quite unlikely to be a good match for your specific needs.

I say this because every project is unique with individual needs and goals, and every remodeling professional is unique too. They all have different specialties, and you need to thoroughly investigate every remodeler you consider using before you invite them to your home for a meeting.

So remember to smile, nod, thank your friend, and put the business card or phone number in your pocket. When you get home and after you throw it away, I suggest reading Sections 5, 6 and 7 of this book so that you'll have no trouble finding a remodeler who's just right for your project and your temperament.

Remember: "Never let anyone else choose your remodeler for you".

The 5% to 15% Rule for Kitchens

One of the very misleading fallacies you'll find on the web is that remodeling project budgets should be set by making them a percentage of your home's value. One source I looked at recently said you should spend 5 to 15 percent of your home's worth on a kitchen remodel. This myth is just stupid.

You'll learn that it takes much thinking and planning, consideration of a myriad of variables, and significant preparation time before setting your project budget (see chapter 12, "The Budget").

The scope and budget of every project are based only on the goals and needs of the owner. So you alone determine the realistic needs for your project, and only you will choose the amount that you spend to achieve those goals. That figure becomes your budget. Never let someone else's silly rule-of-thumb set your budget for you!

CHAPTER 5

Time to Begin...

So far we have looked briefly at the remodeling industry and the sullied reputation it has in the media. We also peeked at the massive size of the industry and the amount of business it conducts each year. Then we reviewed why we remodel, and conversely, why we don't. Finally, I dispelled some of the most common myths about remodeling.

Now it's time to begin your journey into the remodeling process. And like any task, the first step is planning and preparation.

Getting properly prepared to remodel is not rocket science. It's more like taking a high school class. Predictably, there's a bunch of information that you need to learn and understand in order to apply it.

Oh, right. Just like that high school class, there is plenty of homework too! But don't worry, it's fun. And it's essential if you are seeking a successful remodeling experience.

So please take out a clean sheet of paper and a number 2 pencil...

Section 2:
THE REMODELING MINDSET

If you fail to plan, you're planning to fail.

—Benjamin Franklin

To create something exceptional, your mindset must be relentlessly focused on the smallest detail.

—Giorgio Armani

CHAPTER 6

Before You Do Anything

You have this nifty idea to remodel your _____ (fill in the blank). Well, now it's time to call some remodelers and get started, right? NO! Dead wrong.

This is the first of three crucial mistakes homeowners often make. These three blunders instantly elevate remodeling projects to a high risk of failure simply because the owners charge ahead unprepared.

> **Horror Story Avoidance Tip #1:**
>
> **Don't begin the remodeling process without being fully prepared.**
>
> Jumping into the remodeling process by calling in professionals without first doing your own project preparations is the first of three critical mistakes often made by homeowners. Without realizing it, they hand over control of the remodeling project to someone else before having even the simplest plan and preparations in place. The risk of a project becoming a horror story is now remarkably high based on the unknown character, quality and skill of the company partnered with. This is a complete gamble. And considering the dollar amounts involved in most remodeling projects, and how hard we work to earn our money, this is a simply unacceptable error.

Through the years, I have personally helped my clients achieve their dreams. I have led them step by step through the remodeling process, because in most cases, they were unaware of what to do and why. They were lucky that they worked with someone who actually helped them achieve their remodeling goals. And I was able to do this because as a young architect, I was trained to understand people's motives and needs before trying to solve their three-dimensional problem. This is an important step, because without knowing the owner's true goals for a project, the very best that any professional can do is to design a nice generic modification to the home. And that may or may not meet the homeowner's ultimate needs.

This is why you should have a firm, accurate grasp on the fundamentals of your project before you lift a finger to ask for help with your project.

How seriously you work on the assignments (the 10 **Action Items** listed in these next few chapters) will make a huge difference in the success of your remodeling project. Your best effort on these action items will help your professionals to clearly understand the requirements that must be met to produce a successful outcome. If your designer and contractor can "see your vision" as you do, then half the battle is already won.

Based on my experience, homeowners don't enter the process with a well-defined set of goals and ideas for their projects. In fact, the remodeling public typically has no idea what to do, or in what order to do it. They typically call professionals prematurely, thinking they will receive guidance. Instead, by doing this, they blindly give away control of their project (and its ultimate success), to someone else.

Please, **never** give control of your project to anyone else. Only you know what you need and what you want from your project. Only you understand why your current home fails to meet your needs, and what it would take for a new design to successfully meet those needs.

For this reason, there is much to be done before you google local remodeling professionals or ask for any outside help. The preparations you make now, prior to getting others involved in your project, will make or break its success. Nobody else knows your situation, so it's your job to let them know. In order to do that, you must first do some homework!

CHAPTER 7

The Remodeling Mindset

Consider yourself an employer who needs to write an announcement for a new job posting in order to hire a new employee. You'd probably start with the job title and a basic job description. You'd then specify the tasks that your successful applicant will perform, and list any special skills, experience, and unique qualifications they should possess. Finally, you would determine the price you are willing to pay the new employee. This work would be performed prior to posting the job for consideration by potential applicants.

This is the mindset you need to assume when preparing to remodel. You are the Boss with a capital B! You are about to make the most important hire of your career as a homeowner, and you need your job posting to be as accurate as possible. You want to interview only the most successful, pre-qualified applicants for your job. So, your job posting should filter out all but the very best candidates.

Sound farfetched? It's not. You must maintain this mindset throughout the process. Of course your design professional and contractor will know far more than you in their specific fields of expertise, just as employees often know more about the details of their specific job than the boss does. But as an outstanding boss, you hire the most qualified people, manage their efforts, keep everyone focused, and trust the employees to bring their expertise to bear as they perform.

There is no doubt that your project will be guided by your employees' expert advice. But you remain the Boss, and you retain the final say at all times. You monitor all project performance and progress according to the job description and the employment contract.

Even if you have never been a boss before or hired anyone, please don't worry. The information provided in this book will help you get properly prepared to remodel.

Just remember, this should be an exciting time in your life. Remodeling your home is a fun and exciting process, and I am going to help get you fully prepared to face it head on. As such, you, the Boss, will be in control of your remodeling process from beginning to end.

Section 3:
THE PROJECT PACKET

The details are not 'the details'.
They make the design.

—CHARLES EAMES

It's not in the dreaming, it's in the doing.

—MARK CUBAN

CHAPTER 8

Create a Project Packet

The goal of this section is to fully prepare you to contact the industry professionals who will help you on your particular remodeling journey. This is necessary whether you need professional design help or are able to go straight to the correct type of remodeling contractor. Either way, you still need to fully prepare so that your hired pros can help you most effectively.

The best possible way to do this is by preparing a ***Project Packet*** which fully describes the goals and the known details of your project. The Project Packet sets the overall project scope, describes your special needs, and sets your budget, among other things. If you can deliver this information in a clear and concise manner to your chosen professionals, they can more accurately understand your goals and help you succeed.

To do this, you need to begin and maintain a project file so you will not lose track of any project information that you gather as you begin the remodeling process. You'll probably end up with loads of ideas, notes, photos, helpful websites, and all sorts of fun information as you become immersed in your project planning. So take a moment to determine how and where you will collect and organize all your remodeling materials and information.

You will then begin to compile details on project-related materials and finishes that you pre-select (appliances, flooring choices, cabinet door style preference and finish, etc.) so your design pros can craft a clever solution that meets your needs and respects your budget. Your Project Packet is the first big key to your remodeling success.

If you will give your best effort to carefully prepare and compile a first-rate Project Packet—one that clearly communicates your remodeling goals and expectations—as this chapter lays it out, your probability of remodeling success will go up dramatically. Your design and remodeling professionals will have a clear and detailed understanding of your remodeling vision, helping them craft a creative solution for you that will meet or exceed your expectations.

Action Item #1:

Get your laptop ready (or your tablet, or a pad and pencil) so you can take notes as we start going through the Project Packet elements: the Elevator Pitch, the Need List, the Wish List, the Budget, and the Project Scope. Make whatever notes you wish as you read through the information the first time. Keep these all together in the same place, since they will become your Project Packet.

As you reach the individual Action Items for each Project Packet element, reread that section and do the prescribed task. Then afterward, read through your own first draft of the Packet and keep working the material into the best shape possible. Make edits and changes as you read more and learn more. This Project Packet is a work in progress, so stick with it.

Give your Project Packet your full focus and effort. The quality of the information you put together here significantly improves the quality of the custom design solution the professionals can deliver.

TAKE SPECIAL NOTE:
Visit **www.JimMolinelli.com/pp** and download your **FREE SAMPLE PROJECT PACKET**. It can serve as a TEMPLATE you can follow as you create yours!

Next are two different insider suggestions to help you get ahead. These suggestions will make your Project Packet preparations a bit simpler.

Make Your Photos Count!

Take photos of all the parts and pieces you might want to capture and replicate in your project. Wherever you find them, snap a digital photo of each part, each item, each look. But in order to make them count, please type or write very clear notes on each image so you and the design professional know precisely what to replicate from your image. If it was a type of window, great. If it's a particular window seat idea, awesome. If it's an idea for an island layout in your kitchen, perfect. Just be sure you note the exact thing you want the designer to use, so all the other details in the photo can be disregarded!

Be Observant!

Everywhere you go, start looking at the details! When you visit the homes of others, look at their rooms and see if anything inspires you (to do, or to avoid doing). Also, when you're out shopping, look at tile and the designs that can be done with it, whether it's for your kitchen backsplash or the new bathroom. And when you're in the home stores, go up and down aisles you never visit, and see all the items they sell that you might want to try in your new solution. Inspiration is everywhere, so be observant! (And be sure to take photos and keep notes of your observations.)

Action Item #2:

Visit the website Houzz (www.Houzz.com) and make a free account. Then you can start Idea Books into which you can save and annotate images searched from their millions of project photos. Being able to type notes on each image (as noted in the previous Pro Tip) is a huge benefit to help you recall your particular inspiration in each photo.

It's fun to search their site and collect photos that capture little bits of the solution you'd like to see in your home. And when the time comes, you can share your idea book(s) with your architect or design pro!

CHAPTER 9

The Elevator Pitch

Nobody can possibly help you design or construct your remodeling project if you cannot define for them what it is you need done. So logically, the first thing we'll work on is defining your project.

I like your project definition to be short and sweet, but accurate. It also needs to be complete enough to truly convey the essence of what you're planning to do. So, I suggest that you come up with an *Elevator Pitch* project description.

An *elevator pitch* is so named because it is a short, succinct description of your goal or plan, complete enough to convey your message in the brief time it takes an elevator to go from one floor to another with your person of interest onboard.

The first task on your Homework to-do list is crafting the ideal elevator pitch for your project. It's a short and sweet, thirty- to sixty-second speech that summarizes your intentions. And you should practice it so you can reel it off easily at any time.

Keep in mind while writing your elevator pitch, that you're looking for more than "remodel my kitchen" or "revise my master bathroom" or "add a sunroom," which may be semantically accurate but doesn't convey very much information. Try to include a few of the key features involved that make your project description clearer but without rambling. Things like "gut the current kitchen; remove one wall; install new wood flooring, new cabinets, and stone countertops; and add an island with counter seating." This really helps the professional you are trying to work with grasp the scope of your planned kitchen remodel. Or perhaps you say "expand and remodel the master bathroom to include a double vanity, separate soaking tub and stand-up shower, and possibly a separate water closet. I'd also like in-floor heat."

When writing the elevator pitch for your own project, I want you to think about your project and then write out a few lines that describe what it is you are really looking for. Remember, you're not required to solve the design problems or come up with all the answers. You are simply setting the guidelines and parameters that a professional will use to devise a creative solution for you.

During the interviewing process, you will find it necessary to give this information during numerous phone calls and meetings, so go ahead and work on defining what you plan to accomplish in clear and simple terms.

When you have written your first elevator pitch for your remodeling project, print it and save it in your project file. You should read it regularly and edit it as your knowledge grows and your parameters change while you work through the rest of this section. As we learn more, we often alter our initial impressions, so don't be afraid to go back and overhaul your core description if it becomes necessary!

The goal is to end up with a concise, accurate description of your project.

Action Item #3:

Write the first draft of your project's Elevator Pitch **now**, before moving ahead to the next chapter.

REMINDER:
Visit **www.JimMolinelli.com/pp** and download your **FREE SAMPLE PROJECT PACKET**. Use the sample Elevator Pitch as a template for your own version!

CHAPTER 10

The Need List

The absolute core of each remodeling project is the Need List. So let's discuss what the Need List is and how it relates to your project.

A *Need* is any **indispensable** item or feature of the remodeling project that you are planning. A Need is a core element of your project that is so important to you that if it cannot be included, you would not even perform the project.

Ultimately, Needs differ for every person, and for every project. Line up ten neighbors, all of whom own similar houses of a similar vintage, all of whom are performing a kitchen remodel, and I guarantee that the Need List of every family will be different. What makes any project, or even a single room, ideal for one person does not make that same project universally successful for everyone. Each person, couple, or family has unique Needs when it comes to planning the rooms and areas within a remodeling project.

I want you to be aware that Needs and goals are not identical. A Need is a specific item or feature that either gets included or doesn't. Goals, in contrast, are the end result of the entire project. Your *goal* is to remodel the kitchen. Your *Need* might be an island or counter seating in the kitchen. So be sure not to interchange these terms.

Also keep in mind that Needs are not things like a stove in a kitchen, or a toilet in a bathroom. Yes, those are essential elements of any kitchen or bathroom, but they are universal and not specific to your project. Without those items the kitchen or bathroom would simply not work as intended. Here, you and I are focused on Needs, items that that rise a step above the obvious and which customize the room just for you.

For example, in a kitchen, some people would call under-cabinet lighting a need. Some would call a second oven a need. For some, it's informal seating, while for others it's a particular type of countertop material. Can you have a successful kitchen without these items and elements? Sure! But for these owners, who consider these things essential, they are elevated to Need status.

In a master bathroom, a Need could be a soaking tub and a separate stand-up shower, or a toilet in a water closet (separate room). For some owners, separate his and hers vanities are a Need. While others might insist on a no-threshold walk-in shower.

Think about your planned project for a few minutes and ask yourself what are the absolutely essential elements that you cannot live without? What are the Needs in your case? There's no reason to worry about this list—you can't be wrong! Just remember that as you move further along in this book, learning new information, you may very well change some of your Needs, perhaps adding or deleting a few. And if you're doing this project with a partner or spouse, what is a Need for one of you may not be a big deal to the other. But in a case like that, I suggest keeping **all** the Needs on the Need List unless both of you agree to remove them. Perhaps you can note to whom a particular Need is attributed, so your design professional can get the scoop from the correct partner and make the solution a perfect fit.

I find the Need List to be an essential component that even helps make larger, more involved projects more successful. If you don't have one, your architects and designers will provide very generic solutions. So this is the first step to a fully customized solution, one tailored just for you!

And if you're thinking, "I'm not doing a bathroom or kitchen, this does not apply to me or my project," then you're wrong! If you're adding a sunroom or family-type room, there are dozens of things that could be elevated to Need status (TV location, type of window or skylight, fireplace, flooring type, views, planning for specific furniture [like a sectional sofa or recliner], or even a built-in window seat).

Planning a basement finishing project? What about a powder room or bathroom down there? What type of vanity and sink? Is there a wet bar in the basement? An egress window? A new door and areaway out to the yard?

Working on a home office? You might have specialty power needs with dedicated circuits or integrated communications, or perhaps some custom built-ins.

Just working on a mudroom? How about a bench with built-in cubbies or storage for kids' shoes, clothes, jackets, school items? Need extra storage, folding space, hanging space, or a slop sink for the laundry area? Both room types need easy-to-clean floors also.

A screened porch? How about a really strong rigid door with a self-closer piston, instead of a fly-swatter wood door with a spring? Maybe you need a more finished-looking ceiling. Or perhaps you need a way to access and easily replace the screens as they tear or sag? Different types of screen attachment systems address that.

The bottom line here is this: for almost all projects, there are Needs. So the Need List is the first thing you can do to help your professionals understand your interpretation of the project you're planning.

Now that you understand what is on a Need List, and before moving ahead to the next chapter, start writing out your Need List. Remember, it's a work in progress, so you don't have to worry over each item. And as you learn more and get new advice, your Needs and your Need List can be changed. I'm not saying that you should be ready to be talked out of your Needs, just that I've seen homeowners think certain items were Needs, only to find that they had even more effective options or that their perceived Need was just a desire, and proved to be nonessential.

Action Item #4:

Start your Need List now. Write out all project Needs that you can identify, and define or describe the ones that are complex. Perhaps you can find photos that depict your vision of the Need List items. Save or store these in conjunction with your Need List. Remember, you want other people to "see your vision." In order to do this properly, **you** must be clear on your Needs first. Only then can you clearly communicate them to the others helping you design and construct the solution.

REMINDER:
Visit **www.JimMolinelli.com/pp** and download your **FREE SAMPLE PROJECT PACKET**. The Need List TEMPLATE will help you write your version!

CHAPTER 11

The Wish List

So if something isn't a Need, is it unimportant? No way! Just because you didn't consider an item or a feature "indispensable" does not mean you don't want it in your project!

And that's where the Wish List comes in. For our purposes, a Wish List item or feature is anything you really want that is not a Need.

Remember earlier when I said that you may initially declare things to be Needs, then maybe demote them later? Well, the Wish List is where they go unless you choose to dismiss or disregard them entirely.

The Wish List is full of items and features that you would really like to see in your solution, budget permitting. In the end, anything on this list may be omitted from the project because it didn't work well in the design, or you changed your mind, or the budget ran out and the feature was not affordable.

Remember, the distinction between a Need and a Wish is the fact that Needs are indispensable or the project will not happen, while Wish List items are desired and valued, but only make it into the project if the budget is sufficient.

For example, wishes might be things like a fireplace, a vaulted or tray ceiling, a laundry sink in the mudroom, a cabinetry-style pantry, a walk-in clothes closet, a frameless glass shower door, and many, many more.

These features could make you very happy and the project even better, but they have to be worked into the solution by a talented architect or designer, budget permitting.

So if you were debating items being on, or off, your Need List, the Wish List is where they land unless they get dismissed by you altogether.

Action Item #5:

Go write your first Wish List now. List and describe the items and features you'd like to work into the project—budget permitting. Do this without worrying about the order or their potential cost.

Now that you have a working Wish List, you should prioritize it. By this I mean organizing the list so that the item or feature you most want to be included in the project (budget allowing) is on top of the list. Continue priority ranking the rest of the items right down the entire list.

Just as I mentioned that things might move on or off the Need List, you may find that items and features on the Wish List move up or down the list, or even get eliminated, based on your changing priorities. It is not uncommon that items become more or less important as you investigate them and their alternatives. Occasionally, you'll find a different feature that you were unaware of at the beginning, and it can replace what started as a Need List item or highly ranked Wish List item. That's perfectly OK.

In the end, this is a great way to help your design professional understand your thinking about what should be in or out of your ideal project. As you move along in the process, constantly review and revise your Need List and your Wish List, keeping them as accurate as possible.

Another note about the Wish List is this: the quality of your architect or designer will make a huge difference in what Wish List features get included! The most talented designers can sometimes find creative ways to combine elements in a cost-effective way, and that could result in more Wish List items being part of the solution. So when it comes to the design pro you use, look for someone very skilled and creative, but excellent at designing to a budget.

Finally, you will want to learn about the relative costs for items on your Wish List. The reason is this: if the designer is successful at hitting the budget with the basic solution and you can afford to add several things from the Wish List into the plan, you need to be aware of how they will fit based on their cost. If you can get three items on your list for $4,000, or you can get one item, does that affect your thinking? Or would knowing that a real masonry fireplace and chimney might cost $14,000, while a direct-vented pre-fab fireplace could be installed for as little as $4,000 sway your thinking? It goes without saying that these drastic price disparities would make a difference to most people. So, after you make and prioritize your Wish List, try to determine the approximate cost of those items and features so that you are prepared to make your final choices if it comes down to the last few dollars.

Action Item #6:

Go reread your Wish List. Confirm that you would still like to have all the items and features that you listed earlier (budget permitting). Make any additions or deletions that are necessary.

Now, prioritize your Wish List items into the order you want them added to the project. Remember, this is just a first draft. You can revisit this and update the Wish List items and their priority order at any time!

REMINDER:
Visit **www.JimMolinelli.com/pp** and download your **FREE SAMPLE PROJECT PACKET**. The sample Wish List is an excellent template for your own list!

CHAPTER 12

The Budget

After working on defining and describing your proposed project and writing out your Need List and your Wish List, you need to determine what you are willing to pay to accomplish the scope of work you want performed.

But how do you do that? You have no idea what remodeling projects actually cost, right? So how can you set a proper budget?

To answer these questions, I first need to make a very important distinction so you grasp this point very clearly. Cost and budget are not identical. **Cost** is a product of the combination of the materials, the labor price, and the markup (profit and overhead) of the company providing the remodeling. You can't possibly know that number without obtaining pricing directly from a remodeler, and we're just beginning to prepare for the process. In contrast to the cost, the **budget** is the pile of funds from which the homeowner will pay for all remodeling-related expenses. So the cost is determined by the remodeler, but the budget is always set by the homeowner.

In fact, think back to the remodeling mindset analogy I gave earlier about how the employer writes the job description in order to hire an excellent new employee. Part of the job description the Boss prepares is the price they are willing to pay to hire a qualified individual. The price (or budget) for your remodeling project is set by the homeowner in advance of meeting with candidates for their job.

In other words, you set your own budget for your own project! Would it help to have some idea what things cost so that you don't budget $20,000 for a $150,000 remodel? Yes, of course. But common sense should tell you that additions and whole-home remodels don't cost less than a kitchen or bathroom renovation alone.

The logic used to set a remodeling budget is as follows: You have a certain amount of money available to use for your project, whether it's cash, savings, investments, home equity, or a loan. Regardless of how you obtain the funds for your project, there is a finite sum that you could possibly spend. Then you ask yourself how much of that total amount you are willing to part with in order to get your project performed. The answer to that question is your maximum possible budget—**the amount that you are able and willing to spend**.

But before you settle on a final budget figure, there are more factors you should consider. Some of these will affect what you're able to spend, and others might alter what you're willing to spend.

Loans

Many homeowners borrow money to pay for their remodeling projects. You may need to borrow all or some of the funds for the project you're considering.

But before you visit a bank or talk to lenders about your loan, I have some valuable information to share with you. Now, I'm not a loan specialist or financial advisor. But as your personal industry insider, I will share with you how one particular loan type results in remodelers dramatically increasing the contract price. Then, show you how another type of loan could take thousands off the full price of your contract!

I'm not going to discuss every individual loan type available. That topic is outside my area of expertise, and frankly, it's also boring. Go meet with your banker or loan specialist, and you can delve into the details with them.

My purpose in this discussion is getting you the best possible remodeling price without compromising the quality of your remodeler or the end result. And the following discussion and loan advice could help significantly in that regard.

What you need to know is this: In the eyes of your remodeling contractor, there are only two types of payments. They either see the payment as coming from the bank or coming from the homeowner. It's that simple.

So, which method is preferred by remodelers and why? Consider these two scenarios: handing an invoice to someone and getting a check back, or waiting seven to twenty-one days for a bank to issue a payment. Your remodeler prefers the simplicity of being paid instantly by the homeowner. Bank controlled loans involve hassles for the contractor when interacting with a bank and besides, constantly waiting to be paid is frustrating and costly to remodelers.

Another major drawback of bank-controlled loans is that they rarely include a deposit payment to get a job underway. This leaves the remodeling contractor to self-fund the first thirty to forty-five days of the project before the first bank payment arrives. As a result, remodelers not only dislike bank-paid loans, but they also raise their markups and profit margins to a higher level of compensation for essentially funding the first portion of the project.

For this reason, my first cost-saving recommendation to you is this: if you need a loan, always try to obtain a loan that allows you to issue the payments whenever possible. This lets you negotiate a more favorable total price. On bank issued payments, the contractor markup increase could be an additional 5% to 10% of the project. In other words, you could pay about $5,000 to $6,000 more for the same $80,000 project if the bank issues the payments rather than you issuing the payments.

The loan types that allow homeowner control of payments include home equity loans, equity lines of credit, and signature loans. (If you are self-financing your project from investments or savings, you also enjoy this advantage).

My second loan-related recommendation is this: Don't wait. Go talk to your banker or lender now. Waiting until you are ready to sign the remodeling contract will potentially anger your remodeler, who has to put everything on hold and wait for you to shop for and secure a loan. A typical time from the initial bank loan inquiry to the funding of an approved loan can be from 45 to 120 days. Then, if any hiccups occur in the loan things could get even further drawn out. Can you see why this might upset your chosen remodeling professional?

Don't let this happen to you. Discuss necessary loans with your lender of choice and get pre-approved *before* talking to any remodelers. This way you'll know your maximum loan amount (and what your payments will be). After you get loan feedback from the bank, setting your final project budget should be a whole lot easier.

Action Item #7:

All loans take time to arrange. Start loan shopping early in the process to find out what limitations you may have that could affect your loan amount, your loan rate, or the amount of time it takes to approve and fund your loan. This is important information to help you set the budget, but it is also important in the eyes of your remodeler, since it affects how they get paid.

Do this before you interview remodelers, so that you and they both know the payment situation in advance of writing the proposal and signing the contract.

Now I'd like to bring to your attention one other loan type that each of us have at our disposal.

Signature Loans

When we talk about signature loans, we are essentially talking about credit card transactions. The term refers to any loan where a bank knows you have the ability to repay and they will advance you funds based only on your signature, not on collateral. As you might suspect, these loans (especially your credit cards) have fairly low borrowing limits and fairly high interest rates, so they are NOT an ideal way to fund large remodeling projects.

But the flip side of signature loans is that most credit cards these days offer users some type of rewards, such as cash back, air miles, or points. I suggest using your best rewards card to make selected remodeling purchases, then pay off the account balance monthly so it never activates the high interest rates. Use your credit card to buy owner-supplied materials, purchase new kitchen appliances, or pay select subs, like the painter for example.

Pro Tip:

With many credit cards, you get miles, rewards, or cash back for your spending. It's possible to put a lot of project expenses on a credit card and reap substantial rewards, provided you can pay off the balance quickly, avoiding the high-interest rollover charges.

Current Home Value

As part of the loan approval process, the bank determines the value of your home. But when you're setting your budget for your remodeling project, you might also want to consider the current value of your home. There are several reasons for this.

First, knowing what your home is currently worth lets you know precisely what your equity in the home is (current value less amount owed on the mortgage). Second, having an accurate current value gives you a benchmark in your consideration of whether it's better to sell and move versus remodel. And third, it can possibly help you set some limits on the maximum budget for your project. We will now cover each of these factors.

When I teach this information in person, I stop at this point and ask my students how they would determine the current value of their house. But once again, since this is not a live class, I'll just list and explain a few of the ways you might find a current value for your home.

Home Appraisal

The bank is not the only one that can pay for a home appraisal. You can pay an appraiser to do one for you too, and there are two different kinds you can get. The first type, a *restricted-use appraisal* is a limited document with little in the way of a breakdown of costs or supporting documentation, but it gives you your home value, and that's the bottom line. Restricted use appraisals run about $100 to $150. The second and more commonly used type of appraisal is the *summary appraisal*, which gives you more supporting information. This includes interior and exterior descriptions and other opinion and support data the appraiser uses in the evaluation. These typically cost $300 to $400.

Real Estate Agents

It is within reason to ask a realtor to provide you with their appraisal of the current market value of your home. This can be true whether you have an intention to sell in the near future or not.

If you choose to do this, be certain to explain to the agent that you are planning to remodel, not to list and sell your home. After all, you want them to understand that they are NOT likely to conduct realty business with you in the near future.

Pro Tip:

Not all realtors will provide this service or provide it for free, so you may wish to visit a local realty office in person and ask about it, instead of just calling on the phone or making an appointment to meet in your home. If they do agree to give you an appraisal, be aware that they do so to build a relationship should you or others you know need a realtor.

Free Internet Home Appraisals

If you search the web for "home prices" or "home values," you'll find hundreds of links that offer to give you a free home "appraisal" or your home's current value for free. Some actually deliver, and many are scams. However, in most cases they are just out to get your contact information for sales purposes. I strongly recommend that you disregard these.

Home Value Websites

There are a number of websites where you can look up your home on a map using your home address. There you can view your home's lot, building, and even tax data (of course you can do this for other homes in your neighborhood also). Many sites of this type offer their estimated current home values as well. These sites are typically free and many require no registration or membership.

The most recognized site of this type is Zillow (www.zillow.com). Housevalues.com and Trulia.com are two other similar sites. Most of these get their basic information from the state tax records. For this reason, there are often errors in the key descriptors of their listings, and more importantly, their estimated home prices sometimes miss the mark by tens of thousands of dollars. In some areas, their estimates run well below market value, and in others they run high compared to the actual market at any given time. Do not put much stock in the accuracy of the estimated home values displayed on these sites.

You can frequently spot errors in your listings on these sites, but the majority of them show contact information so that the homeowner can submit corrections or edits. Because of the popularity of these sites, you should make the effort to keep your home's listing as accurate as possible.

One similar site that is a bit swifter to update sales and value data, and appears to be more accurate with its pricing is Homesnap (www.Homesnap.com). This site is prevalently used by realtors and consumers to check home prices when buying and selling. Homesnap draws data from many sources, among them forty different MLS (multiple listing service) databases. This site still shows an estimated value of all homes, but it also gives a range of values for other homes like yours that are currently listed or that have recently sold in your vicinity.

PRO TIP:

Beware! Just as you would not list and sell your home for a suggested value that you found on a free Internet website, don't simply trust those same estimated home values for your remodeling purposes either. I suggest that you use them only as a guide. Trust only appraisals from certified local appraisers when buying, selling, or obtaining loans.

Tax Data

All states make their real property and tax data available to residents. Finding out if your state has an online database is as simple as an Internet search for "real property search, your state." There is typically a lot of great information on these databases, often including lot size, home age, square footage, owner data, recent purchase history. They typically show the assessed value of the home as well. This is **not** the current market value of the home; it is the value assigned by the state for tax purposes. For that reason I suggest looking your home's page over, but disregard this as a way to get an accurate current home value.

Cost versus Value

I have already explained how you set a default remodeling budget, as part of the Project Packet you are preparing.

Still, my students usually have two serious questions at this point when I teach this material, so I suspect they may have occurred to you as well:

- How do I really set a budget without knowing anything about the true **cost of remodeling projects**?
- **How much value** do different remodeling projects add to the worth of a given house?

These are both very reasonable questions.

Cost

I believe that it is important to have some idea what real-life projects actually cost. I've seen too many shocked faces when I relate typical real-world costs to homeowners on a first visit. Besides, if a budget is truly inadequate for the scope of work anticipated, isn't it better to know immediately at the start of the process before investing too much time and effort? I think so.

So where can you get honest and accurate information about the cost of typical remodeling projects? If you ask the search engines and read online blogs and articles, you will get an endless variety of prices. You'll also find that web prices are typically ambiguous, with price ranges that are too large to be useful. In many cases, online costs are just opinions, and not very realistic. In the worst cases, they simply reflect popular rules of thumb that are unreliable. And, in my opinion, you cannot rely on the prices you see on television remodeling shows either. So where can you turn?

There is one outstanding source for accurate remodeling cost figures. It happens to be an insider's source, meant for the remodeling industry. It is an annual report compiled and printed each year in *Remodeling Magazine*. The report is called the Cost vs. Value Report (CVVR). The name says it all. It provides answers to both our questions—realistic costs of common projects and how much value is added by those projects.

You can always find the most recent report by typing "cost versus value report" into your search engine. Then click on the link, for *Remodeling Magazine* (www.remodeling.hw.net)

When you arrive at Remodeling Magazine's page, you will see the latest Cost vs. Value Report article. While you're there, feel free to read the article about how costs of projects and their values have changed nationwide over the past year. This is always interesting, but the best information lies in the localized reports.

To access the localized report, you will select the proper region of the country, and then click on the city name desired within your region. In order to view or download the PDF report just enter your contact information. Don't worry, the reports are truly free, and they won't spam you.

To provide this report, *Remodeling* employs realty and remodeling experts in all regions of the US, and in many cities within each region. These professionals establish the costs and values that the report describes. As a result, you get very localized information on different project costs and values for your area.

Some of the listed projects you will find in the report include simple cosmetic and curb-appeal projects, major upscale remodels of bathrooms and kitchens, and even various additions. Most of you will find projects listed that are quite similar to your own, so you can use their projected cost and value as a guide for your project. However, you will need to look closely at their project descriptions to know where their project and yours are similar and different. Then you can adjust the reported cost accordingly.

While you will need to adjust their cost figure so it more closely equates to your project description, this resource provides you with a great starting place for accurate job costs. If you had guessed that your job might cost $30,000, you may have sticker shock when you see the CVVR midrange kitchen cost listed at $54,000, but now you have a trustworthy, solid number.

For almost all homeowners, the real cost of remodeling projects are shocking. In my opinion, it's better to learn about the realistic costs of remodeling right away so you can proceed through the remodeling process with your eyes open. The worst way to learn about real-world prices is from a remodeler's final proposal after many weeks of time and effort have been invested. Waiting till the end and hoping for the best is not a plan I endorse or one you should employ.

As you review the Cost vs. Value Report, read their project descriptions very carefully. Very often they give a square foot size for the project, or they list some finishes that you might not want to use. To the extent that you will select more upscale finishes or perform a larger project, your price will be higher than theirs. To the extent that you use more economical finishes or keep your project smaller than their description, your cost will be lower than their estimate.

Do not simply glance at the first kitchen price you see listed in the report and take that figure at face value and depend on it. If you are careful in trying to compare your project and theirs, the reports provide an excellent way to obtain realistic working prices for your project. Then you will be able to talk to lenders (if necessary) and set your project budget with more knowledge and confidence.

Value

Just how much value can be added by remodeling? Let's look once again at the Cost vs. Value Report, and we'll focus on the VALUE listings this time.

The report asks the hypothetical question, "If you spend our estimated price on the described remodeling project and you sell the home within a year of remodeling, how much will the project raise the selling price?" That is the basis for the value figures that they show.

You should remember that earlier I stated that all remodeling projects add value to the home. I omitted the obvious point that those improvements must be properly performed for my statement to hold true. Also, in homes that have not been properly maintained or updated over time, the value added by remodeling might only bring that home back on par with the values of other well-maintained or slightly improved neighborhood homes. This is not built into the CVV Report, but you need to take it into account for your home.

If you know you'll be moving in the next six years, then you can use the value aspect of each project type to help determine which projects to consider. You're looking for projects that make the home more appealing to the potential buyer and raise the value (read: listing price) by the largest amount. And the Cost vs. Value Report is an excellent resource for this purpose.

It's great to know that 60–75 percent of the cost of a major project gets added to the current value of your home. The longer you live in your home with the new improvements, the more value you receive. Of course, you get the increased total value of the home, but you also get to enjoy the improved function and utility of the home on a daily basis.

Pro Tip:

You may not realize this, but a quality remodeling project remains fresh and "recently remodeled" for as many as ten years after completion!

I've long stated that a great goal for my remodeling clients is that every morning when they use their new bathroom/kitchen/family room they can say with conviction, "Wow! I sure am glad we did this project!" That's what you get for the other 20 to 35 percent of your investment: immense satisfaction.

Now amortize that great feeling over three, six, or even 10 years, and that project has paid off handsomely.

Be sure to watch the values in the Cost vs. Value Report for the types of projects you are planning. And if your planning takes you through fall into winter, be certain to check the newest report, because each year things change. The relative value boost of various projects changes over time. This is one more factor that may help you make the most informed decisions regarding your remodeling budget.

Pro Tip:

Be aware that remodeling an existing room and constructing that same type of room as an addition are not the same thing. Additions always cost more than interior remodels of the same size and scope. The reason is simple: with interior remodeling, you already own the foundation, the walls, the roof, and the mechanical services.

Don't add the cost of "master bedroom remodel" and "master bathroom remodel" together and expect a brand-new master suite addition to come in at that price. It simply won't happen.

Move or Improve?

If you plan to move within five years, you should make all your remodeling decisions with an eye on resale. This does not mean that you cannot remodel a kitchen or bathroom, just don't personalize things too much. Stick to a more neutral color palette, and use traditional materials and looks for your kitchen and bath choices. This gives you several years of enjoyment in your newly remodeled space, and the benefit of selling the house with the term "newly remodeled" in the listing.

If you know that you will be moving in just a couple years, the best advice is for you to stick with cosmetic and remedial repairs and improvements. Bring things back up to full repair, and a state of cleanliness, with excellent curb and eye appeal. In addition to costing less, those projects often have the largest return on investment. If you're in this situation check the Cost vs. Value Report and review the best value projects.

For the rest of you, who are likely to remain in place for five or more years, the full gamut of projects is open to you.

But what if the total cost of the projects you wish to perform runs to the top of your budget? Is it possible that you could also move and find an already-improved property for a price that's equal to the value of your current home plus the remodeling budget?

This is a question that should be asked in almost all large-budget remodeling projects. Even if you answer it by asserting, "There's no way I'm leaving this house," it can be a prudent question. It's not often that moving is the right answer, but you can't know what's possible if you don't ask the question.

If you're looking at spending all your available funds and you can't get everything you were hoping to obtain in your remodel, or if you're fearful that placing your home too far above the typical neighborhood home value is not prudent, then you're a candidate for the following "Move or Improve?" exercise. If not, you can skip ahead to the next chapter.

When you entertain the idea of selling your home and moving, there are many factors to consider before making the final decision. I also suggest you come to a firm decision BEFORE you hire architects or design-build remodelers to help you visualize and price your remodeling dreams. There is no sense spending money designing improvements for a house you'll be selling.

There's no reason you can't explore the costs of moving, to see if the total cost of a new home, in a new location, and suitable for your family, is available, affordable, and a plausible solution for you.

With that being said, let's take a minute now to go over some of the factors you must consider if you seriously entertain the idea of moving to an already-improved home.

Below are four things to take into account when considering a move:

- **Your current location** – Are there features of your home or site that you consider irreplaceable? Are you in a great school system? Near amenities you enjoy (schools, church, work)? Are there friends or family nearby that you're leaving behind? Only you can answer these questions and determine if these factors matter to you.
- **The cost to remodel** – You can now not only set a budget, but also you have some resources to get an idea of the real cost of many remodeling projects. Do your best to estimate what your project might really cost.
- **Your current home value** – Use any of the methods we've already discussed.
- **What you will spend on the new house** – Start by adding the value of your current home and your best estimated cost for the remodeling projects that you are considering.

So, is that it, Jim? Can I now go looking for a new home for sale with that figure in mind? Well, no. Not really. There's more to it, as you will see.

Hidden Costs of Moving

I must introduce some considerations often overlooked by those entertaining the idea of "Move or Improve": the **hidden costs of moving**. Yes, many of these costs go overlooked by those whose preference might be to buy a new home instead of remodeling. None of these are deal-breakers that will swing your opinion one way or the other. But collectively, they can seriously impact your "cost" of moving.

- **Repairs and painting** – Fixing all the little things you've neglected at home, getting it ready to list and sell. These typically include at least some new floor finishes, repairs and painting, but might also include some other cosmetic fixes for better curb appeal and completing any incomplete do-it-yourself projects.

- **Cleaning and staging** – Your home needs to be cleaned, and don't we all love doing that? And in this case, cleaning means really, really cleaning: decluttering, dusting, putting things in storage or donating them, organizing your life which lies around you at home. It's enough to make some people stay put! But this needs doing before opening your home to potential buyers. For the best "first impression" you may even need to pay people to help you with this phase.

- **Paying the realty fees** – Yes, in most cases, you, the seller, pay fees to both realty companies, for both the listing agent and the selling agent of the home you sell. And based on the value of the home, the 5 or 6 percent fee (based on the contract price) can be a hefty chunk of change. In order to weigh this cost, the realty fee needs to be added to the cost of moving.

- **Taxes and closing costs** – One of life's certainties, you cannot avoid the tax man when selling and buying homes either. So be prepared for some taxes and more than a few closing fees to be tacked on to your transaction when selling and buying each house.

- **Packing up a life** – Let's face it, most of us still have boxes of things stored that were never fully unpacked since a prior move. Well, get ready to pack up your family's life to move a few miles up the road. The inconvenience or perhaps the painfulness of having to crate and box everything to move it five or ten miles may be reason enough to stay put. Of course, it's less painful to let someone else box and pack for you, but then there's that cost factor again.

- **Moving** – Once you're packed and ready to go, you rent a truck, pack your belongings into it, and drive across town only to unpack the truck and unpack your life at the other end. Or, you pay a company a lot of money to do it for you. The latter is easier on the muscles, but it will significantly increase the cost of moving.

- **Buying the new home** – Maybe you love hunting for the perfect house, the wheeling and dealing while negotiating a possible purchase, and the uncertainty of your offer being accepted. Maybe not. It can take many house-hunting trips to accomplish, and be a stressful time, and that has a price associated with it.

Additionally, the following seven factors may not as seriously impact your savings account, but they can sure mess with your sanity and well-being. Are they worth it? But you decide.

- **Negotiating two sales** – Some would balk at negotiating one, but to move, you need to sell one house and buy another.
- **Disruption of the routine** – From the moment you get serious about moving, your daily life changes significantly. There're house viewing trips, and meetings with the realtor, bankers, and handymen. There are countless planning sessions for buying, selling, packing, and moving. Kids may need to be registered in new schools. You're moving your utilities and cable. You need to update every online account and retailer, and anyone who sends you physical mail. The amount of time being unproductive or missing work will rise.
- **New commutes** – Assuming you commute to work, you'll have new commutes. If you're looking for more house at a better price, then you're probably moving further away, so your new commute could be longer as well. And those of you in metropolitan areas have to be concerned with the volume of traffic and time it takes to travel your commuting routes. Nobody wants to spend significant chunks of their life in a car, after all.
- **New schools** – Moving the kids to another school is a paperwork headache, that's true. But the real problem with a new school is the emotional impact it can have on the kids: leaving behind friends, associations, clubs, and the known set of teachers, and hoping they can fit in and make a successful go of it in a new situation. Only you can assess how this factor will affect your family.

- **New church** – I suppose it goes without saying that if you move far enough, you need a new location for worship and fellowship. Otherwise you significantly increase the drive time to keep attending at your current location.
- **Outfitting the new place** – Have you considered that you'll probably want to paint a number of the new rooms to suit your style and decor? And aren't there a few of the carpets that you wanted to replace? Well, that's how it goes. While you're not going to remodel it, you're going to fix it up and make it yours, right? So, plan on spending something for these improvements and changes. And don't forget the new furniture you'll need or the new custom window treatments.
- **Griping of family members** – This final issue is the one you'll tire of first, and will be the most frustrating one of all if everyone is not on the same page with moving. The last thing you need while trying to improve the family's situation is infighting and bickering over the move.

Ultimately, only you can place the correct and final value on these factors and what effect they have on your decision to stay or go. Regardless, they need to be considered before you make a choice to move or improve.

At this point, you should recognize that the cost of moving is greater than the worth of your current home plus the amount you were willing to spend on remodeling combined. Tens of thousands more, in fact. And that still leaves you to deal with the emotions and the nuisance factor of moving.

Regardless of your decision, you can now make an informed choice.

Action Item #8

Set your budget. It's often the amount you are both able and willing to spend to accomplish your Need List items. It can be affected by things like real world project cost and value added by the type of remodeling project you are planning; the value of similar homes in your neighborhood, localized sale trends and values, how long you plan to remain in the home and more.

You will want your design professional and your remodelers to know and understand this figure.

CHAPTER 13

Defining Your Project

So far in your **Project Packet**, you have worked on your Elevator Pitch, the Need List, the Wish List, and the Budget. Now it's time to get down to some project-specific details.

Keep in mind that a professional will design your nifty new 3-D solution. **It is not your job or your responsibility to come up with the design or the solution to your remodeling puzzle.** Leave that to the professionals. They get paid to solve the problem!

In this chapter, you will commit many details about your project to paper (or to a document on your computer). The goal is an inspired brainstorming session where you'll write out many of the key ingredients in your ideal new room or rooms. I'll explain a great way to organize those details so they are easy to track and update as you move ahead in the remodeling process.

But first...

Odds and Ends and Other Tidbits

I have a few unique factors to bring to your attention. These are some of my favorite considerations that often seem to help people put their remodeling thoughts in order. Perhaps one or more of these will provide a creative spark that helps you tailor the parameters used for your remodel. These may not fit neatly into any of the categories we've previously discussed. But if any of them inspire you to modify your Need List or Wish List, go for it. You can also make a separate page called "Other Items to Consider" that can be added to your Project Packet for your architect or contractor.

What I know from experience is that the following factors may be either brilliantly applicable to your project, or of no real consequence. You decide if you will pass any of these details and thoughts on to your pros.

- **Your FURNISHINGS drive the size and the layout of the room.** What furniture will reside in your room? Sectional sofas, rockers, and recliners require extra space in public rooms. A billiard table or ping-pong table take up loads of space in a rec room. Is your TV wall-mounted or free standing? What size is the bed? Does the bed have night tables? A headboard? One dresser or two? Chest of drawers? Each piece of furniture requires space to function properly, and also enough space to move freely past it.
- **Would you look at that!** What is the FOCAL POINT of your room? Is it a lovely view you wish to feature? A fireplace? The center island in the kitchen? A television? The fabulous gas range and cooking center? You decide what you want visitors to notice and remember, and write it down! Every room has a focal point anyhow, but by planning it, you get to choose your focal point and not just let it happen.
- **Get a load of that VIEW!** Does your yard have an excellent view that you can take advantage of? Can you orient the rooms, the windows, and the interior layout to take advantage of your view? You can if you make plans right from the start! The opposite is also true if you want to avoid looking in a particular direction from an addition or a remodeled space!
- **Here comes the SUN!** Which way does the sun rise and set? Think before you face your dining room windows to the west or southwest. Otherwise, the setting sun will blind you during dinners (or cause you to leave the blinds pulled shut, negating any view). In your bedroom,

you decide whether you're going to wake with the sun or sleep in a sun-less bedroom. Your designer can manipulate the windows and the room layout based on your choice for sun or for no sun in the mornings!

- **What's that NOISE?** Are there noises you want to hear from the yard? Noises you don't want to hear? Where you place solid walls versus windows will impact the noise you must endure. If you happen to have a waterfall in your pool, or a pond or fountain outside, you may love the soothing sounds they produce, and choose to face your newly remodeled spaces in that direction.

- **What do you LIKE?** Sometimes it's that simple. If you've seen or used features that have worked for you, you can incorporate those into your new solution. Be sure to add these features to your lists for your designers.

- **What NOT to do!** If you've had it and hated it, don't do it again. If something does not work for you, avoid it. Almost goes without saying, but I've said it anyhow. If you don't like a feature, by all means, don't include it!

That's a lot of ideas for your new and remodeled spaces. But each refinement you make to your vision for the new room can result in higher-quality, customized solutions!

Room Functions and Features

The very first time I meet with a new remodeling client, I guide them through their imaginary project to get an idea what they "see." I ask leading questions so I am sure that they have considered even the most often overlooked aspects of that room type. The fact is, each different room has many unique functions and features that need to be listed, easily tracked, modified, and ultimately communicated to the professionals you hire.

In order to get you started with your area by area description, I'll ask stimulating questions while you visualize each new room. This exercise is not about cost or value, it's about listing the new functions and features that you might like in your newly remodeled space. That's it! You will list and organize this information for inclusion in your Project Packet.

You should perform this exercise for every room you are planning to remodel. That's because each room has a very different set of functions and features. As an architect and remodeling professional I always sought client input to help me understand what makes the room perfect for their needs.

Here are three guided examples of the kind of thinking you should do for each new room or area of your planned remodeling project.

Bathrooms

FUNCTIONS: While the typical function of most bathrooms is bathing and dressing related, some bathrooms have additional functions. For instance, if you want a jetted tub or a steam shower, note those. If there is a separate dressing or makeup station in your ideal bathroom, note that. Note whether there will be one user or two at a time in the room. Will the shower be large enough for two?

FEATURES: In a bathroom remodel, the number and type of fixtures make a big difference in the design and the cost. So, whether you have a typical tub/shower combination, or just a stand-up shower, or perhaps a separate tub and stand-up shower, this matters to your professionals. Does your shower need to serve one user or two? Are there multiple showerheads in your shower? Is one a wall-mounted wand? Wands make cleaning the shower a lot easier! They also help women wash their legs more easily when shaving. A step or a niche or a low bench also helps with shaving. But will you ever truly sit on the bench in the shower with the water running? If so, ask for it; if not, save your money. Do you need a niche or a shelf for soaps and shampoos? How many bars of soap or bottles will be stored in the shower? Is there a glass door, a curtain, or is it a walk-in shower? What kind of privacy is required in your bathroom? Are you OK with the toilet in the main bathroom area? Or do you need a water closet (separate room with a door for the toilet)? Do you also want a bidet? Do you prefer a single large vanity or separate vanity basins for each spouse? Will your excess linen and cleaning storage be in the vanity, or in a nearby closet? Will you need a medicine chest? What type of mirrors are you imagining? Can you get from the clothes closet in the master bedroom to the master shower if you're undressed?

Kitchens:

FUNCTIONS: All kitchens have food preparations as their core function. But there are many others that are quite typical. Cleaning! We all clean using products and items stored in our kitchens. I'm also pretty certain you'll have some form of eating take place. Will you eat at a table with chairs, or on stools or chairs at the counter of an island or peninsula? Will the kids do homework in the kitchen? Will you store cookbooks and recipes there? Coupons? Is there a place for your mail/purse/cell phone/tablet? A "junk drawer" that's not in your way? Are there great views from the kitchen? Into other rooms or out to the yard? Surely arts and crafts with the kids will take place in the kitchen? Will you entertain there? Play games? Watch TV? Read? Sort, read, or write mail? Pay bills? Email?

FEATURES: In a kitchen, everyone needs a sink, a dishwasher, a refrigerator, and a place to cook. But will you cook on a range or a cooktop? With gas or electric? Do you need a second oven? What about a microwave? Do you want stacked wall ovens? Is your sink double bowl or single bowl? Is it on the island, or at a window? How is your cooking surface exhausted? Up through a hood and out the roof? Through an exterior wall vent? Or down through a cabinet and into the floor? Do you want a separate refrigerator and freezer? A spare refrigerator?

Will your countertop be tile? Stone? Laminate? Butcher block? Or something exotic like concrete or bamboo? What about your floor material? Sheet vinyl, hardwood, bamboo, cork, and tile are all common on kitchen floors. Will you have a tile backsplash? Granite? Or painted drywall? How about specialty appliances like a mega mixer, blender, waffle iron, bread machine, coffee pot, or toaster oven? Will they live in cabinets, in closets, or on the counter? Where will you store your dry food? In cabinets or a pantry closet? Will you need a spot for a step stool, broom, and dustpan? What about those very occasional items like the turkey platter, deviled egg plate, and cake transporter? Where will those go?

And then we have the cabinets. Are you in love with one particular door style? Maybe a specific wood and stain combination? Or a painted cabinet? Are there features you need to have?

Sunrooms/Family Rooms:

FUNCTIONS: What will you do in this room? Grow plants? Eat? Play Games? Conversation? Fireplace? Television? Play music? Is the room open to the house? Does it connect to the yard? Is it heated and cooled? Is it a "family room" with lots of windows? Does it open to the deck/patio/yard? Is circulation through the room and outside short and easy, or all the way through the room?

FEATURES: Do you envision a glass and steel room that looks like an English greenhouse? Or an aluminum frame and sleek glass—like a modern lean-to? Or are you thinking of just another room that looks just like the rest of the house, but this one has loads of windows? Is the ceiling flat or vaulted? Is it wood or drywall? Will you have an eating table in the room? How about a game or card table? Will there be a piano? Will you use recliners? Rocking chairs? What type of furniture can you envision in the room? How about the floor? Is it wood? Tile? Laminate?

Have you noticed that the simple room names we use don't even come close to describing what really goes on in the room? This is why architects and other professional designers cannot rely on room names to design solutions for our clients. We need a lot of personal input to create a custom solution that addresses your unique requirements.

A kitchen is **not** just a kitchen, and a one master bathroom is **not** identical to another master bathroom. Your specific list of functions and features allows your design professional to craft a custom solution that truly meets your needs.

Homeowners are not trained to think about or visualize rooms the way architects see or describe them. Your understanding of your own project will start growing a great deal as you work on this exercise. You'll be learning a great deal that you never knew. But you'll also become dramatically more observant as well.

Remember: There's no right or wrong, no judgment, no consideration of cost or value, just a "thumbs up" or "thumbs down" about whether you might like a given function or feature in your ideal new room. Later in the process, you will learn more about your options and choices and may choose to edit the details or remove an item altogether.

While you are doing this exercise, you'll find that with some features, you'll want to record additional information. Add those notes after you list the feature. For example, the refrigerator might be French-door style with bottom freezer. Or the cooktop might be six burner gas. Go ahead and add those clarifying notes behind the name of each feature. Every little bit of information will help.

Bear in mind that you don't need to make every decision here and now. If you don't know which countertop material you want, fill in a line for "countertop" and the options you're considering, then choose a specific type later. Or write down "flooring—wood or ceramic tile," and decide down the line. Don't think too hard, and don't worry. Brainstorm and write. We'll organize it all later!

Organize Your Information Room by Room

After reading about the functions and features of some typical rooms, you can easily see that even small remodeling projects have many, many details. To coordinate and organize all your information, I suggest a simple table (or a spreadsheet if you like working digitally).

This next addition to your Project Packet is a room-by-room table that will record and describe as many details about your remodeled spaces as possible. A table is an excellent way to coordinate the details for each remodeled room or area. Your tables will serve as a collection point for all the choices and selections you make throughout the course of your project!

Whether you use a piece of graph paper and a pencil or a computer spreadsheet to record your room by room descriptions makes no difference.

As an example, I have prepared the following sample table. It illustrates a fictional sunroom in the same two-column format that I recommend you use to start organizing some of the many room details for your remodeling project.

SUNROOM Notes and selections
with backyard views, home theater, wood floors, vaulted ceiling
Casual eating, games, reading, conversation, TV

	Feature	Notes and comments (as needed for clarity)
Ceiling	Drywall ceiling (smooth, painted)	1 color
	Ceiling Fan no light	Owner Furnished, contractor installation
	LED recessed lights	Quantity to be determined
Walls	Painted drywall (high)	1 color wall, 1 color trim
	Beadboard wainscot (low)	painted, narrow spacing, vertical
	Tall baseboard (painted)	painted, profile selected later
Windows	Casement style vinyl windows	White vinyl double pane, Low E and Argon. Brand?
	Fixed glass vinyl picture window	White vinyl double pane, Low E and Argon. Brand?
Door	Sliding glass French door to ext.	Andersen Frenchwood. Stained interior
Floor	Hardwood	Same species as adjacent kitchen, matching stain
Contents	Sectional sofa	12' x 9' x 38" tall
	2 adult armchairs	38" x 36"
	2 side tables	17" x 23" each
	coffee table	to be purchased later
	Game tabe	48" square table, 42" high with 4 stools

Use a separate table for each room or area. As you see in the sample table above, place the room name at the top, and then list the most important notes about the room (Need List items or the **Functions** that occur there).

Below the list of Functions, begin your table. In the left column of each row (horizontal line) write one **Feature** found in that room. As you see in my sample table, I organize my **Features** by listing those that occur on the ceiling first, then features on the four walls, then floor features, and finally any room contents. And I organize each room or area in this fashion since it makes it easy to think about each room in the same pattern, and it organizes the table neatly for ease of use.

In kitchens, bathrooms, and laundry rooms, the contents of the room are primarily cabinets, countertops, appliances, plumbing fixtures, and accessories (mirrors, towel bars, shower doors, etc.). But in other types of rooms, the contents are more likely to be the furniture. With regard to furniture, use lines in your table for each piece and list the sizes of the furniture you own. You should also list furniture that you plan to purchase whenever possible so that they can be accounted for by your design professional.

Pro Tip:

In my example, I've added an additional left-hand column that shows the surface or area of the room in which that Feature is located (Ceiling, Walls, Floor, or Contents). This is a logical organizing step that allows me to start listing features at the ceiling of each room, and work my way down the walls to the floor. Then I usually list all specialty items or unique contents for that particular room or area.

This also assists in locating an item when you come to look at the table later to add or update information.

In a bathroom, I treat the shower and/or water closet (if there is one) as separate rooms within the bathroom. This is because the ceiling, walls, and floors are likely to have different features (finish materials, plumbing fixtures) than the main portion of the bathroom.

After listing all the features you can think of in the left hand column, start back at the top of the table in the right hand column and list any notes or comments that pertain to the feature in the left column. Whatever information you currently know about your preferences regarding a feature go here. It can be size, color, style, brand, materials or any other details that help you and your designer understand the feature better. This is a swift and simple way to get started organizing.

When you make notes about the furniture for a room, give the dimensions of the furniture you already own (if being used in the new space). Otherwise, list any known information about pieces you plan to buy. Furniture drives the size and layout of non-kitchens/bathrooms, and this information lets your designer allot the proper amount of space for it in their solution.

After your tables are complete to the best of your current understanding, they become your one-stop source for most of the details about your project.

If you should change your mind on any of the items listed in your tables, at any point in the process, just edit the item and its note in your table. If you decide not to use butcher block wood countertops in the kitchen, but instead are choosing granite, overwrite the space with granite as the countertop material. If you also think you want a particular granite color, then add that information in the note area as well.

As you become aware of other details that you need to select, or which have to be communicated to your architect and contractor, add a new row for those items and keep the tables current.

This is a very simple and flexible way to keep all your choices and selections in one place. Homeowners tend to get overwhelmed by the large numbers of choices and decisions. Tables help keep your choices organized, and they also show you at a glance which decisions you have already made and which decisions remain.

Pro Tip

Since there are hundreds of details in every room, break your thinking down to one room or area at a time, because doing so helps you focus. Don't get overwhelmed. One thing at a time, and it will take as long as it takes. You've got this! Stay focused on one task at a time. When that decision is made, move on to the next task. If you're unsure about a selection, highlight it and revisit it later!

Adding More Detail to Your Table

Below is a look at a portion of a sample table I made up for a master bathroom. Notice that there are many lines for tile. That's because I know that when people finally get to a tile shop and talk to the designers, they usually like to mix a few different types of tile in their overall design. Sometimes they include stripes or decorative pieces (called listellos) on shower walls, or sometimes multiple sizes or colors of tiles, borders, accent tiles, and occasionally different tile shapes. If this is something you consider, simply add more rows for each additional tile type, tile size, or tile color! For now, this is a reminder of one more item you will be selecting before you're done, and you can see at a glance which items you have chosen and which still need your attention.

	ITEM NAME	BRAND
	SHOWER	
Ceiling	Exh Fan in Shower	
	Lights in Shower Ceiling	
	Paint Color Ceiling	
	Ceiling Shower Head	Kohler
Walls	Shower Glass & Door	
	Tile: Shower - wall accent 1	
	Tile: Shower - wall accent 2	
	Tile: Shower - wall field tile	
	Soap storage niches (2)	
	Shower controller	Kohler
	Shower wand	Kohler
	Diverter	Kohler
Floor	Tile: Shower Floor - accent	
	Tile: Shower Floor - field	
	Shower Drain (linear)	

Tile may not be the only multi-line material you run into. Walls can have multiple finishes as well (one or more paint colors, wallpaper, wainscot panels, etc.). There can be multiple types of flooring in a room, and a hardwood floor can have borders or inlays. And, you might have several types of light fixtures as well.

Whatever your rooms call for in terms of Features, give each one a unique line, and fill in what you know about it at this moment. If you know it will be coming in the future, list it and leave the notes blank as a placeholder.

This is how you're going to organize all that information you brainstormed so far in this chapter. Place room name and Functions at the top of each table, with a row for every unique Feature (or material choice, or finish).

If you have items, materials, or features that do not fit neatly into one of the room surface categories, list them last in your table. Do this the same way each time it happens and you'll always find these special items when you're looking.

Action Item #9:

Make a table for each room or area in your project. Set it up with the room name at the top. List the key Functions of the room along with your preferred focal point and any Need List items below the room name.

In the table itself, list all the Features you've considered so far, and just keep adding any new ones that come to mind as you progress through the process. Give each Feature (material or item) a row of its own, and group them together by which surface of the room they relate to (ceiling, walls, floor, or contents) as in the samples shown.

Then in the second column of your table, write any comments or notes you have regarding the Feature listed to the left.

Take your time and work on these carefully because this can give your design professionals a mother lode of information for your project. It not only helps them get a good feel for your thinking and planning, but it also helps you track what you have already chosen with just a glance at any time throughout the process.

The SAMPLE PROJECT PACKET at **www.JimMolinelli.com/pp** has a complete table that you can copy and use as a template for your room description tables!

Pro Tip
Later, when you make more selections and start making final choices, you will have a LOT more information for your table. At that time you can add additional columns for things like the brand, model number, size, color or finish, and other data as needed. If you have other online sources for manufacturer images or data on your selections, you can put the URL link or addresses in the table as well, so it is your one-stop source for all project selection information!

Continue working on your Project Packet, updating and revising the information as time passes. When you go shopping for materials, and as you learn about new options for your project, update and fill in your table. You will be improving the quality of your ultimate solution with each tweak and revision. These tables, in particular, will help you organize all the choices and product information for your project.

CHAPTER 14

Final Touches

The definitions, notes, lists, and tables that you have produced so far will help you keep track of your project's details, and they'll help your design professionals to create a successful custom solution for you.

Before you contact a design professional or a contractor about your project, there are a few important pieces of information you'll want to track down and add to your Project Packet. Each of these can be a digital scan, copy, or print.

- Plot Plan – Each project that requires a building permit and involves exterior additions or structural interior changes will need a plot plan. They are also known as house location surveys. Your architect or remodeling contractor will take the copy you provide and show the permitting authority the new work location and sizes. The title company typically includes a copy of the house location survey in the documents you receive at the settlement of a new home. If you can't find one, many surveyors will create one for between $250 and $500. Realtors often know of local surveyors that can provide realty-quality plot plans at reasonable prices.
- HOA/Architectural Committee Forms – For those of you who live in homes governed by an architectural committee or a homeowner association, you need to contact your board. Verify whether your project will require a hearing. If so, obtain the required forms that your

architect or remodeler will need to help you apply for approval. Add copies of those forms to the Packet.

- Appliance cut sheets (for all sizes/dimensions/specs of your items)
- Manufacturer specification sheet of major material selections
- List of all known current house materials (siding, shingles)

Action Item #10:

Add this set of information to your Project Packet now:

- Add URL links into your table for your already-made selections.

- Add any other loose sheets to the back of the Project Packet.

Pro Tip:

Visit **www.JimMolinelli.com/pp** and download your FREE SAMPLE PROJECT PACKET!

This template will help you tremendously with the creation of your own Project Packet. You can refer to it and mimic its format used.

Of course, you can reread chapters 8-13 as you work through the Packet creation process as well!

Don't forget to add URL links into your tables for your already-made selections.

Your project's success rides in large part on your Project Packet being clear and complete. Do not rush or skimp.

DO NOT MOVE AHEAD IN THE PROCESS UNTIL YOU HAVE A COMPLETE PROJECT PACKET!

Barging ahead without being fully prepared is Critical Mistake #1!!

Section 4:
DESIGN PROFESSIONALS

Design is not just what it looks like and feels like.
Design is how it works.

—STEVE JOBS

The dialogue between client and architect is about as intimate as any conversation you can have, because when you're talking about building a house, you're talking about dreams.

—ROBERT STERN

CHAPTER 15

About Design Professionals

You have now prepared a thorough Project Packet which fully describes your proposed remodeling project, with an Elevator Pitch, Needs, Wishes, Budget, and a table of room-by-room functions, features, and selections. You've also included a plot plan and manufacturer spec sheets/images/data for your appliances and other major choices you've made (like plumbing fixtures, etc.).

The next step will be to decide who you should talk to first.

If you are serious about getting design help, then you want to know which type of designer you need before you start looking for help.

In the following chapters, I'll introduce you to the various design professionals available and give you an idea of their strengths, weaknesses, and some important cost considerations and tips. You will gain a feel for the design pros that might be right for your project, and learn some tips on how to interview them before deciding to hire anyone.

CHAPTER 16

Building Designers

This group of building design professionals helps homeowners with the overall design or the drawing of larger remodeling projects. They can work on interior or exterior projects, additions, or whole-home remodels. While you may use these pros for any size project, they typically are involved in larger, more complex projects, with budgets that can support their expense, or where a professional design touch is essential to the success of the project.

Architects

An *architect* is a professional who plans, designs, and oversees the construction of buildings. The title of *architect* derives from the Greek words **arkhi + tekton**, meaning 'chief master builder'.

Since an architect's decisions affect public safety, architects working in the United States must be licensed in order to practice. In order to earn an architectural license, they must undergo specialized training that includes five or more years of advanced education and several years of internship to gain practical experience. All of that is prior to a nine-part, four-day license examination.

Only those who complete the prescribed education and internship and who pass the examination can obtain a license to practice and call themselves architects.

Active architects must be licensed in each state where they practice. If you hire an architect, always be sure they are licensed by your state.

In most remodeling situations, the architect is the best of the building designers to work with. This is due to their extensive training in all aspects of the home environment. They are trained to respond to the needs of the client, they possess a talent for three-dimensional problem solving, and they are aware of how structural, plumbing, electrical, and mechanical systems interrelate within the design. No other residential designer has the training and skills necessary to integrate those systems in addition to performing high-quality design solutions for the interior or the exterior of a home.

The most significant strength of architects is their ability to perceive and mold the three-dimensional spaces of new and existing rooms together into one unified solution. Unlike ordinary designers, the architect's ability and vision are not restricted by the existing walls and roof of the dwelling. Their solutions tend to be more creative and more complete because of their ability to integrate structural solutions with their designs when adding space or combining spaces. Furthermore, of all the designers mentioned in this book, only architects are permitted to design and certify structural solutions. If you are doing an addition, adding a floor to your home, or combining rooms and spaces together, only architects have the skills and legal qualifications you are likely to need.

With architects, however, there are a few drawbacks you should know about before you hire them to assist with your remodeling project. These shortcomings may include their cost, the amount of time the process takes, and their ability to design to your budget.

Cost – Architects cost more than other types of designers. You have the option to hire them to consult with you (give you advice) at an hourly rate or to draw some preliminary sketches of a possible solution for a low fixed cost. And more traditionally, you can have them do the as-built, demolition, and new design construction drawings, typically for a percentage of the project cost. This fee usually ranges between 5 and 8 percent of your proposed project budget figure.

If you wish to hire the architect to provide supervision of the remodeling construction, expect to pay an additional 3 to 6 percent fee. However, the average residential remodeling projects simply don't have a budget sufficient to cover the cost of the remodeling project itself, let alone the additional cost of the architect.

Time – Architects do their interviews, field measurements and as-built drawings, and schematic designs; then they produce the drawings and specifications needed for bidding and permits. This entire process is done before the homeowner meets with or contracts with a remodeler. Therefore, the entire design and drawing process with an architect from the time you sign a contract with them can be as little as thirty days and as long as a year for complex projects. This amount of time may not be fully anticipated or understood by homeowners, especially if their only familiarity with remodeling is based on TV show remodeling. In that case, homeowners assume that the design and remodeling process is very speedy, but this is not the case in real life.

Hitting the Budget – Finally, while architects are very good at devising creative 3-D solutions based on your needs, they are terrible at estimating the cost of their designs. Please listen to this again carefully: architects are BAD estimators of the cost of the work that they design. Few, if any, will admit this, but I'm telling you this fact from painful personal experience. Don't blame architects as a group for this failing. They simply are not trained as estimators. Their skill set is very large but does not include remodeling estimating.

In most cases, architects will listen to your design requests and your budget and generally agree that the budget is satisfactory for the scope of work. But I'm telling you to expect the *real* price of their design, when bid by a remodeling contractor, to be from 10 to 50 percent above the budget. If your budget was $100,000, you might pay from $5,000 to $8,000 for the architect's design and then still be told the remodeling cost would be $125,000 or more. In such a situation, your total expense could be $25,000 to $40,000 over your declared budget.

In my experience, it is simply impossible to trim as much as 20 percent or more from any design, period. To remove that much cost from a remodeling project, it needs to be redesigned or the project scope needs to be reduced. Truthfully, to reduce an over-budget design by as little as 10 percent requires significant compromise on the stated design goals and will leave homeowners terribly disappointed: there is just no way to feel enthusiastic about a gutted, shrunken project that was reduced in scope because the initial design was well over budget.

And I have yet to see a contract that required the architect to redesign the project for free to make it work within the budget. As unfair as it seems (and is), do-overs require you to pay additional fees.

Designers

The use of the title *architect* and the representation of oneself as an architect is legally restricted to licensed individuals as previously discussed. However, other terms such as *architectural designer* and *designer* are not legally protected. I will refer to all those others who provide architectural design and drawing services as "designers" for the rest of this book.

In the US, independent, non-licensed individuals may perform design services outside the professional restrictions, including providing design and remodeling services on houses and other small residential structures.

With designers, you have no idea about their background, their education, or their training. Truthfully, they don't need to have any of those to call themselves a designer and charge for their services. There is no association or governmental authority that registers or regulates them. For this reason, many designers are just self-taught individuals who have several years' experience building or selling remodeling. They may simply know many of the typical methods of modifying and altering homes and have a computer with drafting software on which to draw their plans.

The only significant benefit of using a designer when you need remodeling design is this: cost savings. Compared to a licensed architect, they will be less costly. A designer could save you about 50 percent or more compared to the cost of a licensed architect for a similar scope of work.

The drawbacks of using a designer are pretty significant, however. There is no set of requirements for their education, training, internship, or licensing. So you get what you get in terms of skill and quality. There is just no way for you to know the full extent or nature of their skill. Additionally, they generally have no estimating skills or the ability to design to a budget, so expect the real cost of their work to come in well above your stated budget. Finally, designers are neither qualified nor allowed to certify the structure of the solutions they propose, nor can they sign or stamp permit drawings. This means you may need to pay an architect or an engineer to certify or stamp the drawings or the structural solutions in addition to paying the designer. This all but negates their most significant benefit.

Being completely honest, there is another problem to mention. You have probably driven around your town and seen additions that look bad. Odd looking boxes that are often out of character with the original house. They scream "I'm an addition". You've seen them. Almost without exception those additions and remodels were drawn by designers who lack the aesthetic sense and design abilities necessary to make an addition look original. And isn't that what you really want? Your remodeling project is likely to be one of the largest purchases of your life, especially if it is an addition. In my opinion, it's always worth choosing the most skilled design professional you can afford.

Are all designers are unskilled? No. Many individual designers have gone through architectural programs, and some might have many years of meaningful experience. The problem is that the average homeowner has absolutely no way to assess the skill or education level of any particular designer. Since there is no way for you to know who is well qualified, it's best to avoid them as an option for your remodeling designs and drawings.

Draftspeople

There are thousands of folks now who offer drafting services to the public. Most these days are using some variety of computer software to produce plans, elevations, sections, and even 3-D views for their clients. If all you need is to get a layout drawn, this is an economical way to accomplish that.

However, like designers, these individuals are not licensed, and therefore their level of education and training is unknown.

For most of your projects, I can see no practical reason to hire this set of specialists. Anything that they offer is also available from other professionals with more knowledge and experience.

CHAPTER 17

Interior Design Professionals

There are two sets of designers we'll discuss here: interior designers and interior decorators.

In general terms, interior designers create highly functional spaces based on the customer's preferences and behaviors. Decorators, on the other hand, fashionably manipulate the furnishings and finishes of an interior space.

Interior design related projects usually involve the content of rooms (cabinetry & tops, built-ins, furniture, etc.), but they seldom involve the technical trades and aspects of construction such as plumbing, HVAC, electric service, or structural manipulation. As a result, the projects that interior design professionals usually do are interior only, and non-structural.

Interior Designers

Twenty-seven of the fifty states now have mandatory licensing or registration requirements for their interior designers. However, the term *interior designer* was deemed too generic to restrict or protect, so the states protect the terms **registered interior designer** or **certified interior designer**. In each state, there are specific educational and/or examination requirements for these design professionals as well. And additional states continue to add registration for their interior design professionals. The current list of state registration details can be found here: https://www.asid.org/content/state-licensing-regulations.

Interior designers are trained to design creative interior spaces that are also safe, functional, and compliant with building codes. Their skill set and services go well beyond simple color selections and furniture, which will come as a surprise to many homeowners.

In fact, their contribution can be as simple as jobs needing the clever re-arrangement of space, to projects that require technical expertise like window and door placement, acoustics, and lighting. But their skill set does not typically include exteriors, the major trades (HVAC, plumbing, and electric), or structural design. This limits their ability to alter load-bearing walls or design additions without an architect's assistance. For this reason, when working on major projects, interior designers often team with architects or remodeling contractors.

If you need someone to design an addition or a whole-home remodel, or you are removing structural walls, you'll likely need an architect. But for design advice on things like room sizes based on furniture layouts, textures of finishes, lighting, color, and interior room design, interior designers could be the best choice design pro.

And while they are not typically able to do the structural and other trade-related designs (which can exclude them from being the only designer of major remodeling projects), they can work together with architects to collaborate on the spatial and interior design for all project types.

Interior Decorators

Decorators, unlike interior designers, are not licensed or registered professionals. There is no educational or training requirement for people to call themselves an interior decorator and offer their services. Typically, these individuals offer to help homeowners decorate the interior of their homes or remodeled spaces.

Their range of services routinely involves designing or advising on the treatment of the surfaces in rooms (textures, paint colors, wallpapers, blinds and curtains, flooring materials, etc.), and the furniture and accessories to achieve a particular style or look. These designers typically have contacts in both the supply and installation trades, and they can help get their designs priced and installed for you. Sometimes they are aligned with specific brands, from which they have significant discounts or exclusive agreements to use those products. Be sure to inquire about this if you consider using a decorator.

CHAPTER 18

Specialty Designers

There are a number of specialty designers that only work in one specific area. The most common specialists are kitchen & bath designers, which include both certified and uncertified practitioners. Other designers you might need or consider are lighting designers and tile designers.

Kitchen & Bath Designers

These individuals specialize in kitchen and bathroom design. Kitchen and bath designers are not licensed, so the term is not restricted. And that also means anyone can design kitchens and bathrooms, including those who are untrained or uneducated in the field. The vast majority of kitchen and bath designers are not formally trained.

Generally, these designers can help you with almost anything kitchen and bath related. They can help design the basic layouts, do detailed cabinet design, work with you on plumbing fixture selections, tile designs, etc. In other words, if it has something to do with kitchens, or with bathrooms, these designers can help.

In most of the cases you'll encounter, these types of designers are much more narrowly focused. For instance, if you go to a location that is primarily a cabinet shop, they'll also have countertops, often flooring, and probably some plumbing fixtures. But ordinarily, the designers there will be all about laying out and detailing the cabinet arrangement. These days, they all use computers to compose the layouts, show you the pretty 3-D images, and then price and order the cabinets.

On the other hand, some kitchen and bath design specialists are not affiliated with a showroom or retailer, but remain independent. They typically will offer even more in terms of overall aid to the consumer, with a fuller set of design services.

Whichever type you choose, the most important distinction with the typical kitchen and bath designer is this: experience. Those who have done this for a number of years, who pride themselves on knowing all the details of their cabinet lines, and who stay abreast of appliance specs and trends will be far more helpful.

To call anyone with less experience and skill a "designer" is truly a misnomer. For instance, every cabinet sales location is staffed with "designers." The reality, however, is that they are really salespeople that use nifty computer software, look up the cabinets in their catalogs, and try to sell as much product as possible. This is what you'll see in most shops and home centers you visit.

Try to find a designer who has more than a few hours of training on their fancy software, as well as a rudimentary grasp of the factors affecting quality kitchen and bath designs, takes work. One way to ensure you get someone well trained and qualified is to seek and work with a certified designer.

Certified designers are people who have been instructed by national organizations that issue training courses and seminars, and which certify that their trainees meet a certain quality standard. What the designers earn through these courses is not a licensing or even a registration by the states. But it is a guarantee that the certified individual has undergone a fairly rigorous regimen of classroom training before meeting the certification criteria.

The National Kitchen and Bath Association (NKBA), founded in 1963, is the national organization that certifies kitchen and bath designers. They have over 60,000 certified members (CKBDs, Certified Kitchen and Bath Designers; or CMKBDs, Certified Master Kitchen and Bath Designers). NKBA also accredits many college and university design programs so students who graduate have a leg up on the certification process. NKBA's CKBD certification requires at least sixty hours of approved classroom education and three to five years of full-time experience, followed by passing an academic design exam.

Hence, many privately-owned kitchen and bath shops have a certified designer or two on staff. Some of the corporate shops will too, though you'll have to seek them out specifically. Some of the rest of the employees may be seeking certification, or just working as cabinet salespeople. Being a designer implies bringing both knowledge and experience together with creativity to conceive a solution that can delight and meet the basic need. The thing to keep in mind here is this: don't settle for a salesperson; seek out a certified designer, or at least a designer aspiring to become certified.

Also, be aware that in any one cabinet/kitchen shop or store the selection of brands/lines of cabinets, plumbing fixtures, appliances, and flooring offerings will be limited. Don't be surprised if a shop or designer has perhaps four or five brands, each with one or two lines of cabinets. Generally, they will have one builder or entry level cabinet brand, two or so semi-custom brands, and a couple full-custom brands. This allows them to cover the vast majority of situations a homeowner or builder client can present to them.

Just know that it's likely that your flooring, appliances, and maybe the countertops for your kitchen will come from elsewhere. For your bathroom, you'll probably order plumbing fixtures from a plumbing supply shop due to their ability to showcase more products and maintain more expertise, being a single-line shop. The same is likely the case with flooring and lighting.

While a one-stop shop for design and all the materials is a great idea, it would be impractically large and terribly expensive to bring that many products and experts together in one building. However, your certified designer should have enough expertise that when you tell them what you have in mind for flooring, tile, appliances, or fixtures, they can design with that in mind, and even help you select the perfect matches where the selections dovetail into the cabinetry.

As with architects or any other professional, you need to shop around! All people and their companies come with different philosophies, talents, personalities, etc. Only you can determine if the people you choose to hire are easy to communicate with, can see your vision, and have the expertise and easy manner necessary to help you with your project.

Tile Designers

There are no licenses or certifications for these folks. However, find a tile salesperson with many years of experience, a grasp of their lines, and who shows a talent for design, and they can help you mix and match materials, colors, sizes, and shapes into a nifty and cohesive layout for your floors, showers, or kitchen backsplashes.

When looking for a tile designer, your best bet when you walk into a larger shop is to ask for the most experienced designer they have, and see how their advice feels. There's no other way to know how good they are except to talk to them and perhaps see samples of their work (or call references).

Like the situation with cabinet designers, tile designers often work in shops that have six or eight manufacturers and a lot of individual shapes and sizes in each line. But nobody has "all tile" in their catalog or showroom. So if there's something specific that you've seen and want to consider (a particular tile size, shape, style), bring a print of it or a clear, large digital picture or web page showing it so they can help you with their most comparable tile.

Lighting Designers

High-quality lighting design enhances the architectural experience. You don't want to just settle for a fixture in the middle of each room's ceiling. Don't just let your remodeler design your lighting, and don't do it yourself.

Then who do you use? If you don't hire an architect, seek out a high-quality lighting designer with lots of experience in residential lighting at the best lighting shops. These people are not licensed, registered, or certified, so it's a crap shoot what their education, training, and experience are. But walk into a shop and ask to see their top residential lighting designer—and that should do the trick. By doing this, at least you won't get a salesperson; you'll get a talented designer who can take the plans that others have drawn for you, and enhance them.

Undoubtedly, you won't need or even like all the types of high-tech lighting that are available today. But the improved methods for lighting kitchens these days compared to just fifteen or twenty years ago are amazing. Dimmable LEDs in the 2700–3000K range are everywhere and can be used as task lighting from the ceiling, from under the cabinets, or from fixtures. The bulbs (lamps) last much longer, are cool to operate (little heat produced), and cost pennies to run even when lit all day long.

So explore the world of options open to you in a lighting showroom or design studio, and have fun!

CHAPTER 19

Relative Costs

There are some rules of thumb you can apply to the relative cost of design professionals. They go like this:

> Architects cost more for the same task than an interior designer, and both cost more than a certified specialty designer. While they are all registered or licensed or certified, architects can do more and have a broader professional skill set and therefore cost more than the others.

Within each category (architectural, interiors, and specialists), those who are licensed, certified, or registered are all costlier than those without formal education and training in those fields. The main reason you would choose an untrained, uneducated, unlicensed professional is if you know of them personally and you are convinced that their design opinion or aesthetic is perfect for your situation—and all you need is an opinion, not a complete design or set of permit plans.

However, if you need plans for the project, and if they will need to be certified in order to obtain a building permit, the architect is the only residential design specialist that can do that for you. If you hire anyone else, you'll still pay for the architect or an engineer to "seal" the permit drawings. In this case, it pays if you to hire the right professional for the project, or have them collaborate on the new structural solution with whomever else designs or draws the plans.

Additionally, design professionals can charge based on an hourly rate, a specific task, or a complete project. Which one you choose (and YOU should choose, not them) is based on the extent of work you need performed. Opinions and quick ideas are great for hourly hires. Quick hand sketches and simple designs or a few notes on materials and suppliers are examples of scope-based work, for which they will set a fixed fee. And if you need a full design, with bid or permit documents and assistance with bidding or obtaining materials or contractors for the work, that's the full monty. You will get advice, a preliminary design, some modifications, a final edited design, all necessary project drawings, and documentations—all for a set fee. Each professional will price these differently, so ASK them about their fees for various scopes of work when you first interview them.

It is important that you always know what you're getting in exchange for your payment! Get it in writing, and sign a contract with the pro you choose. The agreement should say what they are providing (design services, permit plans, documents, bid specifications, prices, etc.). And if there are to be revisions to the initial design, it should say so. The pros don't want to perform endless edits, so the language should state the limits on revisions in simple terms. If you don't understand their terms and jargon, ask for the terms to be in plain English. You must understand what you will receive in exchange for the fee you pay.

CHAPTER 20

How to Hire a Designer

It helps to know what to expect before you make the call and set up a meeting. In this chapter, I'll give you a number of tips and suggestions that will help once you decide you do want to talk to a design professional about your project.

First and foremost, you want to hire individuals and companies that have been doing this for several years. While everyone needs a first client or their first large project, you don't want your project to be their first experience. Besides, businesses that have endured for six or seven years already are past most of the difficult financial hurdles and are often well established in the community with other professionals and supply sources.

With that in mind, here are some other thoughts that will help you before you contact any designers about hiring on for your project:

- Go for the best person with the best credentials in the area of expertise that you need. If you're after help with interior color, you don't need an architect, you need someone who does walls and colors every day.
- When you need help with tile patterns or a cabinet layout, don't waste time with a higher paid generalist, go to the expert. Get the big design from the pro, then get the specific design from the specialist.
- Architects, designers, interior designers and decorators, and many specialty designers can be hired either by the hour or by the project/job/design. Whenever possible, get a full-job price quote. Make

sure it covers the design and the drawings, and the rights to use them as you see fit. Hiring designers for open-ended design (by the hour) can get VERY expensive, and you have no control over that. It helps to have some maximum price limits built in.

Before you hire ANY designer, see other designs they have done for projects similarly priced to your own. While you might not like the style or the colors—as those were the choices of other homeowners—be sure you like the cleverness and the manner of the designer you choose. Also, be sure they are tried and true. Call those former clients (more than one) and be sure that working with the designer was an easy, pleasant experience.

Pro Tip:

Nearly all design professionals offer a free initial meeting to discuss a potential project. Some will do so at your home, others at their office. Take full advantage of that time to thoroughly interview them and assess their skill and personality. Do not feel pressure to hire anyone immediately. Always sleep on it. Finally, call references and be sure they had great communication and an open working relationship with the pro you are considering.

Also keep in mind that design professionals come in all shapes, sizes, genders, and personalities. Be certain you select one with whom you can speak plainly, one who sees your vision through your eyes and is not trying to steer you in their direction. Be sure you have a good rapport with them, because two-way conversation and idea sharing are essential. And remember, there are hundreds of others who will be thrilled to work with you, so feel free to turn down anyone that is not easy to talk to or work with.

Finally, don't work on a handshake, and make sure you are very, very clear on what you're getting in exchange for the fee. Get it in writing, and sign a contract with them. If there are revisions to the initial design included, the contract should say so. Professionals don't want to have endless edits, so the language in the contract should say that in simple terms. Again, I can't stress this enough: know what you're getting.

PRO TIP:

If you need advice and not a full project design or a complete set of permit drawings, then just pay for advice! You can usually hire any of the professionals discussed here for an hour or two of consultation.

Have an architect come to your house and advise you which walls are bearing walls and need structural solutions for their removal (and which don't). Or ask them for a simple hand sketch for a possible arrangement of the addition, or the combined kitchen, eating, and dining rooms.

Once your remodeling is nearly complete, bring a decorator out to talk about finished flooring, paint colors, wallpaper, and window treatments—and do it as a consult, not a full design. One or two hours with a few notes on their suggestions and sources and brand names should answer your questions and not commit you to a large design fee with more drawings and cost than you truly require. Pay them to consult if consultation is all you really need!

CHAPTER 21

Design It Yourself

My advice on do-it-yourself design is this: DON'T. Instead, trust the professionals for a thorough and clever solution to your problem. Since professional designers do this for a living. they're simply better at solving three-dimensional problems and meeting needs than you will be.

That said, I love nothing more than having a savvy, well-informed, educated homeowner to work with. And you can become significantly more in-tune with the nuts and bolts of your project and the plight of your design professional when you measure and draw a solution for yourself. You'll get a feel for the room sizes, wall thicknesses, door and window locations, cabinet/furniture sizes, etc.

However, if you are going to draw your own solution, I'd suggest picking up a great piece of 3-D residential design software for your computer. The software I've used for about fifteen years is Chief Architect. Chief makes a fabulous, inexpensive, homeowner-friendly, easy-to-learn software that is intuitive and easy. Their software also has a thirty-day free trial (with some limitations). This software is in the Home Designer Series, and I'd suggest the Architectural version ($199 as of this printing). Other products are available, some at much lower prices, but the learning curves and complexity of the products means you'll never really get it to work — a waste of time and money.

If you do try measuring your existing home and designing a potential solution for your project, I have one overriding piece of advice: Don't drink the Kool-Aid! By that I mean, don't fall in love with your solution. It's just an exercise. For fun. Do it for the experience and knowledge to be gained. Then work with your design professional, who will design it significantly better, taking into consideration many more variables, to craft the perfect customized solution for you.

Section 5:
REMODELING PROFESSIONALS

There is no greater feeling in business than building a product which impacts people's lives in a profound way.

—ELLIOTT BISNOW

CHAPTER 22

About Remodelers

The single biggest mistake a homeowner can make is to hire the wrong remodeler. That bears repeating. **The single biggest mistake a homeowner can make is to hire the wrong remodeler.**

Doing this leads to more problems, delays, cost overruns, and project failures than all the other mistakes you can make combined. If you re-read that opening sentence, it sounds pretty obvious, right? But you might be thinking, "OK, Jim, it sounds good, but how do I avoid hiring the wrong remodeler?" That is the *perfect* question to ask, one which this section of chapters on remodeling professionals answers.

What the public does not know is that there are many various **types** of remodeling contractors. Some do large volumes of work, while others do small volumes. Some take on only specific kinds of projects. Still others have business models that make them more or less attractive for certain types of projects. Because of the numerous factors you must consider when choosing the remodeler for your project, the chapters in this section introduce the major types of remodelers and provide you with the information needed to match a remodeler type to your project.

Once you know the right type of remodeler to consider for your project, you only want to interview, and ultimately select from, the most qualified contractors of that type.

Horror Story Avoidance Tip #2:

You MUST identify and hire only the right TYPE of remodeler for your project.

Remodeling companies come in many different sizes and with many different specialties. You can't get the right results if you choose the wrong remodeler.

Pay very close attention as we cover remodeling company TYPES (Chapter 24 through Chapter 29). You will need to identify the right remodeler type(s) for your project. Only once you know the right type of contractor for your job can you start selecting home improvement companies of that type to interview and ask for proposals.

Only work with the most professional home improvement contractors possible. All contractors who do remodeling for a living are NOT all true professionals. They may all get paid to work, but not all companies perform up to a professional standard. The best remodelers make a very good living performing excellent work and making their customers happy. They have done so for a number of years, proving themselves with an excellent track record and longevity in this difficult business.

Furthermore, true professionals have a very caring approach to their work, to their customer relationships, and to the law. The remodelers you consider must all be licensed (where required by law) and insured. They must always pull the required permits for your project and obtain all required inspections. Never work with any unlicensed remodeler (where licensing is required) or anyone whose current insurance policies you have not verified. And never consider using a contractor that suggests going without a building permit or inspections when those are required.

Obviously, obtaining permits and getting inspections add some time and costs to a project. But doing so helps ensure that your remodeler is working within approved code standards. For this reason, it is wise to think of these codes as your local jurisdiction looking out for your welfare, and by extension, helping protect your investment.

CHAPTER 23

Licenses and Insurance

Remodeling Licensing

Some of you live in states or jurisdictions where remodeling contractors are NOT required to have a remodeling license. As a result, your job in verifying the quality of your prospective hires will be more difficult. You'll need to do a little extra work to verify that they are a stable company, serious about their reputation, with a long tenure in the community and a lot of happy clients.

Below is a quick rundown of the licensing requirements of all fifty states in the US, at the time of publishing:

- Twenty Eight states in the US require remodelers to obtain a state-issued license before they can perform any home-improvement work. Working on homes without a license in most of these states is a violation of the law punishable by fines and/or jail time. The licensing requirements vary by state, and you should look up your state licensing board to learn more about your state licensing requirements.

- Idaho, Iowa, New Jersey and Washington don't license home improvement contractors, but they "register" them instead. This is at the state level, and for all home improvement contractors. Registration is not as strict as licensing, but it means that the state maintains control over the industry and the practitioners. As I cautioned above, if you live in one of these states, only work with "registered" remodelers, and check them out with your state agency before inviting them to your home for an interview!

- In ten states, they do not license remodelers on the state level but do so at a local level. The jurisdiction may be a city, a county, or a town, but in order to operate legally, home improvement contractors still must to be licensed. Not all cities, counties or towns require licensing.

- Very limited local registration or licensing in selected cities and areas occurs in three states: Kentucky (Lexington/Louisville only), South Dakota, and Wyoming. Outside of the municipalities requiring registration, there is no current regulation of the industry in these states.

- Five states: Maine, New York, Oklahoma, Texas, and Wisconsin, have NO licensing or registration at the state or local level.

Unless you live in one of the five states with no licensing or registration, you should *always* call or go online to determine if your area required licensing or registration. If so, always verify that your contractor is licensed or registered, that their license number matches what they showed or told you, and that their license is current. This is your first and best method of protecting your money and your home.

Furthermore, if your state has either local or statewide licensing, DO NOT EVER work with unlicensed contractors. It is a recipe for disaster. In fact, in many cases, states that license remodelers disallow court cases brought by homeowners against unlicensed contractors, removing your legal recourse. It's seriously bad business—avoid it totally. There is no outcome that is worth taking such a huge risk with your project and your money.

Liability Insurance

All remodeling contractors need to carry liability insurance. Though claims against remodeling companies are relatively rare, when they do occur, they are usually large and significant. The liability insurance they carry protects YOU, the homeowner, if they do something that causes damage to your home or property.

Examples of such incidences could include fires or flooding due to mistakes or negligence. If the remodeler tries to remove tree limbs or trees which fall and damage your home, those go against the liability policy. If they alter the structure, causing the second floor or roof to fall or become damaged, that too is a liability issue. Even the very safest and best remodeler could make a mistake or have an accident occur. And regardless of the type of damage, your homeowner's insurance will not cover your remodeler's errors, so be certain their liability policy is in place.

In order to do this, you should ask to get a copy of their declaration sheet, which shows the legal name of the company, the address, and the policy size, among other information. Then verify that the policy covers the same company whose name is on your proposal/contract. Also verify that the policy is CURRENT (in date). If it will expire before your project is done, insist that the remodeling company get you a copy of the new policy when it renews, and then verify that it remained in force. Finally, make sure their policy has at least a $2 million total coverage. In the event there is another project going and two jobs have claims, you don't want to have the coverage amount of the policy run out paying for the other claim and leave you hanging.

Workers' Compensation Insurance

Workers' compensation insurance covers injuries to the workers of the remodeler or to the individual subs the remodeler hires to work on your project. If this policy is not in place (or current), then an injured worker can sue you and get a settlement from you personally or from your homeowner's policy. Avoid this bad situation and be certain your contractor has a current workers' comp. policy. Ask to see a copy of the current policy along with their liability policy so that you can verify their coverage.

It is also important to know that based on the number of employees and the business model of the company, some remodelers and subs are NOT required to have a workers' compensation policy. If you are told this by a remodeler you are considering, please check the regulations with state remodeling or insurance officials before agreeing to work with them. Waivers of required workers' compensation coverage usually covers only sole proprietors and other very small companies.

While on the subject of injury, do yourself a favor and remove obvious hazards before work begins, to eliminate any frivolous claims against you by an injured worker. Make sure there are no personal belongings scattered about the yard and work rooms, and that there are no obvious accidents waiting to happen.

Pro Tip:

Always ask each remodeler that you interview for the following four things:
- A copy of their remodeling license (if req'd in your state/jurisdiction)
- A copy of their liability insurance coverage
- A copy of their workers' compensation coverage
- Three referrals who have done similar projects (comparable scope or cost)

You do NOT need these delivered at your first meeting. But, if you have still not received them all by the time you are ready to review proposals and choose your remodeler, then DO NOT USE THAT REMODELER!

Homeowner's Insurance

While the contractor's liability policy protects you against remodeler negligence and accidents, and their workers' compensation policy protects against jobsite injuries, neither of those protect your home and your belongings against anything. That responsibility falls on your homeowner's policy.

One often overlooked task when people remodel is to contact their own homeowner's insurance agency. It is prudent to increase the coverage amount of your policy by the cost of the project you are performing (or at least the value-added amount of your project). The house will be more valuable when the project is completed, so, your insured value or total coverage should be adjusted up to cover your home's full new value. It might increase your premium slightly, but it could save you a tremendous amount of grief if anything went wrong.

When a project is underway, most people do not understand what materials and products are a remodeler's responsibility, and which are covered by the homeowner's policy. If the lumber piled in the driveway is stolen, who pays for it? What about cabinets or appliances in the garage? So here's a rule of thumb. Products attached to your home, in their proper, final location become your responsibility at that time. Up until then, those materials and products are covered by the contractor's insurance policy.

Pro Tip:

Contact your homeowner's insurance company and raise your policy coverage limits by the cost of your project when work begins so that you are not underinsured in case of a claim.

CHAPTER 24

Design-Build Remodelers

What Is "Design-Build" Anyway?

The term *design-build* refers to the joining together of the architectural design team with the construction team. The idea was first used in commercial construction when developers wanted to reduce the time it took to get a project designed and constructed, while remaining on-budget during the process. The huge additional benefit to them was how the cooperation between these two camps allowed the design to be estimated early and accurately and then re-estimated at all stages of re-design. This keeps the project budget in check throughout the process.

In the more traditional construction process, the architects do all their work first, get paid, and then put the construction drawings out for bids. The architects and contractor are not on the same team figuratively or literally. Traditional projects take longer to get under construction due to the linear process of designing the complete project and following that with estimating and then construction. Because of this linear process, these project designs are often significantly costlier, and the process itself is also more costly, due to paying two separate sets of professionals.

For these same reasons (a streamlined process with faster delivery coupled with a lower, more accurate cost), some larger remodeling contractors started offering design-build services to homeowners in the 1990s. And since the 2000s began, "design-build" has become the hottest marketing phrase in the remodeling industry. In fact, you can hardly look at a remodeler's advertisement or website these days that does not tout their services as design-build. So, you might wonder, is it really possible that all those remodelers are truly design-build companies, combining architectural design and construction? No. It's not.

The truth is, few of today's remodeling companies who claim to be design-build use architects to do their designs and permit drawings. And almost no so-called design-build firms have architects on staff. This begs the question: "If they are not using architects, then who is doing the designing?" And that, my friend, is precisely the question you should ask every time. Don't turn over the design of your large remodeling project to just anyone. Always make sure of their design credentials.

As a rule, architects and design-build remodelers only get involved in larger projects, since the budget for most small projects cannot support the cost of the architect's design fees. The architect gets paid regardless of how simple or how complex their involvement is, and the remodeler needs to generate enough money to pay the architect. They do this by charging design fees to the clients or by specializing only in larger, more profitable projects. Most design-build companies I know do both these things—charge fees and work on larger projects.

However, some traditional remodeling companies (discussed in detail in the next chapter) can operate as design-build remodelers by partnering with outside architects. In this way, they can offer true architectural services to their customers, without having a high-priced architect as a full-time employee. Remodelers with this arrangement always charge fees for all architectural services. But even though homeowners pay both design fees and the full remodeling price, some benefits of the design-build process remain in place. They still have a cooperative "team" concept, increased speed from the start of design through construction, and more on-budget projects.

Beware!

Like I mentioned earlier, the majority of today's "design-build" remodelers are not. Instead, they are traditional remodelers who produce medium or large projects and just use the title "design-build" to attract clients. No architect is involved in the process. Once again, the question to be asked is this: "Who does the designing if not a licensed architect?" And once again, that is the correct question to ask. The sad answer is that some unlicensed designer on the remodeler's staff, perhaps with some CAD or drafting experience, does your design and drawings. But despite the company calling themselves design-build, no architect is involved, and you are not getting true design-build services or benefits.

I cannot recommend that you use a generic remodeling company calling themselves "design-build", but which does not use an architect for their large projects. Your project design will only be as good as the talent of their "designer." And there is no way for a layman to discern this. If your planned project is large (a whole-home makeover, a multi-story addition, a new floor added above your current house, or a large addition involving multiple interior rooms), my suggestion is to either hire an architect and bid the project out or hire a design-build remodeler with a licensed architect. It's worth the price you pay to get professional design paired with top-quality remodeling experience.

Cost Implications

The cost of using a design-build remodeling company is very similar to or slightly more than that of a traditional large-project remodeling company. If the design-build company's prices are slightly higher, that is likely due to the fees charged by the licensed architect or due to a business model that results in higher overhead. Otherwise, the total price is essentially the same as other similar-sized remodelers.

If the design-build remodeling company partners with an outside architect, the fee they charge for the designs and permit drawings will be based on the architect's cost. Most times they try to make these fees more customer friendly than those you would pay when working with the architect directly. For simple design sketches or schematic ideas, the price could range from $500 to $1,500. For design and permit drawings, it might reach $2,500 to $4,000 (or more for complex projects). This is lower than what the same architect might charge for separate design. Additionally, the remodeler gets owner feedback and provides estimates of the evolving design, keeping the project closer to budget than on ordinary architect plus remodeler projects.

Furthermore, sometimes the design-build remodeler will offer pricing where some or even all of the design fee is credited against the cost of the remodeling contract. This is a win-win for the customer and the remodeler. So, if you are doing a large or complex remodeling project and are considering an architect for the design, check with some highly-rated design-build remodelers first. You should always inquire up front about their design fees (what those fees cover and who owns the rights to the design) and ask whether they credit the cost of the design against the cost of the remodeling contract.

Drawbacks

While design-build (DB) remodelers offer many advantages to their customers, there are a few drawbacks when using a DB company, of which you should be aware. These drawbacks include the following:

- **Choose Just One** – You can't get ideas, designs, and prices from several DB companies and then choose who to use for the remodeling. This is largely due to the fact that there are almost always significant design fees just to get these folks to partner with you on your project. Once you put a few thousand dollars into the design and permit drawings, it's not generally to your advantage to break the relationship and shop elsewhere. Neither is it advisable to hire two or three DBs to all provide preliminary designs and estimates and then choose which you prefer to use. The obvious reason for this is the up-front design fees and contracts necessary to get them each involved.

- **No Bidding** – Most uninformed homeowners think, hear, or read that they should get several "bids" in order to know their project is priced well. I'll deal with the accuracy of that line of thought later in the book. But the bottom line is this: you can't compare prices with the design-build model. Instead, you need to do your company investigations up front before you sign the initial design contracts and become a partner with the DB remodeler you have selected. Part of your investigation of each DB company you consider is how often their clients' projects come in near the initial budget.

- **Ownership of the Design** – Typically, even if you pay the design fees, the architect and/or the remodeler will retain the rights to the design. If this is the case, you cannot walk away from the partnership after the design and drawing phase and take the drawings and hire another remodeler to construct your project. This is a big deal since you'll have spent the design fee without the ability to use the drawings (without paying an additional amount for that privilege). My advice is to ask every DB remodeler (or their architect) about the rights to the design and drawings, as well as if your design fees provide you with ownership of the design and the right to use the drawings as you choose. Obviously, asking the question raises a red flag to the remodeler, since they fear that you are only interested in an inexpensive design and you might walk away and build the project with another company. But you need to know this information before you sign or pay anything.

PRO TIP

What do you get for your money? It's critical to know what set of design-build services and products you get in exchange for your design fees. What's more critical is finding out BEFORE you sign and pay anyone. The last section explained that you need to get the rights to use the design. That's one thing you must receive for your fees. You also need to see and understand what services and products you are buying, and see these spelled out in an agreement that you can review ahead of time. For instance, just how many design ideas or design revisions does the agreement include? You can't expect endless revisions, but you might not like the look of the first design. You may need some veto votes and revisions during the design phase, without invoking additional fees. Also, with regard to the products of the design process, do you get the typical set of permit drawings and a written specification with allowances? If their design is a Google Sketch-Up 3-D electronic model, then it does you no good—unless you use that remodeler for the construction of the project. So, in the event you do not proceed into the remodeling phase, you must know what you have bought with your design fee.

Your Best Bet

Design-build remodelers are essentially medium and large-project traditional remodeling companies that use architects for their designs. Those architects could be employees but are more likely independent professionals that partner with the remodeler for this exact scenario. If you are doing a larger, more complex, and longer duration projects, real design-build companies are probably your best bet. For example, if your project budget is $65,000 (or larger) or your project includes major modifications to the structure of your home or is a large addition, then you will be well served with the design-build remodeler. While they often do awesome kitchen and master bathroom projects, they usually do them as part of larger projects. So only contact true DB remodelers if you want the architect-designed project and have the budget for it. Or, if you're willing to pay a little more to get professional design and top notch remodeling – then this is your answer even with smaller projects. But if every dollar of a smaller budget needs to go to the actual construction, then look for other, less costly answers.

CHAPTER 25

Traditional Remodelers

Traditional remodelers make up the majority of all remodeling professionals. They'll perform a very wide range of projects, from one- or two-day duration projects up to jobs costing hundreds of thousands of dollars.

For the sake of our discussions, we'll break them down into slightly smaller groups to discuss. This will be the same way you'll consider them when the time comes to select remodeling companies to interview for your projects.

To start, remodelers can be analyzed or grouped in three main ways: by revenue, by the size of staff/number of employees, and by typical project size. Surprisingly, remodelers with the largest annual revenues are typically companies that do siding, roofing, windows, gutters, or other small projects for thousands of clients per year. However, this is of no practical value to us at this time. The size of the staff or employee base of a company likewise does not help us discern which company is worthy of consideration for your particular project needs, but this fact *will* come back into play later on. That leaves typical project size as the final distinguishing factor between typical remodeling companies.

With that in mind, and so I can help you select the right companies to consider for your project, we will break traditional remodeling companies into large, medium, and small categories for the following discussions. This means that their typical or average project will be high priced (large), medium priced (medium), or low priced (small).

Large-Project Remodelers

For this book, the distinction of "large project" will cover jobs with a price range of about $75,000 and greater. These tend to be the same "size" projects that architects may be involved in, or that design-build remodelers would also perform. In fact, when homeowners hire architects to draw complete projects, large traditional remodelers and design-build remodelers are often called on to bid on those projects. The singular difference between this large-project remodeling company and a true design-build remodeler is the lack of an architect on staff or in partnership with the company to perform designs for the clients.

As a result, their designers are often regular employees who wear other hats as well (like owner, salesperson, or production manager), so you need to beware that you cannot be sure of the design abilities, design experience, or design training of the staff of traditional remodelers. Because of this, these companies would not be your first choice when high-quality design is a critical factor for your project.

In most cases, these companies' bread and butter projects are likely involving more complex projects, often encompassing new additions along with some interior or exterior remodeling. Projects that exceed $75,000 are large projects by almost anyone's definition. But if you are considering an addition and whole-house remodel in the $250,000 range, you'll obviously want large-project remodelers with lots of experience at similar-sized jobs. (I'll spend time talking about this later when we talk about selecting the best contractor for your project.)

Now, to be clear, just because large-project remodelers do larger projects, this does not mean they are necessarily large companies. Remember, "large" refers to job size, not company size or revenue. Such a company might do one or two projects a year, but the projects are always large-budget jobs. Conversely, they could do four or five projects at a time. That is often the indication of larger company staff size and revenue. However, again, for our immediate need, it is not critical. We simply want to be able to match your project budget and complexity to the right type of remodeling contractor.

This type of remodeler, the large-project traditional remodeler, routinely works on higher cost projects than other traditional remodeling contractors. And when you're needing a more complex project constructed, you want a company that does it routinely and with great success.

Medium-Project Remodelers

Just as we used project size to define large-project remodelers, we'll do the same for medium- and small-project remodelers as well.

Let's start with medium-project remodelers. These companies typically perform projects from $30,000 to about $75,000. As a result, their project scope differs from large-project remodelers.

Medium-project remodelers don't typically perform two-story additions or whole-house remodeling projects, and seldom if ever add a new floor above an existing home. While they might do so occasionally, their bread-and-butter project is a smaller, less complex project.

For the most part, they do conventional additions with some other interior and exterior revisions thrown in. They might perform a basement finishing project complete with a bedroom, bathroom, or kitchenette. You might use them for a new bedroom suite over an existing garage. And more commonly they perform kitchen additions, kitchen remodels, and significant-sized interior remodeling projects. They will also take on multiple smaller projects in combination, done under one contract.

Small-Project Remodelers

Small-project remodelers typically work on jobs from about $5,000 to $40,000. They might work on projects such as powder rooms, hallway bath remodels, budget kitchens, screened porches, basements, and small one-room additions. These listed projects are not exclusive to small-project remodelers (both medium-project remodelers and handymen could perform some of these projects as well). It's simply that these projects routinely fall within the sweet spot in which small-project remodelers operate.

How to Differentiate Between Traditional Remodelers

In order for you to interview the best-fit remodelers for your project, you have to be able to determine their typical project size. Knowing their average project cost will allow you to select only companies that work regularly on projects with budgets like yours. And that's exactly your goal: you always want to hire a remodeling company that is a perfect match to your project.

Don't ever worry that your project is redundant or that it could fail to challenge your chosen remodeler. It absolutely *is* redundant, and it likely will not challenge them! But a remodeler with a long history of successful projects of your type should still be thrilled to perform one for you. Furthermore, the best companies already have a hundred similar projects to their credit, and they got into the remodeling business to do precisely those projects! You can rest easy knowing that they are perfectly prepared to take on your project.

Truth is, you always want to hire a company that has performed and will continue to perform the same project you want to do. Why? Because they will be the most accurate in pricing and constructing the project. They also know how to avoid the most common errors inherent in your project type. And that expertise will save you money, time, and grief, especially when compared to hiring the wrong remodeler.

So how can you determine the real "size" of a traditional remodeling company?

Of course, you can call and ask "What is your typical project size?" But if you get an answer, it's likely to be misleading. Contractors always want you to think they are bigger than they are (especially when they don't already know your project type or budget). So, you cannot depend on the accuracy of the answer to this question.

Instead, I'll give you two questions that the company WILL answer. And those two answers will allow you to determine their typical project size. Why will they answer these two questions honestly? Because these two questions give them an opportunity to brag! Remodelers love that.

Questions:
- How many projects do you perform in a typical year?
- What is your typical yearly revenue?

Once you know their annual dollar volume and their average number of projects per year, simple division tells you their average project size.

Ideally, you want to find a remodeling contractor who does your TYPE of project regularly and whose average project size is well aligned with your budget. You almost always want to avoid contractors with a smaller typical project size than yours. This becomes even more critical with larger projects and budgets. Remember that it's always better to hire a costlier specialist than to give a too-small company with less experience a project above their ordinary level. While all remodelers rely on the goodwill of homeowners to try larger projects and improve their skills, your job is not the time to let someone learn on the job. You should hire someone for whom your project is an everyday event which they can execute with predictable ease and success.

For this reason, hiring a company with a greater typical project size than your project's budget might be to your advantage if their increased skill and expertise does not add too much overhead cost to the equation. (We'll discuss how the remodeler's company structure and overhead affect you in the next section.)

But for now, remember, there are **two separate steps** in identifying a remodeler's fit with your project. First, that they truly do a LOT of projects of your type. And second, that their average project size is similar to or possibly a little above your budget size.

CHAPTER 26

Specialty Remodelers

Specialty remodelers are companies that choose to specialize in a specific portion of the remodeling industry. Here are examples of some of the more common specialty remodelers:

- Kitchen & Bath Remodelers
- Deck & Screened Porch Remodelers
- Basement Remodelers
- Landscape & Hardscape Design and Remodeling
- Pre-fab Sunroom Remodelers
- Closet & Storage Specialists
- Cabinet & Casework Specialists

Bear in mind that in this chapter I'm speaking only about remodeling companies that are specialty remodelers. Don't be confused by stores that sell these parts or pieces or provide some of these services (and may even have their own subcontractors who can install their products). Also, be aware that these specialty remodelers have all the same licenses, registrations, or certifications that their design-build and traditional remodeling counterparts are required to have. They simply work in one specific area of focus where they often have significant expertise.

For homeowners considering projects of these types, hiring a specialty remodeler could provide the best combination of expert advice or design, specific knowledge about their specialty, and lower overhead costs.

My one caution when considering a specialty remodeler for your project is this: in some cases, these companies have relationships with specific brands or suppliers of materials. So visit with them and determine which cabinet lines, appliances, and tops they may be limited to if you are planning a new kitchen. For bath projects, the cabinets, tops, tile, and plumbing fixture lines they work with may be limited. Likewise, the landscape company may use just one or two brands of pavers, lawn furniture, or lighting. Just be sure to check it out so that you are happy with your options before you sign with them or make a commitment.

If you're planning a kitchen, bathroom, or new landscape/hardscape project, you may also have the option of using a certified kitchen and bath designer or landscape architect, based on the staff personnel at the various contractors you consider. If this is a significant factor for your kitchen or master bathroom, in particular, be sure to only seek out companies with an NKBA designer on staff.

CHAPTER 27

Single-Line Remodelers

Single-line remodelers are companies that provide one service only. You hire them directly to do their "thing" for you. Essentially, they are a subcontractor to you.

The single biggest challenge with these companies will be scheduling. If you need several of these companies to come in one after another, you're really asking for schedule problems. Most of the time, general contractors have a difficult time scheduling subs that they use regularly, so you can certainly anticipate the same thing.

My second concern with some single-line contractors is that their scope and skills are so limited that they do not, or cannot, provide you with a "complete" project. For instance, a granite contractor can make and install a beautiful stone top but cannot hook up your new disposal and faucet and will not do paint touch-ups. You'll need to have those ancillary tasks performed separately. Another example is that siding contractors cannot perform any new electrical wiring changes as part of their projects. What this means is that you simply need to be aware that many single-line contractors limit their scope of work. So be sure to ask what associated tasks you will still need to perform or arrange to have performed in addition to what they will be doing.

Here are examples of some of the more common single-line remodelers:

- Gutter & downspout contractors

- Gutter covers contractors
- Siding contractors
- Roofing contractors
- Replacement window & door contractors
- Painting contractors
- Carpet/flooring installation contractors
- Granite/countertop contractors
- Basement waterproofing contractors

Unlike all other remodeling contractors, these companies are not all required to be licensed or registered remodeling contractors (in areas with licensing and registration). So it becomes your role to check out their reputation and past performance even more thoroughly so that you only hire providers with the very best references and record of performance.

CHAPTER 28

Handymen

It is important to explain here the distinction between handymen and small traditional remodelers. It is a duration- and complexity-based difference.

Handymen typically specialize in repairs and short-duration projects that require just a few hours, or at most a few days to complete. They perform tasks that you cannot perform yourself (be it a lack of skills or lack of time).

Think of handymen as "honey-do-list" specialists and you won't be far off.

Projects around the house that you might call a handyman for include the following:
- All types of small physical repairs to the home
- Honey-do-list items of all kinds
- Minor drywall work or repairs
- Painting touch-ups, small paint jobs
- Installing a new door or storm door
- Changing locks or door hardware
- Adding or replacing skylights

Just remember, if you live in a jurisdiction with licensing or registration of remodeling contractors, please be certain any handyman that you hire is in compliance.

It is also important to know that when working with handymen, problems in understanding the scope of work are very common. To avoid these, you should prepare a clear Project Packet, and also insist on a written or typed scope of work along with the contract you sign. Never accept verbal prices without documentation. Always work with a contract so you have that degree of protection.

CHAPTER 29

Others

There are a handful of "others" who could potentially cross your mind with regard to remodeling projects.

These might include:
- Carpenters who moonlight
- Friends and neighbors
- Family members
- Friends of friends
- You

My simple advice to you in all these cases is this: don't do it. If you want professional results and the value that comes with them, then please hire the right professional. Having a truck and a hammer or a cell phone and business card does not make people professional remodeling contractors, so unless you're having someone make you a doghouse or birdhouse, just say no to this option. Use only appropriate professionals, whom we have already reviewed.

Trust me when I say, it will cost you FAR MORE to start a project with the wrong person or company and then complete it with the right company than it would have to hire the very best pro the first time.

And if you plan to do it yourself, prepare to take at least twice as long and spend three times what you think it will cost. Besides, spouses have a very limited tolerance for errors and incomplete projects.

Section 6:
HOW TO INTERVIEW REMODELERS

You can't get the right results if you choose the wrong remodeler.

—JIM MOLINELLI

Choosing the right remodelers to interview is vitally important if you want a successful project. Then, only the best of those companies you interview should provide you with proposals.

Obviously, you should only choose remodelers that perfectly fit the type and cost of project you are planning. And a contractor must check all the boxes in order to make it onto your interview list. But which boxes must they check?

CHAPTER 30

Only Interview the Very Best

If you want the best results, you'll want to choose from the best remodelers. And the best remodelers differ for every project and every situation. But one thing is constant: to have an opportunity to select the very best company for your project, they need to be in the mix. So be sure to select the most highly qualified home improvement contractors to interview. Doing so makes it easier to get a great fit later on.

As you prepare to invite remodelers to come to your home and interview with you about your project, there are a number of factors you need to consider before you can confirm a company as an interview candidate.

Licensed or Certified Remodelers Only

If your state, city, or jurisdiction licenses or certifies home improvement contractors, then only work with those who provide you with proof of their current license or certification. Additionally, if there is a licensing body, it behooves you to visit them online or make a call to verify that any contractor you are considering is, in fact, licensed. Don't risk your project with a company that avoids the most fundamental requirements of the profession. [See Appendix 3 for information about remodeling licensing by state].

Experienced Only Need Apply

While every company and every business owner needs a break to move up and try their first project of a particular size or type, I suggest you let them learn on someone else's dime. Don't let your house and your project be the learning ground for anyone. Only choose experienced remodelers. Make certain they have been in business six to seven years or more so they have proved to be financially stable. Also, verify that they have done an extensive number of projects of the same type as yours (bathroom, kitchen, major addition, basement, etc.). Of course, you will explore this further during your interviews, and afterward with their references. But make sure they meet with your approval on this count before you place them on the list of invitees.

Do They Specialize in Your Project Type?

It's essential that the remodelers you choose do numerous projects of the same type as yours. If you're doing an addition with a master bathroom in it, they need to do a lot of master baths and similar-sized additions. Same with kitchen remodels, or basements, or whole-home remodeling. Whatever you are getting ready to do, you only want to talk to companies that do what you need and do it often. You should see evidence of it on their website or their advertising, verify it when you first call, and then verify it again in person when you interview them. This is critical.

Match Their Average Project Size with Your Project

Once you can verify that a remodeler does enough projects of the same type as yours to be considered a specialist at them, you want to make sure their average project size matches your project size. Early on we prepared the Project Packet, and one key element of this is your Budget, which has been tempered by all your project requirements, your availability of funds, and the real-world cost of similar projects. Using this number, you need to determine the typical project size for each company you invite to interview, as I instructed in chapter 25.

While I nestled the explanation of average project size in the section on traditional remodelers, it applies to ANY remodeling company. You want your project size and theirs to be very close. A mismatch with a company whose average project size is SMALLER than your own is a recipe for disaster and to be avoided. A mismatch with a company that has a much larger average project size than your own is to your advantage in terms of getting a skilled set of craftsmen, but it's also likely their margins are higher than those of a well-matched company.

Bear in mind that an average project size is comprised of many jobs. Some will be smaller than the average, and some larger than average. Some firms have more projects in their average, some have fewer. An average price is not a precise figure. You may find that a reasonable range includes prices within 10 to 15 percent of your budget.

My advice to you is to do your level best to find a company with a lot of projects like yours and a lot of projects in the same price range as yours. If they have checked off these boxes in addition to the couple listed previously, they're the kind of remodeler you will probably invite for an interview.

Explore Unique Circumstances Early

If you have unique circumstances or needs that may rule out some companies, it's best to find out as soon as possible. Since unique circumstances are, well, unique, I can't possibly explain them all, but I will give a few examples.

One example would be if you wish to use the direct-pay option (where you pay subcontractors directly with your checkbook or credit card) for your project. In this case, you should investigate that option with the company's salesman before setting an appointment, and then review it again during the interview so everyone is clear. Another example would be that your schedule has unique deadlines that affect the start or end of a project (a wedding being hosted in the backyard next summer, old friends visiting for two weeks from Germany, you're all away on vacation for a month, you need to live in the house and stage the project in two distinct phases). These types of situations would need to be discussed in advance, and again in the interview.

Another unique condition would be if you have a friend or family member who owns a company that you want to participate in the project as a subcontractor (because they are giving you a "deal"). In this case, you must be sure that the remodelers that you select to interview will work with your relative. Some may not. Many spend years cultivating relationships with their subs and don't want to work with anyone else. They also have no control over your buddy or brother-in-law as far as scheduling and quality go.

If you need your remodeler to pause mid-project to allow YOU to perform a phase of the project, you MUST get that approved in advance. Messing with the schedule, especially in a non-skilled, open-ended time frame, could well eliminate a lot of your best choices—so pick and choose your unique circumstances carefully.

These are just a few examples that can guide you. But if you have these or any other unusual needs or requests, you will want to call or drop by the remodeling company's office to ask in advance. It's best to find out early if your special needs are a problem that precludes you from working together, before wasting everyone's time.

Compile a Short List of Candidates

Regardless of the source of the remodeling companies you start investigating as potential interviewees for your project, you want to get to a manageable number. An interview could take you one to two hours with the introduction and review of your Project Packet and your questions for each representative. They too will want to ask you questions, see your project location, and perhaps take photos and measurements, so you don't want to invite too many companies to participate. It's easier to select your highest regarded three or four firms and hold interviews with them first. This will limit the amount of time you need to take away from your routine in order to meet these folks.

Also, if at any time, for any reason, you learn information about a company that means you no longer wish to consider them, you should tell them right away. "Thank you for coming out to meet with me about our upcoming project. For a number of reasons, I do not think your company will be a good fit for our project. I do appreciate you taking the time to meet with me," will suffice. There is no need to complete the entire interview if you know there is not a good fit. There are dozens of excellent remodelers that will be thrilled to work with you. Just call another good candidate and move ahead.

I'd suggest that you get two to four proposals. You can get more if you wish to invest that extra amount of time to interview and vet them. And certainly, having more prices from well-qualified companies can help establish the "right price" for your project (disregard the high and low proposal prices and see where the majority of those remaining fall—that's the "right price").

Now that you have a short list of interviewees whom you'll invite to your home, and assuming that your Project Packet is complete and ready to go, it's finally time to set up those interviews. Contact the top few companies on your list of vetted remodelers and ask them to set appointments to meet with you and discuss your project.

Remember, in a design-build situation, you cannot get the proper design-build experience if you ask them to "bid" projects (if they even honor that request). DB companies typically charge a design fee up front to come up with a solution using an architect, so you need to partner with one firm and go through the process with them as a team. However, you should meet with and interview three or four, until you find the ideal fit of architect and remodeler with your project needs. Then saddle up and go with the best one.

Now you know how to select the best remodeling companies to interview.

The next chapter introduces the best collection of cost-saving measures I know. You may want to use one or more of these methods to help reduce the cost of your project. And be sure to have your mind made up on these options prior to meeting your remodelers so that you can discuss them in person!

CHAPTER 31

Controlling Costs

In remodeling, the old adage definitely applies: you can choose any two of the following attributes: quality, cost, or duration.

Of course, everyone wants to pay the lowest amount possible and get the best job possible. The problem is that only an industry-savvy person can discern what is truly the least possible amount and best possible outcome in any given situation. What I recommend when doing a remodel is that you should look to spend the least amount *necessary*.

Buying on price is the third most common reason for remodeling project stress and failure. There is always a reason that the lowest price is the lowest price. In my experience, you don't want to learn about that in a first-hand manner. In fact, perhaps the other old adage is *most* appropriate in remodeling: you get what you pay for.

In this chapter, I show you the best ways to reduce the cost of the project. Additionally, I will explain how to minimize the variability of prices from different remodelers in a bid situation. These suggestions will not make the companies you select and interview offer you identical prices, but they will result in a lower and more comparable set prices.

Horror Story Avoidance Tip #3:

<u>NEVER</u> choose your remodeler based on the lowest price!

There is only one scenario when this could possibly work out OK. If you select three or more fabulous remodelers with remarkable reputations and perfect track records, and they are all the perfect type and size for your project, and then if every single proposal price you receive comes out within 10% of one another—then you can select the low-cost company. Otherwise toss out the low-price option. The risk of going low-price is **not** worth the minute savings over the correct priced proposal.

You get what you pay for. In this case protect your home and your family and pay for the best company. Cheap contractors are **not** how you save money.

Always Use Allowances

In all mid-size and larger projects, you want to control costs using allowances. In simple terms, allowances are little piles of money that the remodeler will set aside within the estimated contract price to buy items or services used in the performance of your project. Allowances can be used for a myriad of items or services. Some of the most common ones are listed below:

- Cabinets
- Countertops
- Appliances
- Light fixtures
- Plumbing fixtures
- Flooring materials
- Tile
- Exterior doors & windows
- Electrician costs
- Plumber costs
- HVAC costs
- Specialty features (cable railings, fireplaces, etc.)

The simplest thing you can do to help hold your costs down and get valuable feedback about the remodelers you receive proposals from is to have them all declare the allowance figures for all these items being used in your project. Why will this help you? Let's take a look.

In the absence of guidance from you, the price each company gives you will include a different amount of funds for the purchase of those items and services. Some companies will want to minimize those figures so that they also minimize the bottom-line cost and look more attractive to homeowners shopping based on price alone. Other remodelers will include larger amounts for cabinets, tops, and flooring so that you get a better-quality selection or higher-cost choices for your significant selections. But if you don't know what amounts were set aside, you would never know that the lower priced proposal did not include enough money to purchase the items you want and that the higher priced option accounted for those selections adequately.

When you ask remodeling contractors to declare the allowances included in their proposed prices, you can see who is allotting more and who is allotting less for the different allowance items included. This helps eliminate many of the problems associated with the lower bids. Owners who sign a low-priced contract only to find out later that there was not enough money set aside to buy the cabinets and tops they desire, have no choice but to pull out the checkbook and pay additional costs mid-project. What happens if you have no more to spend? Or if the bank loan does not cover the additional expenses? In a case like this, you're stuck, and you are at the mercy of the contractor, who can now charge extra for everything you "add" to the contract. You may find yourself in an impossible situation if you sign a contract without having the allowance amounts declared.

When all your bidders declare their included allowance amounts, you can easily see what the spread of allowed costs is. And you can follow up and ask, "Why are your cabinet and top allowances so low?" or "Can you show me what brand and line of cabinets that allowance will purchase?" You can also ask about seemingly higher allowances. This gives you a chance to learn about and manage costs BEFORE ever selecting the final contractor and signing a contract.

When you use allowances, you limit the most variable expenses of the project, and you will often find that the remaining expenses should be reasonably similar across the board. In other words, the actual cost of materials and labor to perform the project should be quite similar from one company to the next. The same is true for their cost of other subcontractors. Consider the following table.

	Townhouse Kitchen Remodel		
	Estimate #1	Estimate #2	Estimate #3
Materials and Labor	$6,610	$6,610	$6,610
Overhead & Profit	$11,047	$12,694	$14,636
Allowance Items	$13,500	$16,470	$20,000
Total Proposed Cost	$31,157	$35,774	$41,246

This table shows the identical small townhouse Kitchen with a small island. The ONLY difference in these three prices are the three different allowance levels. The cost of the cabinets, countertops, and hardwood flooring were priced at modest, average and slightly upscale levels in the three proposals. The large variation in the total cost illustrates how dramatically a few line items change what the homeowner sees from different companies. Knowing what allowances were included in a proposal, you can do a little math to normalize the proposals. If you add $3,000 plus 50% markup to #1, and subtract $3,500 plus 50% markup from #3, you find out that these three different proposals are nearly identical. But if all you ever saw was the Total cost, you would **never** think these proposals could be equivalent. This is why you should always insist that allowances be used and declared in every remodeling proposal you accept.

When you normalize prices this way in the real world, they will seldom be identical. But after adjusting for allowances, you can learn a lot! The price difference after adjusting is almost exclusively due to the different markup (overhead plus profit) for each company.

All businesses cover costs like rent, phones, utilities, vehicles, advertising, insurance, employee benefits, administrative salaries and other non-project related costs by charging overhead. Overhead is added on top of all labor, material and subcontractor costs within your contract. Typically, small companies have small overhead expenses and large ones have larger overhead expenses.

Every item or service that is included in a remodeling proposal (or contract) also includes a markup that is comprised of the remodeler's overhead expenses plus their profit margin. A company with larger overhead will always cost more for the very same project than a low overhead company.

Adjusting for allowances lets you see the markup differences of the bidders in dollars. It's a nice piece of information to have. But based on my explanation and your observations of each remodeler's advertising, website, vehicles, specialty employees, office/showrooms, etc., you probably could surmise this already. This last calculation simply confirms it.

A significant additional pricing benefit can be gained when using allowances if you simply declare to the bidders, "I want you to use the following allowances in preparing your proposals" (and then give them a list of allowance figures to use when estimating). When all your bidders use the exact same allowance figures those items and services, it equalizes the single biggest price variable between proposals (eliminating too-high and too-low allowances). It also stabilizes their markups. Since a markup is charged on every dollar included in an estimate, reducing the values used in the estimate also reduces markup costs by the same percentage. This practice will limit the normally large variability in total markup as you saw in the prior example.

Taking this to the extreme, if you told everyone to allow just $1,000 for new cabinets and $1,000 for new countertops (figures that are absurdly low), what have you done? You have reduced the allowance figures of a typical kitchen by perhaps ten to fifteen thousand dollars, and also limited the amount of markup included. This lowers your contractor-based costs to a much lower total figure. Just be aware that when you do this, YOU are still responsible for paying the additional costs between the allowed amounts and the real-life price of cabinets and tops (or whatever allowance category you might set limits on). But if you are self-funding your project, this is very much in your favor. With some bank loans, this might not be possible. It only works when the homeowner has control over disbursement of funds.

Other Cost-Cutting Options

Once again, before you invite remodelers to your home and ask them for proposals, you have the following four cost-cutting options to consider employing to help you reduce your total project cost.

Remove It from the Contract

Identify anything you can arrange yourself, with little or no expertise required, and remove these things from the scope of work. "What?" you might ask. Let me explain . . .

If you are comfortable going to Sears, Home Depot, Lowes, or any other local appliance shop and signing an agreement to purchase your own appliances for the kitchen remodel, then why pay your contractor extra to do it for you? In some cases the contractor discount on an item type (like cabinets) is so large, and the fact that they have a strong working relationship with the supplier is so important, that you should use their vendor for your purchase and keep it in the contract scope.

But the discount cost to the remodeler for buying most appliances, carpets, light fixtures, bathroom accessories, etc., is so small as to be nonexistent. And their markups are from 20 percent to 60 percent, so it is to your advantage to remove those product costs from the contract for net savings to you. Besides, the local carpet shop or appliance dealer is usually set up specifically to work with homeowners, and provide free delivery and installation. As a result, you can almost totally eliminate markup and profit on all appliances and carpets in your project. In modest kitchens, that may save $1,000, while in upscale kitchens, you could save up to $15,000 or more. Why pay your remodeler to "sell" you products that the vendor is happy to sell you directly? Keep in mind this is ONLY for products and services where a working relationship between the vendor and the remodeler is not required.

For services like painting, tile installation, electric, plumbing, HVAC, or hardwood flooring, your contractor knows the subs and suppliers well and has relationships that should allow them to control the schedule and any callbacks much more easily than you could manage. Leave coordination of the professionals to the professionals.

Supply It Yourself

There are a number of things that you can and should simply supply yourself. These things are almost all taste-driven choices that are required in your project but play a significant part in the final look you are trying to achieve.

In most of these cases I suggest that you inform your remodeler prospects that you intend to purchase and supply the following items for them to install:
- Cabinet knobs/pulls/handles
- Framed mirrors at vanities (not plate-glass mirrors)
- Bathroom accessories: towel bars, paper holder, robe hook, etc.
- Ceiling mounted light fixtures (NOT recessed, in-ceiling items)
- Ceiling fans
- Wall-mounted lights (vanity, sconces, or exit door lights)

This is not done for cost savings, but because it gives you complete control of the final look that you desire. All these choices are taste-driven, and your impression is the most important one. Besides, architects and remodelers are never right. If they allow $200 for a fixture you would spend $110 on, you think they are driving up the price. If they only allow $50 for an item that you would spend $150 for, you think that they are low-balling you. And if they buy a light fixture or mirror for you, there's no doubt it would not be the one that you would have selected!

In short, though these expenses are often a small figure, perhaps in the hundreds of dollars, they make a large impact on the final look of the project. So buy these items yourself, supply them or have them delivered to the house, and have them installed by your chosen remodeler.

Do It Yourself

If there are portions of the work that you really want to do yourself, and for which you have the skill set and experience, then you can inform your prospective bidders that you intend to perform these services.

In my experience, the only service that owners have performed successfully was painting. This does NOT require years of training to do, and it can save hundreds to multiple thousands of dollars based on the size of your project. If you (perhaps with a group of friends) buy all the paint and supplies required, along with some pizza and drinks, you can paint an entire project in an evening or a weekend. Whether you rent the finest equipment available (talk to the nearest professional paint/paint supply store) or do it by hand with brushes and rollers, there are great savings to be had.

Pro Tip:

Paint before the finished floor is in place whenever possible. You don't want to risk spills or drips on your new hardwood, tile, or carpet if it can be avoided.

Pro Tip:

Paint kitchens before the cabinets are placed. You can get a prime coat and one or two finish coats in quickly and easily without having to worry about those thousands of dollars of cabinets you might scratch or drip on. After the cabinets and tops are installed, all you have is a few touch-ups that can often be done (carefully) with a brush and a steady hand.

One thing people always ask if they can do to save money is demolition. Why? I think it's because busting walls, cabinets, and floors with a sledgehammer is fun. At least it looks that way on TV, right?

But the real cost of demolition is not in the busting of walls and cabinets. It's in the back-breaking work of hauling the bits and debris out of the house and getting it to the dump. If you're not prepared to clean up and dispose of all the debris, then doing the demolition is not a way to save costs or time. And most importantly, when you're taking apart walls, ceilings, etc., you probably don't have the skills to deal with the plumbing and electrical services in many of the rooms we remodel, so don't touch those. Please leave that for the pros.

Besides, the company you hire does this for a living. They'll do it faster, better, and cheaper than you can.

Finally, it's not in your best interest to "do" part of the actual work yourself. Many contractors don't want the customer (or their friend, family member, or coworker) providing integral services in the middle of the contract. It's a recipe for disaster. If "you know a guy" and want to get "a deal" on a particular phase of your project, my advice is this: don't do it. But if you insist, then alert all the remodelers you interview about your intention to do such-and-such a phase yourself or to have so-and-so do that phase. At least your early disclosure prior to their estimating and proposal writing allows them to adjust the schedule and cover the contingencies. It's always better to ask permission in this case. Never spring a surprise like this on your remodeler after the contract is signed, or you could be in for a difficult time.

Direct-Pay Option

This option is only applicable if you are self-funding the project (you, not a bank, are making all payments). It also requires the cooperation of your remodeling contractor. It MUST be brought to their attention early in the interview process in the event that they choose not to participate. That could mean finding another firm to interview if anyone is hesitant to allow this option.

I first used the direct-pay option with clients during the economic downturn, in an effort to be much more cost-competitive and to stay busy. Customers loved it for reasons you'll understand in a moment. I kept signing customers, and they got a top-quality company at a much more affordable price.

This option is the single biggest cost savings advice I can offer you, and it is without risk. In fact, this tip will not alter the quality or the look of your project one iota, but could save you five, ten, fifteen thousand dollars or more on an upscale kitchen remodel, a large addition, or a major remodel.

The direct-pay option works like this. You ask your remodeler to obtain prices, quotes, and bids from their regular vendors and subcontractors for some of the following big-ticket items:

- Hardwood or tile materials
- Cabinets
- Countertops
- Plumbing fixtures
- Exterior doors
- New windows
- Electrician (materials and labor)
- HVAC (materials and labor)
- Plumber (materials and labor)

And you let the remodeler know that you intend to pay their vendors or subcontractors directly (instead of you paying the remodeler and them paying the vendor). The remodeler presents you with the price quote, invoice, or bid from their sources, and you use your checkbook or your credit card to immediately pay the costs.

Because you agree to work with their regular vendors and subcontractors, your contractor knows that they can maintain input and control over the orders, the schedule, and the quality. However, when using this option, you should also suggest to your remodelers (or expect them to suggest to you) that they place a 10 percent markup on the list of direct-pay expenses as a management fee to offset their time obtaining pricing and ordering the DP items on your behalf.

How will this benefit you? The largest benefit is a significant cost savings. With the total cost of the list of direct-pay items and services out of your contract, your savings are approximately equal to the overhead percentage of the remodeler. Smaller remodelers with lower overhead (20 to 25 percent) result in slightly less savings to you, while larger remodelers (overheads from 30 to 60 percent) would result in much larger savings. So, doing this with upscale and large projects through design-build and large traditional remodelers could result in very large savings. How large? The combined cost of just semi-custom cabinets and stone tops in a nice kitchen could cost $20,000. This means your savings could be $6,000 at a 30 percent markup or $10,000 at a 50 percent markup. The cost of doors and windows, HVAC, plumber, and electrician could also easily hit $20,000 to $40,000 or more on large projects, meaning additional direct-pay savings of up to $20,000 if you use higher overhead remodelers.

There is a second significant benefit of using the direct-pay option. As mentioned earlier (when I told you about signature loans), using your credit cards to pay for remodeling expenses has its privileges. You not only enjoy the direct-pay overhead savings outlined above, but you reap the benefits of the card you use to make those payments (cash back, airline miles, or points). You actually save on the initial contract, then again whenever you make your direct-pay payments using your card! Just be certain that you pay off the entire balance of that card monthly to avoid the high interest charges.

If this direct-pay option is something you desire to use for your project, then you should only obtain proposals from remodelers who are willing to cooperate with you. The only way to find out who will agree to do the direct-pay option is to ask them. So be certain to bring it up during your initial interviews. I think it's an important item to place in the introduction of your Project Packet as well so they cannot misunderstand your intention.

While the direct-pay option sounds very one-sided in favor of the homeowner (it really does offer very large price breaks to those who use it), there are some benefits to the remodeler too. First, the involved subs and suppliers get paid immediately by you. Typically, they invoice the contractor about thirty days after service and get paid another thirty days after that. And let's face it, the remodeler has a few less bills and payments to worry about! Second, remodelers who employ this option often make more sales by remaining more price competitive. And, they also lower their income taxes and their insurance fees slightly (both of which are based on the total dollars of revenue through the company). Don't get me wrong, the homeowner benefit is huge by comparison. But if it means making the sale and getting a project or losing the sale to a company that will cooperate, many remodelers will agree to work with and use this option. Just be sure they know about it up front. **Never** spring this on a contractor as a last-minute suggestion.

Pro Tip:

For projects where you control the payments (not the bank), you should attempt to use the Direct-Pay Option (DP) with your remodeler. In these cases, the contractor lets you pay for selected big-ticket items, subs, and materials directly to their regular vendors. When you do this you receive reduced or eliminated overhead (markup) on the DP products and services, allowing you some substantial savings.

For the contractor, this is better than the almost certain disaster if you insisted on buying and supply the parts and pieces on your own. The Direct-Pay Option allows the contractor to maintain control of the orders, performance, schedules, etc. And they are always more comfortable working with suppliers and subs they use regularly. Your major benefits are substantial savings and trade pricing.

Frankly, it would be a real mess if you tried to arrange all these purchases and deliveries on your own. Instead of you trying to purchase doors, windows, cabinets, tops, flooring, tile, or plumbing fixtures; and instead of finding your own electrician, plumber, painter and HVAC company; let the pros arrange the deals, and you simply pay directly and save.

And remember to use your credit card whenever possible on these purchases to get a double benefit: card rewards (cash back, points or miles).

Buying and Supplying Your Own Materials

For myriad reasons, I don't recommend you do this because you simply don't have the same number and quality of contacts and sources that your remodeler has. You don't work with the vendors regularly so that you can get immediate help and cooperation when needed. You also don't get trade pricing like your contractors receive.

I suggest using your remodeler's regular suppliers, vendors and subs whenever possible. Take all the help and guidance their trade partners have to offer. Not to mention the cost discounts.

Ignore "price clubs", outlets and bargain stores. The quality never compares with the lines and products at your remodeler's regular vendors. And when something happens mid-project, you want them to make the calls and solve the problem. God forbid if your cabinet order was wrong, or a critical part was missing and work stops 3-4 weeks while parts have to be tracked down.

I've shown you many ways to save money without affecting the quality of the end product. Don't gamble on cheap products or vendors. Don't compromise on the quality of your results. You get what you pay for.

Remember: Price, Quality, Duration. You can choose any two.

CHAPTER 32

Prepare to Interview

This chapter should be a review and serve as a final checklist for you to make sure you are ready to meet with prospective remodelers to discuss your project and request a proposal.

Here are several important reminders:

- Only work with professionals (licensed, permit using, highest quality).
- Only work with established firms (six–seven years or more in business).
- Only work with insured firms (liability and workers' comp).
- Select the right type of remodeling company for your job and budget.
- Select only remodelers whose average project size is similar to your budget figure.
- Interview only remodelers who regularly perform your project type.

If each company you are ready to interview ticks all the items in the list above, you are choosing from an elite group of remodelers. Now it's a question of interviewing them to determine the nuances of how each company operates, how they look at your project from their perspective, and how they accept and assimilate your Project Packet (including the budget).

WHAT TO ANTICIPATE

The answers to the questions you ask, the interest they show in working with you on your project, and the quality of rapport you have with them during your meeting will help you choose the one or two companies with whom you would prefer to work.

Look for enthusiasm from them about your project and your preparedness. Look for their professionalism in the questions they ask you so they can better "see" your vision for the project. Also, evaluate an overall feeling from their salesperson or designer. Will you be comfortable working diligently with them on the small details of your project? Were they interested in YOUR opinion and answers? Or were they more intent upon telling you how wonderful they are and how easily they can handle your project?

It's not uncommon for homeowners to rule out one or two of their four initial interview prospects because they were made to feel insignificant. Or perhaps they failed to get a warm, fuzzy vibe from a remodeler's representative. Or maybe the personality of their salesperson was just odd. Their rep might have arrived late and been unapologetic or seemed impatient to be done and get going. Sometimes you can't even articulate precisely why someone impressed you or failed to impress you. But what you need to keep in mind is that the simple goal of each interview is this: you want to decide whether you would sign an agreement with that company if the design and price work out well. If the answer is "yes," then you await their proposal and look forward to their presentation.

After a remodeler has designed and estimated a solution for you, it's probable that they will want to sit down again and show you the solution while selling you on hiring their company. That second visit is an additional one- to two-hour time investment. I suggest you only have them return if you would hire them (assuming a clever design and an acceptable price tag). Don't waste more time on candidates that you are not willing to hire.

The truth is, there are dozens more companies that would be thrilled for the opportunity to work with you. Be willing to "toss aside" companies who leave you with an awkward or negative feeling!

PRO TIP:

Be the Boss! (With a capital B.) Sit behind your massive imaginary desk while you hold your new employee interviews. Review with each applicant the required job qualifications (from your Project Packet items) and the price you wish to pay (Budget). **Ask them to explain why you should hire them. Ask them to explain why they are the best option for your project.**

Your goal is to obtain proposals from the best-qualified candidates only. It's simple really: Are they truly qualified? Do they impress you? Would you like to work with them if their design is good and their price is fair? You've got this, Boss!

Pre-Interview Checklist

Make sure the following items are fully prepared and ready to go before your interviews begin:

- Project Packet is printed and complete:
    - Brief description
    - Need List
    - Wish List
    - Budget (with any limiting factors/loan info)
    - Room x Room Description Table(s)
    - Plot Plan
    - Already made selections (finishes, cabinets, appliances)
- You have vetted each company you will interview:
    - Licensed/registered (if required)
    - In business at least six to seven years
    - Full liability insurance ($1 million or more per event)
    - Workers' comp insurance (if required for each company)
    - You know their average project size
    - You know how often they perform your type of project

If you are ready, call and schedule those appointments, Boss!

CHAPTER 33

The Interviews

You're now scheduled to meet the representative of your selected remodelers (the salesperson or architect) at your home for the first time. Your pre-qualifications are complete, and your Project Packet is ready to hand out.

Now there's just one thing to focus on: the initial interview meeting and the questions you need to get answered from each remodeler who's applying for your job!

Obviously, you'll introduce yourself, and they'll do the same. But rather than traipsing from room to room showing them the rooms to be remodeled, I suggest that you sit and discuss the project first.

Here are some suggested agenda items for your first meeting:
- Sit and introduce your project.
- Present your Project Packet.
- Give your elevator pitch description.
- Review the Need List, clarifying anything unclear.
- Review the Wish List, clarifying anything unclear.
- Present your budget. "I'm able and willing to pay up to $XX,XXX to accomplish my Need List with a creative solution." And if your budget is FIRM, please make that very clear.
- If a loan is involved, tell them about that now.

- Discuss their company's method of payments (including payment size and typical payment scheduling).
- Review the Room by Room Description Table.
- Review any other project selections you've made.
- Include your plot plan.
- Ask questions:
    o Employees or subcontracted crews?
    o How many employees? Overhead only employees?
    o What subs do they use in projects like yours?
    o What hours/days do they work?
    o How long from signing a contract to starting work?
    o Provide proof of insurance (liability + Workers' Comp).
    o Provide several similar job referrals.
    o Arrange a jobsite visit (current client).
    o How many jobs run at one time?
    o How many jobs per year?
    o How much total remodeling revenue last year?
    o Have you ever been to court or arbitration? What were the circumstances?
    o Who are my points of contact when the project is underway?
    o How do we communicate during construction?
    o If changes arise, how are they handled? Are there administrative charges for *change orders* during the process?

If your state has contractor licensing or registration, there may also be a licensing agency that offers some consumer protection benefits. You could find out if they log official complaints against remodelers or if they mitigate disputes between owners and remodelers. It's also common that many states and jurisdictions have advice for consumers when hiring local remodelers.

If you find your state or local website that a company you are considering has a complaint against them (or a negative review on Angie's List or another reputable remodeling site), now is your chance to ask about the circumstances of that complaint so you can learn about how it was resolved. A poor review or a complaint is just a red flag to ask a question, not a reason to eliminate an otherwise good candidate from consideration. However, multiple substantiated complaints or a number of very poor reviews would probably rule out using a particular company.

At any time after the initial knock on the door by your prospective remodeler, feel free to ask them about the other personnel in the company and the roles they all hold, emphasizing the ones you might interact with. Always feel free to ask to meet any other personnel, including the owner, if that would make you more comfortable with choosing that particular company.

After your Q&A session, your interviewee will need to see the room or rooms where the work will take place. Take them into the areas of the work to see the scope of the project. You should also be prepared to show them the main electrical panel, the main water supply shut-off valve for the home, and the main waste line (the latter two if a bathroom or kitchen is involved). If they need to look at your furnace or AC equipment, they will ask you (be prepared if your project involves an addition or new HVAC equipment.)

As mentioned, they will need to photograph and measure the rooms and areas where the work will take place (including the outdoor areas for any additions that are planned as part of the project). You'll want to make sure the areas to be visited are easy to walk through and free of major clutter and obstacles.

The final moments of the interview are also very important. You must make it clear that they can email or call if anything in the Project Packet needs further clarification. I suggest asking a question like this: "Now that you've seen my Packet and seen the room(s) and had a little time to consider the project, what is your opinion about the proposed budget for the scope of work I have requested?"

This answer will give you their gut feeling for the adequacy of your budget based on the scope and on their experience. If they are already certain you asked for too much, they'll say so now. If they honestly believe they can perform for your budget, they'll also let you know that. Don't CHANGE anything at all based on their answer. This was so that you get a feel for each company you ask for a proposal.

Your final questions of the day are these: "How long will it take you to design a solution and prepare your proposal?" and "When will I hear from you again and receive your proposal?"

If you're a detail-minded person, you can email each rep after they have visited and thank them for coming out and spending time with you discussing your project. You can let them know how excited you are about the project, and close with something like this: "And we look forward to meeting with you again _____ to review the design and the pricing." You simply fill in the blank with the date or time frame that they told you would be needed to get your price and proposal ready.

If You Use Architect + Remodeler

If you used an architect to prepare designs and drawings in advance, then you only need to present those items to your bidders when they visit. You still ask about their companies and subs, workers, and other details listed above, but there will be no measuring and no need to design a solution. They will only need time to prepare the estimate and get you a proposal. That process might even be handled by your architect in some cases.

As you may have noticed, the process is a little more streamlined in the architect + remodeler model. You'll simply wait to get all the bids back and won't have to review the various design options, since you did that with your architect in advance.

If You Use Design-Build

Once again, you'll hold an in-depth Q&A interview with each firm in your home, present your Packet, and ask all the same construction-related questions noted above. In this case, you'll not be asking for designs and proposals from them since that would entail multiple design fees in most cases. However, you will want to ask as many questions as necessary to give you a good understanding of the company's philosophy and work methods, like with any remodeler. You can also ask about the design process, the typical timelines (durations) for projects like yours, ownership of the designs and drawings, and the other things mentioned in chapter 24.

Finally...

There are no stupid questions. So just ask. No matter what it is.

We all tend to forget things, and there will be SO MUCH information, so take notes and write the answers to your questions down. You could use a voice recorder if you want to review it later or keep notes.

It's never the end of the world. You can always follow up with a phone call or an email to ask a forgotten question, clarify a fuzzy point, or verify something you can't remember from their visit.

Make a note about each company when you finish your interview about whether they impressed you and would be a good fit, or if you feel for any reason that they should not be considered further. Don't carry an underwhelming company any further. Cut ties and select another firm to interview. You won't hurt their feelings. In fact, you're saving them and yourself a lot of wasted time at a minimum. And most importantly, you eliminate any misery and poor results that can come from a bad fit.

There is always another excellent candidate out there to consider. Never settle for less than good enough.

Section 7:
CHOOSING YOUR REMODELER

If you pay peanuts, you get monkeys.

—CHINESE PROVERB

The only thing more expensive than hiring a professional is hiring an amateur.

—RED ADAIR

You have made tremendous strides thus far if you have been working along with my suggested plan of action. You defined and refined your project's scope. You then clearly communicated the critical details of your project vision for your design and remodeling professionals to use in order to develop a clever solution. Finally, you met with and thoroughly interviewed a number of remodelers who could help make your imagined remodeling project a reality.

Now we've arrived at the heart of the matter: who will you hire and why?

In the remaining chapters, I'll help you understand the important factors to consider while you deliberate on whom to choose. I'll suggest reasons why you might select one contractor instead of another. I will also discuss the nine hundred-pound gorilla in the room: the price of the work.

CHAPTER 34

Evaluate the Proposals

Once you select the small handful of remodelers that you would consider working with, confirm with them when they will present you with a proposal. In most cases, this will include a design with some drawings or images that let you see how they envision your newly remodeled room(s). This should be a written document with the project-specific details and a price.

You should NEVER accept prices or proposals verbally, regardless of whether it's in person or on the phone. Similarly, a scribble on paper—even company letterhead—is also a no-go. And if they simply send your price by email and cannot make a professional attempt to explain their ideas and price, then rule them out. Never forget that there are dozens of other companies that would be thrilled to take on your project. There is no reason to ever settle for proposals (or workmanship) that are anything less than professional.

The proposals you see should be organized, neat, thorough, and easily understood. It's probable that most remodelers will want to present the proposal in person so they can explain their design and the nuances of their proposal to you and answer any questions or objections you may have. It's also possible they took a direction with their design that you might not love. If this is the case when they pitch their solution in person, they can read your response and will likely offer to revise the solution and the proposal to better suit your preferences.

Keep in mind that the larger and more complex your project, the more involved the design will be. If that is the case for you, it may take remodelers and designers several meetings to craft a clever design that meets your needs and your budget.

But once your contractors have finalized their design solution, you should expect their proposal rather promptly afterward. You should always ask, on each day that you meet with a representative, "When will you be getting back to me with the next design/edit/proposal?" You never want to be waiting and wondering. Always have them set the next appointment before they leave the current appointment, or at least give you a date by which they will accomplish the next step and get back with you. And hold them to it! Part of your evaluation is not just the quality of the solution and the price but also their respect for you and your time. Being on time for meetings and delivering proposals in a timely manner ought to be part of your evaluation.

When you reach the point where you know they will be preparing your proposal, there are some things that you want them to include. Be sure to specifically request these five items:

- Written description of the scope of work
- Bullet list of items added & omitted from prior version
- Itemized list of all allowances included
- Itemized list of any owner-supplied items and services
- Itemized list of anything NOT included but necessary

This way, when you get the final proposals from your selected contractors, you will be able to compare them more easily with one another, making your final decisions a little simpler.

CHAPTER 35

Mind Your P's and Q's:

Remember hearing the phrase "mind your p's and q's" when you were in grade school learning to write? Well, in an entirely different context, it applies once again as you consider the results of your remodeler interviews.

In this case, there are five P's and one Q that I want you to mull over: Professional, Prompt, Proposal, Preference, Price, and Quality. I suggest that you make a simple scoresheet and assign each remodeler you are considering a score for each of these categories. Give a score of ten to the company that most impressed you in each of the six categories, and then assign the other remodelers a score of nine or lower based on your impressions.

Below you will find a brief explanation of what to look for in each category.

Professional

Each contractor should exhibit the very best qualities of a professional company. Their literature, their website, cars or trucks, personnel, offices, and paperwork ought to be professional in appearance and practice. They should have great pride in their stature in the community and industry, have their insurance and registration (or license) in order, be properly insured, and have excellent communications with you. Every contact with them should leave you feeling confident in their ability to help you through this process and perform your project successfully.

Prompt

Punctuality in this industry is critical. It is quite common for individuals to get detained and run late. Lots of seeming "emergencies" pop up in the course of running remodeling projects. But common courtesy and a healthy respect for you and your time should never be far from the remodeler's mind. If someone is running late, they should always call before they are actually late, inform you of their intention to still make the meeting, and give you an ETA of their arrival. It was my habit on those rare occasions where things cropped up to call more than ten minutes before the appointment time and let my customers know I was already on the way but would arrive a few minutes past the appointed time. I then apologized for being late when I met them at the front door. And almost every time I did that, do you know what happened? They thanked me. I was late, and here they were thanking me. Because they were appreciative of my courtesy and desire to be punctual and prompt.

You cannot yet know if the other workers in a particular company will be prompt and timely, but the initial sales people and/or designers might give you an indication if punctuality is a valued trait.

Proposal

Was the proposal they presented to you handwritten on a napkin or a three-ring notebook page, or typed and professionally presented on letterhead? Did they make a phone call with their "price," or did they take the time to clearly propose the scope of work, the cost of that work, and any options and extras?

Was the proposal neat? Was it clearly written in words and terms you understood so that both you and the remodeler could have a clear understanding of the proposed work to be performed. Did it look clean and professional?

The job of the proposal is to clearly define the entire scope of work—what is and what is not included. It should list all the major material types being used in the project, all the major finishes, allowances for the big-ticket items included, and a list of things NOT included as well. There should be no ambiguity. If you are unclear about anything, have it revised so it is totally clear and understood by both you and the remodeler. It will become part of the contract between you and them (along with the permit drawings), so you want it to be perfectly clear— all black and white with no gray areas. A well-crafted, very clear proposal is a significant indication of a detail-minded, customer-oriented professional.

Preferences

This one is as simple as it may seem: Which company impressed you more? With whom did you have a very easy rapport? Who was able to see your vision clearly and help you refine it? Whose design was most exciting to you? Which company offered you the best combination of value and cost? Who was able to educate you about their solution and the way they would approach the process?

By now you have probably noticed that price has not yet been considered. We will, of course, get to it next. But these four other "P" factors are all very important in making your decision. What these other factors tell you is more about the relationship that their company tries to build with each customer. For example, one of the professionals you interview might score perfectly in these four categories and only have the third best price. In my experience a high score in these four areas is vitally important and worth paying a little more for. So I suggest that you review and score those you have interviewed for your project carefully on these first four 'P' parameters.

Price

What will it cost? The fact is, it's very easy to rank the "bid" prices you've received. But you should consider a few other things along with their price. Was their price under or near your budget figure? If it went above your budget figure, did they offer you some alternatives to bring the price down? Were there options presented to you that would result in a more on-target price?

There is no way to know with certainty that any price is accurate, complete, or fair. And believe it or not, remodelers make a lot of mistakes in estimating, and sometimes in doing very simple math. What you are looking for when considering several proposed costs are finding those that are closely grouped. As a rule, you might like to see prices be within 10–12 percent of one another (within $5,000–$6,000 for a $50,000 project, or within ~$10,000–$12,000 for a $100,000 project). In such cases, I would consider those prices "equivalent."

You may have heard folks say you need to get three prices to be sure you get a fair offer. I believe that's wrong. If you really, truly want to shop based on price (which I advise you **not to do** – reread Horror Story Avoidance Tip #3), you may need to obtain at least four or five prices from equivalent remodelers. My logic is this: The highest price of four or five bids should almost always be discarded. While I truly believe that "you get what you pay for" and "quality costs money," you will not often choose the highest price (of 4 or more). In fact, the high price is usually high for a reason. If a company is very busy and does not need another project at that exact moment, they typically raise their profit margin so that if they get another project, it is handsomely profitable. Another potential reason for a too-high price is a mistake by the estimator. But I don't suggest that you entertain the highest bid out of four or five companies unless you've fallen in love with their design and professionalism.

Just as I said, "there is a reason that the highest price is high", there's also a reason that the lowest price is low. The most common reasons for a too-low price (more than the ~10 percent difference I mentioned) is an estimation mistake. And trust me when I say, you do not want to be halfway into a project when your remodeler realizes that they will lose money on your project due to their error. Work could slow down or stop, and they could direct their best efforts toward more profitable projects to keep the cash flowing. Even worse is if they intentionally price the project low just so they could win the bid, because they are hurting financially and are desperate for funds. In any event, being contractually bound to the low-bidder too often places you in a precarious position. The phrases "over a barrel" and "between a rock and a hard place" come to mind.

You almost never want to select the lowest or the highest price, for the reasons I've mentioned. After eliminating the low and high bids, you should find that the remaining prices are reasonably close together. That is probably the most accurate price range for your project. Again, those two or three prices should fall within about 10 percent of one another.

If you employ my earlier suggestion and require your remodelers to disclose all allowances in their estimates, you eliminate the single biggest normally-hidden variable between companies. That's because the cost of that handful of big-ticket items (and the 20–60 percent markup on them) result in the large spread between the bid prices, in most cases. But when you know all the allowance figures, you can see the obvious differences between each bidder's proposal amount. And don't forget that each remodeler also marks up those allowances—making the difference even greater! This easily accounts for 5–15 percent differences in proposal prices! With a pencil and a calculator, you can normalize the bid prices to the "average" allowance figure (as I demonstrated back in Chapter 30). Then the difference between their proposed prices will now primarily reflect the different overhead and different business models of your bidders.

Quality

While you never need to pay "top dollar" for remodeling, you probably remember the old adage I spoke of earlier: you get what you pay for. And that's never been truer than in remodeling. Ask yourself, can the very best of the best be the lowest price? Possibly, but it's quite unlikely. And for the reasons I already stated above, the highest price is not likely to be the very best quality offer for you either. If you were to consider five proposals, the best deal in terms of accurate pricing and quality will be in the middle three prices, in my opinion. That's not guaranteed, but the highest-quality companies make fewer mistakes and seldom will bid on jobs if they don't want them or are not well suited for them. Therefore, it's unlikely they will be the highest or lowest price.

The other way you will learn about the overall quality of the products produced by your bidders is through their references. In the next chapter I'll provide you with some questions you should use when meeting or talking to past clients, so you can learn about the quality and work habits of the remodelers you're considering for your project.

Then, after you've taken into consideration your calls to referrals or visits to job sites, you can assign a score to your various remodelers for their overall quality—the quality of their organization, and of the products they produce. Remember this: they should produce excellent results and very happy customers.

PRO TIP:

There are three significant variables in every remodeling project. They are quality, cost, and duration. You can only control TWO of these three variables. The third variable is controlled by your remodeling professional.

In most cases, homeowners have a finite budget, so they opt for low-cost. Most owners also fear a never-ending project, so they choose shorter durations. But then they realize that puts quality under the control of the contractor and many are reluctant to give away quality. So, what do you do?

The answer is simple: I believe that you choose high quality. Then, by selecting an excellent contractor, you can expect a reasonable duration and maintain a fair cost.

CHAPTER 36

How to Use References

One of the most important steps you can take to protect your remodeling investment is to talk to several references for each company you consider hiring. It sounds cliché, but this process can tell you even more about how a company works with their customers than several interviews with the company representatives themselves. There is just no substitute for being able to ask almost any question of a former client to learn more about the contractor and their work habits and treatment of the project and the customer.

For example, imagine if you were to call a reference and ask the following questions: "Did you like working with Company XYZ?" and "Would you use them again?" Of course, we all expect to hear these two answers: "We loved them!" and "Yes! We would call them again if we did another project!" If you receive any other answers than those, the remodeler who gave you that reference should be immediately eliminated for being stupid. Every reference should be a raving fan of the company that gives them as a reference.

Also keep in mind when conducting these reference interviews that the goal is to ask smart open-ended questions that allow the homeowner to answer honestly without incriminating the contractor or themselves for choosing that contractor. Below I've given you some questions that will get you some excellent insight into how each of your prospective remodelers has worked with their customers. The answers will truly help you differentiate between the companies you're considering.

Questions for References

1. When something went wrong, how did they handle it? Were you contacted for your opinion and input? Was the issue resolved to your satisfaction? (*Something always goes wrong, so this is a great way to gain insight into the problem-solving mindset of each remodeler. It also tells you if the company is highly proactive about remedies or if customer prompting and interaction is required.*)

2. Were they on-site daily? Did they keep regular hours? Did they alert you in advance when they would not be at your house working for a day or two? (*These questions give you a feel for the punctuality of each remodeler and the day-to-day schedule for the foreman/lead carpenter/staff.*)

3. Did they respect your home, your belongings, your yard? (*You're looking for insight into whether they protected other rooms, furnishings, cared about dust and muddy footprints, didn't break things and knock over artwork, fixed ruts in the grass, and generally took care of the place as if they lived there.*)

4. How easy were they to contact when you had a question or concern? By phone? Email? Text? The foreman, or the office? (*It's important to know how easy it is to contact a company and whether they respond promptly and with proper concern and urgency when questions are asked or a need arises.*)

5. When you asked about any changes to the project, how responsive were they to your inquiry, and were they generally receptive to mid-course changes? (*Things always arise that you cannot foresee. You want to know if you are selecting a company that is willing to make a change that you want, or add or delete something from the project without hassles [assuming you ask before it's impossibly late for the requested change].*)

6. Is there any advice you would give me if I hire them to do a similar project for me? (*Leave it open-ended and see what you can learn. If this*

question comes late or last, you're more likely to get an answer other than, "No, they did a great job.")

Asking all these questions of each reference you call will require about five to ten minutes of your time. But what you learn will be so valuable that it could easily sway your preference from one company to another that has a finer reputation among their former customers.

Because this is such an integral step, you don't want to wing it. Have the questions written or typed out so you can take notes. The subtle distinctions in the answers from company to company will surprise you.

And whatever you do, please don't skip this step. It's far too important. You're about to spend tens of thousands of dollars, and the information you discover will help protect your investment and should also go a long way toward putting your mind at ease as you make the final choice of one company over another.

Think about it: you would never make any other purchase this costly without spending all kinds of time and effort researching and learning all about the investment. So don't fail to spend a few minutes insuring that you hire a firm that will make you as happy as they've made their other clients. The fifteen to twenty minutes it takes you to call three references per remodeler is a tiny effort with a huge payback and valuable insight about your final few candidates!

CHAPTER 37

How and When to Negotiate

Back in chapter 31, I addressed a number of ways to save money on your projects. Those methods were to be used when you were just starting to meet with your contractors and were planning your project's future. Those were all about saving money, but they were not ***negotiating***.

After you've interviewed your best prospective contractors and you know who you WANT to work with, or perhaps which two remodelers you wish to select from, this is the one and only time in the process where you should negotiate.

In my experience, you get only one opportunity to ask for a deal or a concession on the price. The best time to do this is when you've narrowed your selection down to one or two choices, and I'll give you my suggestion for the best possible method.

By this point, you should know that a remodeler's total fee to you is comprised of their costs (labor and materials), overhead (costs of non-project related business expenses like rent, utilities, cars and trucks, office staff, etc.), and profit. The profit most remodelers shoot for is 10–15 percent on top of their combined costs and overhead. If they have estimated your project accurately and perform the project efficiently, they will make closer to 15 percent profit. If they have made any errors in their estimate or if they produce the project inefficiently, then their profits are reduced, perhaps significantly.

The reason I bring this up now is that when homeowners ask for price concessions, they often ask for far too much of a "discount." What does that mean? Well, if your project "price" from a remodeler is $50,000 and you ask them to sign for $45,000, you have asked them to give up about two-thirds of their profits if they price and produce the job perfectly. If they are an honest company that prices their work fairly, they cannot just eliminate two-thirds of their profit because you asked them to lower their price.

As a rule of thumb, all price concessions from an honest contractor will probably require a reduction in the scope of work, the use of smaller allowances, or other such trade-offs. If you have set a realistic budget and their final proposed cost is in line with your budget, you're not likely to agree to a lesser scope of work, and they are not likely to agree to a lower price for the same scope of work.

About now you might be thinking, "Jim, why are you calling this chapter 'How and When to Negotiate' and then telling us there is no wiggle room in the proposal price with which the remodeler can negotiate?" That's actually a fair question. I was simply trying to show you that a pure price reduction is **not** the way to approach your one and only negotiation.

Instead, I have three suggested methods that are far more likely to result in a better price or better value for you, without reducing the scope or the quality of the project.

Ask for a Price Reduction

The object here is to use the lower price from a contractor you are willing to work (preferably your second choice) in order to get the best deal possible from your higher priced but preferred contractor. This does not mean asking both contractors for lower and lower prices. Remember, I mentioned that you only get to ask a remodeler one time for any deal or concession, so this needs to be performed only after some careful forethought. It works best when your preferred company has the higher priced proposal than your alternate selection.

This is performed by you after interviews are complete and before you invite anyone to meet to contract review and signing.

Speaking to your preferred, higher priced contractor (in person or by phone—no texts or emails, use verbal communication only), let them know you prefer to work with them above the other companies you interviewed. However, another contractor with whom you would be willing to sign, has offered a lower price. Then you make this simple statement: "Their price is $XX,XXX (give them the REAL lower cost but do NOT name the other company). If you can do something to bring your price more in line with their price, then I'm prepared to sign with you instead."

By stating it very simply and open-endedly, without declaring a particular final price or the amount of the "discount," you intentionally leave the entire solution in their hands. Knowing that you are willing to sign with should motivate them to suggest a discount or concession. But once you have asked the question, you shut up. You don't say another word until after you get their response.

Pro Tip:

In negotiations, the first one to name a figure loses. If you ask for $5,000 off the price or ask them to do it for $55,000 instead of $60,000, the obvious response they make is to cut your difference or your suggestion in half. So don't suggest the solution to them; instead suggest that you want them to make an improved offer in exchange for you choosing them as your contractor.

It's possible they will say, "No. I'm sorry, we estimated this as precisely as we could and this already is our best price." But it's more likely that if they want your project, they will make you an offer that puts their price closer to the other bidder's figure. No matter what the response is, you need to accept that negotiations are now over. Take it or leave it. In our scenario, that means you either pay the offered price from your preferred remodeler, or you select your second-choice remodeler and accept their already lower price. Your reply will be either, "OK, I accept that offer," or "I'll need to consider whether I can pay your price, or if I will select the offer from my second-choice remodeler. I'll have to let you know my decision when I've made it."

This simple method almost always earns you a cost compromise from your preferred contractor. It may not be a lot of dollars, but they typically attempt to make their higher price more attractive.

And after this plays out, you typically get the really good contractor at the lowest price, or you get your favorite contractor at a better price than they initially offered.

Ask for a Round-Down

In the event that you have only one remodeler you wish to work with (or you choose to work with the lower priced of the two even after the "best offer" from the higher priced company), here is your best option for a price reduction from them. Remember, their profit margin is about 10–15 percent, so your "ask" needs to be no more than one-half to one-third of that amount. What I found was that the easiest way to go was to ask instead for a "round down." On a lower cost project, round down from $18,800 to $18,000. On a larger project, suggest a round down from $83,000 to $80,000. If you shoot for 3–5 percent and hit a nice "round number," you'll be successful in most cases.

Just keep in mind that you're naming a price in this case, and the first person to name a price loses in negotiations. The way I suggest you work this is as follows: "I'm prepared to sign a contract with you for the current scope of work if the contract price is $XX,XXX." In this way, you are not inviting more negotiation; it's an unspoken 'take it or leave it' offer. One warning: if they say, "No, we cannot do that" the discussion is over. You need to be prepared to accept their regular offer or walk away and use another contractor. This is a one-time opportunity, and you only make the offer knowing what your decision is in advance—then stick to your guns.

Add to the Scope, but Hold the Cost

Surprisingly, the very best deal you can get is to pay their asking price. What do I mean by that? Well, after you've gone through all the steps outlined in the book, you're convinced that they are a legitimate professional remodeler. For this reason, you can't really balk at their proposal cost, right? And maybe you're not a "negotiator" willing to ask them to cut their price because you know that's cutting into their profit margin. But there *is* a way you can profit and still pay their asking price.

You see, in most larger projects and in many medium ones as well, you discuss many options along the way before arriving at the final scope of work reflected in the proposal. Some items on your Wish List are discussed and omitted for purely financial reasons, perhaps. But this is the stage of negotiation when you can drag that list back out and see if there is one special thing on that list that you REALLY still want to include.

My suggestion is that you tell the remodeler of your choice, "I'm prepared to sign with you and pay your full proposal price, but I'd like you to include that _____ we discussed earlier. If you add that in at the proposal price, then I'm ready to sign the contract." You need to be judicious and make sure that the amount of the extra item or work you ask for is not more than 10 percent of the project cost. You also need to be prepared for the contractor to counter-offer. When I negotiated as a remodeler, I often said things like, "I'll give you the labor to install your additional skylight, if YOU pay the actual cost of the skylight," or "That lift-top window seat would cost about $4,000 in materials and labor. I'll split that cost with you, adding only $2,000 to the price but doing the seat in the same manner we previously discussed." In this way, you are getting MORE PROJECT at little or no additional cost.

If you have a small ask or a little extra money and you have one or two special items that you'd like to add into the scope of work, this is the time and this is the method to get those included for free, or at a steep discount.

The reason you ask now and the reason your remodeler is likely to accept is two-fold. First, you're prepared to sign the contract. And they don't want to lose a sale by saying 'no'. If you've been a nuisance-free client throughout the process and they are interested in your project, they'll work with your one-and-only request for a concession. Second, if you're asking for a several hours of labor and common materials that fit easily into the flow of work for the big project, then only the purchase of specialty items or materials actually add to their cost. In that case, they might ask you to pay the item cost, but they'll eat the labor and overhead.

Examples of this are that they ask you to pay for the skylights, but install them free. A tray ceiling is all lumber and drywall, so they'll likely just say yes. A tile backsplash in the new kitchen won't cost them much time and labor, but they might ask you to supply or pay for the tile itself. If not free, these small additional costs get you more project for the same dollar and are a great way to bulk-up your project just before signing the contract.

Only ONE OPTION Applies

Please remember, you can only try ONE of these methods with any remodeler you consider hiring. You can't ask for a round-down AND an add-on. You can't ask them to cut their price to approach a lower bidder and then also ask them to round down. Because of this, you'll need to consider your situation and the relative placement of your remodelers to one another in terms of total cost, before you choose which method of negotiation you wish to pursue. And while it goes without saying, I will mention it anyhow: be true to your word. Don't ask for a concession with the caveat "if you do this I'm prepared to sign the contract" and then fail to follow through. You would immediately drop a remodeler that went back on their word to you, so don't do it to them.

CHAPTER 38

Remodeling Contracts

In case you've forgotten how bad the industry reputation is, please reread the early chapters of this book. My advice is that you must always sign a contract when you remodel, if for no other reason than to protect your investment. I think we can all agree that most remodeling costs are large, probably larger than you realized. Don't risk that amount and more on a "feeling" or on the word of a remodeling salesperson. I'm not suggesting that all remodelers are liars and scoundrels, far from it, but the advice "trust but verify" certainly applies here.

Before I discuss the most common remodeling contract details, let me mention the two contract types that are NOT written by the contractor in cooperation with the owner: (1) contracts that are written by an architect (AIA 101/107), or (2) contracts written by a bank (with bank-controlled disbursements). In these cases, the homeowner and contractor have little say about the contract terms and payment schedule and simply sign the documents and become parties to the agreement. Control over the process is maintained by the contract agent (the architect or the bank), though it is possible the architect or bank will work on the draw schedule or disbursement terms directly with your contractor. If you use an architect or have a bank-controlled loan, you can discuss the terms of your particular contract with your architect or banker.

My final note before we dive into contract information is that I am NOT an attorney. This is NOT legal advice. You should feel free to consult a lawyer when presented with your contract offers from your own remodelers. This chapter is to familiarize you with the basics of remodeling contracts so you can scan them and have a reasonable understanding of some key sections.

Typical Remodeling Contract Requirements

The following items relate to features or sections that any reasonable remodeling contract should contain. Become familiar with these, and be sure to ask your remodeler for a blank or "draft" contract to review in advance of receiving their proposal. This will give you time to read it over and modify any necessary items. In the event the contractor is reluctant to alter their agreement for you, this may affect your final selection regarding whom you hire.

Information on Parties to the Contract

A legitimate contract identifies all parties to the contract by name, address, and contact information (phone, fax, email). In most cases, this includes the contractor and the homeowners. A contractor's license number should also be displayed if you reside in a jurisdiction with licensing or registration.

Total Price and Payment Terms

The agreed-upon total price of the contract needs to be clearly displayed. All individual payments (called draws) need to be clearly listed, detailing the amount due and the milestone in construction that triggers each draw payment.

In most cases the homeowner and contractor can negotiate the size of the payments and the milestones that trigger them so that money is being paid only as progress on the project is being accomplished. It is recommended that a very large initial payment or deposit be avoided. A rule of thumb is for the deposit to be one or two times the regular payments, and the final payment to be one or one-half times the deposit amount.

My experience is that draws or payments due weekly to bi-weekly allow the homeowner to feel comfortable with the progress in construction. This setup also provides regular cash flow and incentive for the contractor to maintain the scheduled flow of production.

The final payment, or a portion of it, should be held back until all punch-list items (last remaining details as the project winds down—best if it is a written list signed by both parties) are completed.

Dates

Any contract needs to be dated when signed (the date of contract origination). All contracts should also include start and completion dates, or a start date and project duration. In some cases these dates are unknown, so the start date may not be a date but something like "within a week after the building permit is issued" or "to be determined." The duration of a project might be stated as "13 weeks" or "12 days" or "4 months." You can ask your chosen remodeler to put in the terms that are most suitable for your situation.

There will usually be a limitation clause in case of disasters, strikes, wars, acts of God, etc., that allow the schedule to be expanded. If you wish your project to be completed by a particular date, that needs to be specifically included in the contract along with a penalty clause in case of failure to do so.

The date of the contract production often occurs on the first page with the parties and payment terms. The contract signing dates are usually on the signature pages where both parties sign and agree to the contract. The project start and end dates may appear elsewhere; be sure to look them over.

Permits and Inspections

If you live in a jurisdiction where permits and inspections are required, then you must include a clause in the contract that states the contractor is responsible for obtaining all required permits and inspections for the project.

Scope of Work and Drawings

The contract is not the only document that you might need to be concerned with. Any design or permit drawings and separate specifications also need to become part of the contract. If the drawings and specs are separate documents, they should be referenced in the text of the contract as being part of the contract or agreement between parties. They should be mentioned specifically by name, and dated. Those names and dates should exactly match the names and dates on the documents themselves. It is possible on smaller projects to literally type all the specifications into the contract itself. Both methods are fine. Just be sure that the exact set of drawings and specs you are agreeing to are fully referenced in your contract.

If you have auxiliary drawings such as from a cabinet manufacturer or supplier, those too should be incorporated into the contract in this manner.

Materials

If your project will be using very specific brands, models, materials, or colors of materials and equipment, they should be called out. They can be written out in a section of the contract, they can appear in the project specifications, or they can appear on the project design drawings. Read through this set of selections so that you are sure the choices you want to be included are the ones in the contract.

Warranty

Every contract should include terms of the warranty granted by the remodeler. Minimum warranty information should include the following:

- duration of the warranty period (time)
- any maintenance required as a condition of the warranty
- the remodeler's obligations to the homeowner during the guaranty period
- the procedure a homeowner follows to obtain warranty service

Dispute Resolution Clause

The very best dispute resolution protection you can have is to select a remodeler who always honors their obligations to their customers and avoids litigation and arbitration at all costs. Discussing areas of concern is so much swifter and easier than fighting about a resolution. So call every reference and ask how problems, misunderstandings, and disagreements were handled. Then choose a contractor that has never been sued or taken to arbitration. This is your first best protection.

Below we will discuss the two primary methods of dispute resolution used by remodelers: the courts and arbitration.

Going to Court

Courts are slow and very expensive. And even if you win your case, you'll spend more winning and lose more in downtime and enmity with your contractor than it's worth, in my opinion. And don't forget that in many cases, the initial result can be appealed. The only real winners in litigation are the lawyers.

Arbitration Clause

An arbitration clause in a home improvement contract should include the following:

- The name of the organization that will conduct the arbitration
- Any mandatory fees that will be charged to the parties
- Whether the arbitrator's findings are binding

Typically, the dispute resolution clause requires a separate signature page from the contract. This is based on the requirements of each jurisdiction.

Making Changes

All remodeling contracts need to discuss how to make changes to the contract. Once it is signed, it is a binding legal agreement, so altering it has to be addressed. Typically, remodeling contracts are altered by a *change order*. A *change order* is a brief (often single page) document that sets the scope of the change and the price change of the change, and is signed and dated by all original parties.

Changes can be additional work, the omission of work that was in the initial agreement, or just a change of some facet of the project—even if it does not require a financial adjustment.

Be certain your contract has a way to alter or amend the contract and that you understand how it works, if there are any administrative fees, etc.

Date of the Contract

A home improvement contract must contain the approximate dates when the performance of the home improvement will begin and when it will be substantially completed.

CHAPTER 39

Final Thoughts

You now have at your disposal all the tools needed to plan and coordinate any remodeling project successfully.

You can properly perform the following eight tasks:
- Prepare a complete Project Packet
- Choose any design professional you might need
- Identify the right type of remodeler to interview
- Thoroughly interview your selected remodelers
- Review their remodeling proposals carefully
- Select the best remodeler for your needs
- Negotiate your best possible final price
- Review the remodeling contract
- Sign up for and begin your remodeling project!

Eliminate the Three Critical Mistakes

There are three critical mistakes that lead to the overwhelming majority of remodeling problems. Avoiding these mistakes is not difficult, you just need to keep them in mind and follow the process laid out in the book. I flagged each one and taught you how to avoid them as I presented the process. You can always refer back to the "Horror-story Avoidance Tips" in the text. Here they are once again:

1. Never start the remodeling process without preparing fully.
2. Don't choose the wrong TYPE of remodeling company.
3. Don't select your remodeler based on lowest price.

Invert this list, and you have a fabulous and simple guide to remodeling success!

- Prepare thoroughly in advance.
- Only select the correct type of remodeling company for your project.
- Make your final choice of whom to work with based on all the factors of a project (design, quality, references, rapport, creativity, communication, longevity, awards, professionalism). Oh, and price too.

Remember to be the Boss (with a capital B) throughout the process, and remain in control of your project. Perform that role well, and hire an excellent employee to work for you. Then take a step back and let them do what you hired them to do: construct an awesome new project that will add great value to your home, bringing you improved function, beauty, and delight for years to come.

ASK-ME-ANYTHING!

Sometimes...
you still have questions or concerns,
even after reading a book like this.

———

Now you can...
Ask the
Remodeling Professor!

Jim offers **1-on-1 video calls** and
gives **clear answers and action steps**
for your specific situation!

Jim is a life-long industry insider and
remodeling expert who is impartial,
and whose only interest is your success!

———

SCHEDULE YOUR CALL NOW:
www.JimMolinelli.com/call

List of Horror-Story Avoidance Tips

Tip #1 - Don't begin the remodeling process without being fully prepared.

Tip #2 - Identify and hire only the right type of remodeler for your project.

Tip #3 - Never choose your remodeler based on the lowest price.

Action Items

Create Your Project Packet

Action Item #1:	Prepare for your **Project Packet**
Action Item #2:	Visit Houzz.com, open free account, collect ideas
Action Item #3:	Write first draft of **Elevator Pitch**
Action Item #4:	Write first draft of **Need List**
Action Item #5:	Write first draft of **Wish List**
Action Item #6:	Prioritize Wish List
Action Item #7:	Start shopping for **Loans** if you need one
Action Item #8:	Finalize your project **Budget**
Action Item #9:	Make **Room by Room Table**
Action Item #10:	Add Final Touches to Project Packet

APPENDIX 3

Remodeler Licensing & Registration by State*

Remodeling license/registration status of the 50 states*:

State	License/Registration?	Notes	Group / Board / Agency
Alabama	YES	Prime/Sub	Alabama Home Builder's Licensing Board
Alaska	YES	General (residential) / Subs	State of Alaska Department of Commerce
Arizona	YES	Homes & Remodeling	Arizona Registrar of Contractors
Arkansas	YES	Remodeler & Home Improvement	Arkansas Contractors Licensing Board
California	YES		California Contractor State Licensing Board
Colorado	Yes - Locally only	Local (County, City, Region) Licensing	
Connecticut	YES	Remodelers AND remodeling salespeople	Department of Consumer Protection
Delaware	Yes - by City/County	City/County level licensing	Department of Finance, Division of Revenue
Florida	YES - State and local	State OR City/County licensing	Construction Industry Licensing Board
Georgia	YES	Residential Improvements over $2500	Georgia Board of Residential & General Contractors
Hawaii	YES	General Contractor & Subs, over $1000	Department of Commerce and Consumer Affairs
Idaho	YES - registration	REGISTRATION, not licensure	Idaho Bureau of Occupational Licenses - Contractors Board
Illinois	Yes - by City		
Indiana	Yes - by City		
Iowa	YES - Registration		Iowa Division of Labor
Kansas	Yes - Some Cities	Select cities only	
Kentucky	Yes - 2 cities only	Lexington/Louisville city registration only	
Louisiana	YES	$7,500 + need licensed remodeler	Louisiana Licensing Board for Contractors
Maine	NO		
Maryland	YES	contractors, salespeople, & subs	Maryland Home Improvement Comission
Massachusetts	YES		Office of Consumer Affairs and Business Regulation
Michigan	YES		Department of Licensing and Regulatory Affairs
Minnesota	YES		Minnesota Department of Labor & Industry
Mississippi	YES	remodeling jobs over $10,000	Mississippi State Board of Contractors
Missouri	Yes - Locally only	City, County, Township licenses only	
Montana	YES		Montana Department of Labor and Industry
Nebraska	YES		Nebraska Department of Labor
Nevada	YES		Nevada State Contractors Board
New Hampshire	Yes - Limited locally	Some LOCAL level requirements only	
New Jersey	YES - Registration	Not a license, just registration. Mandatory.	New Jersey Division of Consumer Affairs
New Mexico	YES		New Mexico Regulation & Licensing Department
New York	NO	Permits and regulations at municipal level only	
North Carolina	YES		North Carolina Board for General Contractors
North Dakota	YES	Improvements over $4000	North Dakota Secretary of State
Ohio	Yes - locally	County/City licensing & permitting	
Oklahoma	NO		
Oregon	YES		Oregon Construction Contractors Board
Pennsylvania	YES		Department of Labor & Industry
Rhode Island	YES		Contractors' Registration and Licensing Board
South Carolina	YES		South Carolina Contractor's Licensing Board
South Dakota	Yes - Limited locally	Local registration may be required	
Tennessee	YES	projects over $25,000	Tennessee Department of Commerce and Insurance
Texas	NO		
Utah	YES		Utah Division of Occupational and Professional Licensing
Vermont	Yes - Locally only		
Virginia	YES		Division of Professional and Occupational Regulation
Washington	YES - Registration		Washington State Department of Labor & Industries
West Virginia	YES		West Virginia Division of Labor Contractor Licensing
Wisconsin	NO		
Wyoming	Yes - Limited locally	Some City/County registration	

*At the time of original publication. Please check your state/city/area before you remodel

PLEASE HELP OTHER HOMEOWNERS

Please do me a favor?

Leave a brief **review** of

on

It makes a huge difference!

Don't let your book gather dust when you're done.
Please pass it on to someone else who can also benefit!

ABOUT THE AUTHOR

Jim Molinelli (the Remodeling Professor) is the quintessential remodeling expert. He has earned three different architecture degrees and holds a Maryland architectural license. He has also taught on the architecture faculty at Texas A&M University.

After leaving Texas, Jim entered the design-build remodeling field, where he spent the past twenty-five years helping Maryland families remodel. His unique designs have garnered more than fifty remodeling awards. He also received the Maryland Governor's Citation for Meritorious Service two times, once in 2006 and again in 2016.

Since 2002, he created and taught local 'Prepare to Remodel' classes for homeowners through Howard Community College. That led to both this book, and his innovative online remodeling course *Remodeling Success Blueprint*!

He and his family live in the suburban Washington, DC area. He enjoys travel and golf, and is an avid baseball fan.

Jim also does occasional live workshops and classes, home shows, and speaking engagements. You can contact Jim via his website:

Made in the USA
Coppell, TX
02 March 2020

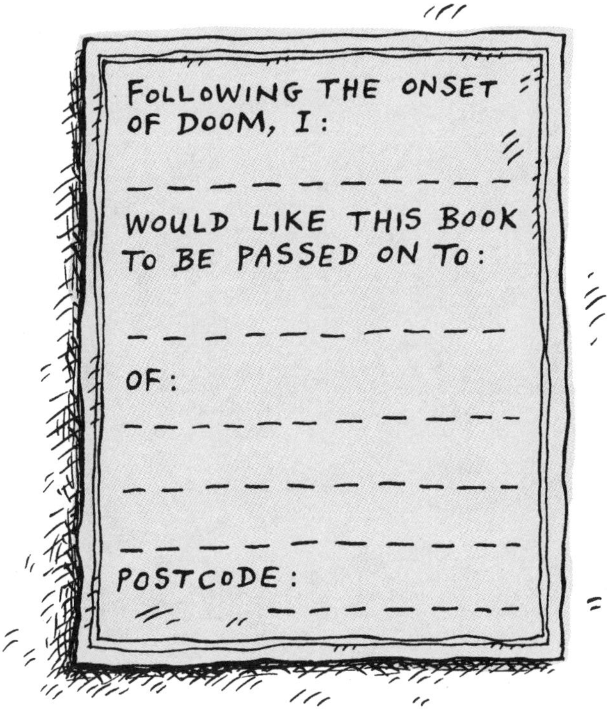

FOLLOWING THE ONSET
OF DOOM, I:

_ _ _ _ _ _ _ _ _

WOULD LIKE THIS BOOK
TO BE PASSED ON TO:

_ _ _ _ _ _ _ _

OF:
_ _ _ _ _ _ _ _ _

_ _ _ _ _ _ _ _ _

_ _ _ _ _ _ _ _ _

POSTCODE:
_ _ _ _ _ _ _

THE COFFEE TABLE BOOK OF

THE COFFEE TABLE BOOK OF DOOM

Steven Appleby & Art Lester

A PLUME BOOK

The authors wish to express their heartfelt gratitude
to those who have made this book possible through their contributions,
their expertise and, perhaps above all, their forbearance.
They include: Pete Bishop, Lloyd Clater, Rosemary Davidson, Nick Battey,
Simon Rhodes, and Jo Unwin, our agent.
Special thanks to Gilly Fraser, Nicola Sherring and family.

PLUME
Published by the Penguin Group
Penguin Group (USA) Inc., 375 Hudson Street, New York, New York 10014, U.S.A. •
Penguin Group (Canada), 90 Eglinton Avenue East, Suite 700, Toronto, Ontario, Canada
M4P 2Y3 (a division of Pearson Penguin Canada Inc.) • Penguin Books Ltd., 80 Strand, London WC2R 0RL, England • Penguin Ireland, 25 St. Stephen's Green, Dublin 2, Ireland (a
division of Penguin Books Ltd.) • Penguin Group (Australia), 250 Camberwell Road, Camberwell, Victoria 3124, Australia (a division of Pearson Australia Group Pty. Ltd.) • Penguin
Books India Pvt. Ltd., 11 Community Centre, Panchsheel Park, New Delhi – 110 017,
India • Penguin Group (NZ), 67 Apollo Drive, Rosedale, Auckland 0632, New Zealand
(a division of Pearson New Zealand Ltd.) • Penguin Books (South Africa) (Pty.) Ltd., 24 Sturdee Avenue, Rosebank, Johannesburg 2196, South Africa

Penguin Books Ltd., Registered Offices: 80 Strand, London WC2R 0RL, England

Published by Plume, a member of Penguin Group (USA) Inc. Originally published in Great
Britain by Square Peg, an imprint of The Random House Group Limited.

First American Printing, October 2012
10 9 8 7 6 5 4 3 2 1

Ⓟ REGISTERED TRADEMARK—MARCA REGISTRADA

LIBRARY OF CONGRESS CATALOGING-IN-PUBLICATION DATA
Appleby, Steven.
  The coffee table book of doom / Steven Appleby and Art Lester.
    p. cm.
  Includes index.
  ISBN 978-0-452-29866-8
  1. End of the world—Humor. I. Lester, Art. II. Title.
  BL503.A67 2012
  001.9—dc23
                                            2012018102

Printed in the United States of America

Warning

Perhaps by the time you read this book
some of the Doom scenarios included will no longer be
global threats. Maybe the human race will have
acted together to contain greenhouse gas production
and tree felling. Or they will have developed a
laser shield to deflect incoming asteroids.
Perhaps not.

All the facts and theories in this book have been checked
as thoroughly as possible. We humbly apologize
for any errors that may have crept in.
After all, we are human—as we assume you are.

FACING THE FUTURE:

This book is dedicated to the Earth.
We hope that its end will be exciting for
anyone who happens to be
passing by and stops to watch.

Dear fellow mortal,

Imagine that you're sitting on your sofa leafing through this book, when you feel an odd vibration. Ripples start to shiver across the surface of your teacup. Puzzled, you strain your ears. Then you hear a distant rumbling. Barely audible to begin with, the noise grows louder. And nearer. The sound is unfamiliar at first, but then you realize what it is.

Hoofbeats.

Don't go to your window and peer through the curtains. Don't tempt the Horsemen of the Apocalypse by showing your face.

Doom is no longer far off in the distant future. It could arrive as early as Tuesday morning.

And there's nothing you can do except read on...

    Yours anxiously,

       The authors

DOOM—What's That?

Do we even have to ask? Everyone knows what Doom is. We've never actually seen it, and lots of predictions anticipating it have failed to materialize, but it's been with us since the cave days. It was there with us when we hid under the covers as children, and it flashes into view every time we switch on the evening news.

fig a — CURTAINS

Don't look out!

Everyone knows: it's curtains.

Here's a dictionary definition:

> **Doom:** (dû:m), noun.
> Fate or destiny, especially adverse; unavoidable ill fortune; ruin; an unfavorable judgment or sentence; the Last Judgment, at the end of the world.

It seems we all know about Doom because, as the definition confirms, it's our destiny; it's unavoidable. That's why religions are full of it. In theology, talking about it is called eschatology, or the knowledge of the "end times." Because it's linked to the Last Judgment, Christian, Jewish and Muslim holy books describe it as a final payoff for unbelievers. Infidels will all be wiped out—usually horribly—while the good guys will be saved. If you're a certain type of fundamentalist, you're just waiting to be "raptured," or maybe beamed aboard a spaceship. But even modern, secular types have Doom anxiety. You bought this book, didn't you?

For nearly everybody, it's all about guilt. When things are going along pretty well, it's natural to think they can't last. Walking along a pavement on a sunny day is an invitation for someone to drop a grand piano on your head. We feel that something must be wrong with the way we're living. Using all that energy, buying a second home while some people are sleeping in cardboard cartons, eating strawberries at Christmas dinner. It's all too obvious: we're heading for a fall. Aren't we?

CARVING THE CHRISTMAS STRAWBERRY

We cling to our Doom anxiety like a Linus blanket. Maybe we know that living without Doom would be like a soccer match without a final whistle, a sandwich with no bread, a murder mystery with no villain. Unimaginable. Worse: boring.

So we look fearfully at the skies, listen for rumors of new dread diseases and nuclear accidents from behind the sofa, and take an aspirin every morning. We know that if there was no Doom, we'd be forced to invent it.

How Do We Know Doom Is Coming?

Prophecies. We can be sure that prophets have always had a stab at predicting the end of the world. Most of these have been lost in time, but the present count of known prophecies stands at 147.*

DOOM
↓

St. Ambrose of Milan predicted in AD 378 that "the end of the world is upon us," but that was during the sacking of his homeland by Goths.

Sextus Julius Africanus predicted the end of the world in AD 500, but later changed his Doom date to AD 800, just to be 100% sure.

The Bible gave us the Four Horsemen of the Apocalypse, right at the end of the book. It has had many notable advocates, such as Isaac Newton (Doom date: 2060), the Venerable Bede (Doom date: 2076) and Nostradamus (Doom date: 3786).

In 1997 a group of end-of-the-world aficionados predicted Doomsday at the approach of the Hale-Bopp comet and achieved personal Doom by committing suicide.

Though there is no agreement, a grouping can be seen between next Tuesday and approximately AD 3900. Many of the earlier prophets suggested round figures for Doomsday, such as AD 500, AD 1000 and AD 2000, perhaps assuming that God, too, employs the decimal system.

* The most recent, at time of going to press, is that of a Californian radio evangelist who predicted "rapture" of true believers on May 21, 2011, to be followed by world destruction in October of the same year.

TIMELINE SHOWING WHEN THE WORLD IS PREDICTED TO END...

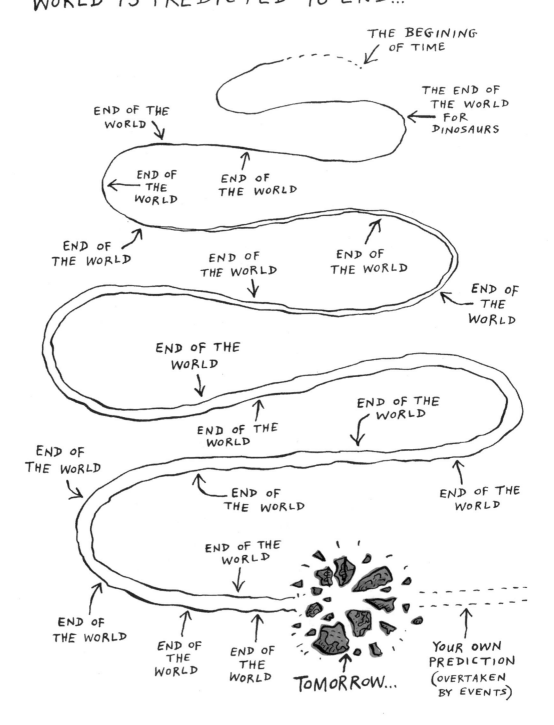

Our next date with Doom appears to be in December 2012. That's according to the ancient Mayan calendar, which ends then after a period of civilization lasting 5,125 years. Strangely, this appears to concur with a prediction made by St. Malachy in 1143, who said the world would end during the tenure of the 112th future pope. The current pontiff, Benedict XVI, is the 111th, and he's 83 years old.

December 21, 2012. Write that date in your diary.

Science. Once Galileo started messing around with lenses and had the first good look at the stars, we began to hear from astronomers and other scientists. They've been identifying ways we might end ever since.

The white-coated prophets of the laboratories have produced dozens of nightmare scenarios. These range from hideous new diseases to collisions with lumps of rock in space and invisible death rays.

Eerily, many of their most recent predictions tend to point to the year 2012.

Intuition. We human beings are the only creatures that have a sense of time.

So we just *know*.

You might think that the enterprise of science, with its method and its facts, would inoculate us against the most extravagant doomsday obsessions. But it doesn't. If anything, it just gives us more to worry about.

Scientific American, September 2010

Contents

Asteroid Strike

What are the odds that Earth will someday be impacted by an object from space?

100%.

In fact, every day over half a million pieces of rock from space enter the Earth's atmosphere. Of course, most of these are harmlessly burned away by the atmosphere and become "shooting stars." But some will get through and wind up as paperweights on the desks of scientists.

A bigger chunk of rock (a swimming pool–sized object) sailed between the Earth and the Moon in the summer of 2010. We didn't know about that one until it had passed. Somewhat larger objects of 100 meters (like a soccer pitch) would destroy cities. There are known to be more than 100,000 of these in our cosmic neighborhood.

Recently an object called Apophys, with a diameter of 270 meters, has turned up. At first it was thought that there might be a collision with us sometime in 2024, but it now seems that a near miss is more likely. What is a problem is something called a "gravitational keyhole," a zone of just a few meters that can

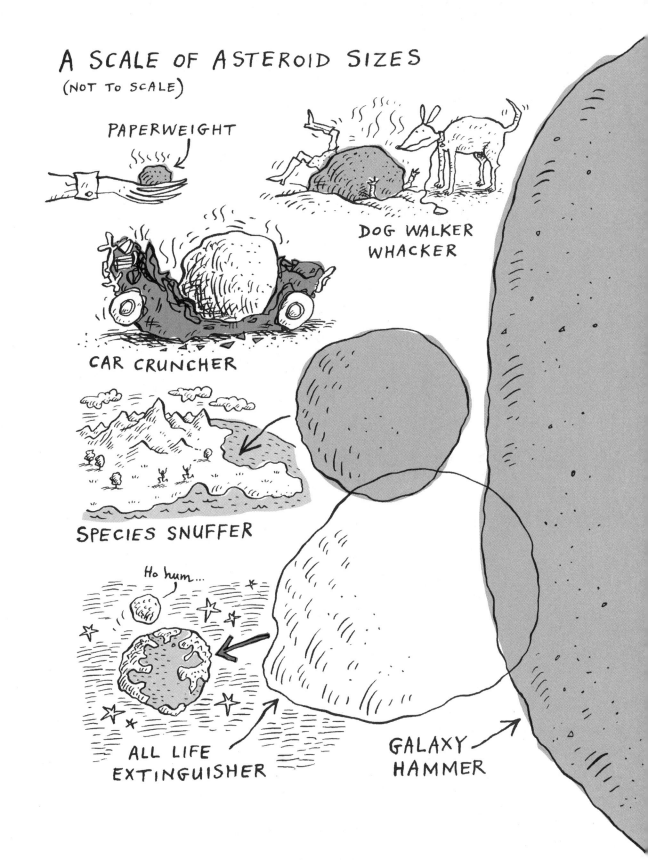

alter the trajectory of an object passing through it. That would mean a return of Apophys in the year 2036. And next time it might not miss.

IN ORDER TO FULLY APPRECIATE THE LIKELIHOOD OF THE EARTH BEING HIT BY LARGE ASTEROIDS, WHY NOT REPLICATE THE SOLAR SYSTEM IN **YOUR OWN HOME!** YOU REPRESENT THE EARTH...

CRACK!

Ouch!

SIMPLY:

i – HANG CROCKERY, PANS AND OTHER ITEMS FROM YOUR CEILING.

ii – WALK ABOUT BRISKLY WITH YOUR EYES CLOSED.

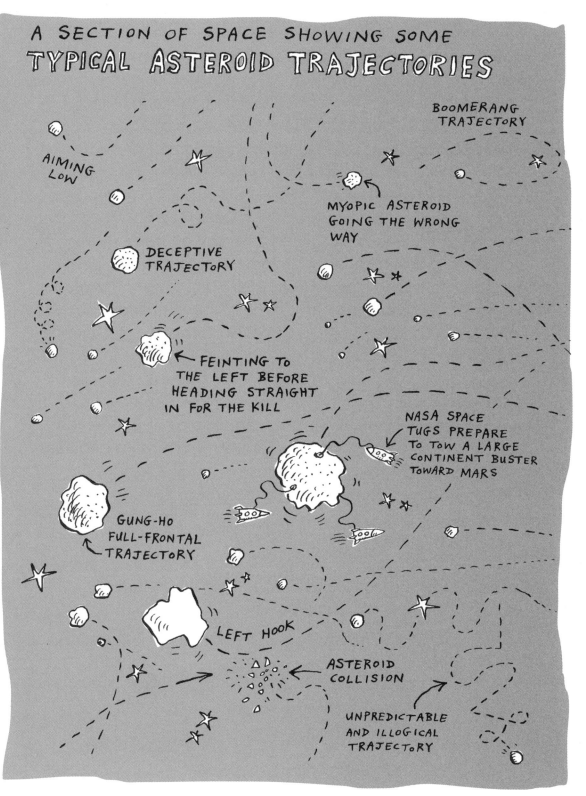

If Apophys enters the atmosphere it will be traveling at 50,000 mph and explode with the force of 30,000 Hiroshima bombs, making a crater about the size of New York. It will generate high-speed winds that will flatten buildings in much of the planet and may raise the temperature of the air to an unbearable level. Massive tsunamis would affect all coasts, and the likelihood of an artificial winter is great.

According to the Task Force on Near Earth Objects set up in 2000, there are about 1,000 known nearby asteroids with diameters of greater than one kilometer, any one of which is capable of causing global destruction. These big lumps of rock are known as "species busters." One of these, called 1950 DA, has a good chance of hitting us in 2880, according to *Science* magazine.

What can we do about it? Scientists have proposed deflecting Apophys with nuclear weapons, blowing it up, and even inventing a "space tug" equipped with plasma engines. Then there is the "Yarkovsky effect," in which focused solar heat causes the asteroid to shift its trajectory. So far nobody has got further than the theoretical stage, so nobody knows if any of this will work.

Experts say we still don't really know what's out there. An impact could happen at any time.

Like tomorrow.

While we're worried about what might happen to the Earth in a collision, how do we know that the near-Earth object might not have worried inhabitants of its own? And what steps might they take to deflect us?

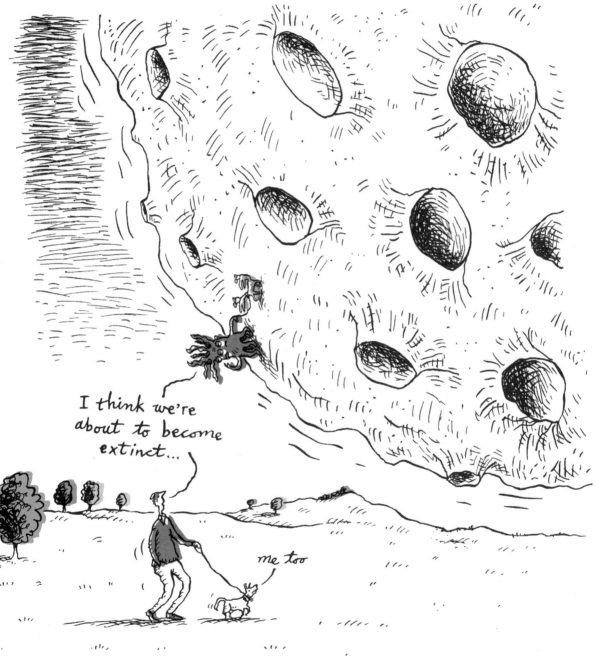

Gamma Wave Pulse

Earth is a sitting duck for pulses of destructive energy that come from so far away in the cosmos that we can't even detect the source.

Gamma rays, the most powerful form of radiation, are created from the decay of radioactive material. Sometimes they appear as the result of a supernova explosion, such as that of the Crab Nebula, which lit up the sky in 1054. When stars explode, or when black holes get tetchy, they emit this super-strong radiation in pulses that last for fractions of a second to several minutes.

These pulses travel at the speed of light through space and pass through every solid object they encounter.
Unlike visible light, they cannot be seen or their images captured in mirrors.

Because they have the shortest wavelength of any known form of radiation, they are the strongest. A burst can release more energy in 10 seconds than the Sun will emit in 10 billion years. The rays kill human cells, which is why they are used in cancer therapies. If a gamma wave burst were to strike the Earth, much of the protective ozone layer would be stripped away, leaving all life susceptible to ultraviolet and other harmful forms of radiation from our own Sun.

Gamma wave pulses are not rare. According to NASA, they are continually occurring in various parts of the universe, popping like flashbulbs every few seconds. Optimistically, astrophysicists until recently have believed that such a flash only happens within our galaxy every few million years.

However, the explosion of the small neutron star known as SGR 1806-20 in late 2004 was a surprise event that disrupted communications satellites and caused other effects still being argued in scientific circles (see pages 187–186). Another surprise finding by glaciologists in 1987 of isotopes of beryllium-10 in ice samples showed that large waves of cosmic rays have impacted with Earth in much more recent history.

Still, it doesn't happen very often.

Does it?

Earthquakes from Outer Space

Can earthquakes start in outer space?

Some scientists are beginning to think so. When a star collapses into itself, huge amounts of energy in the form of gamma rays are released in fairly narrow bands. As they travel, gamma rays form gravitational surges that move faster than the rays themselves.

The earthquake of Boxing Day 2004 caused a huge tsunami in the Pacific that killed more than 240,000 people. By far the largest quake of modern times, it registered 9.4 on the Richter scale. Just 44 hours later, a gamma ray burst struck the Earth. This was over 100 times more powerful than any previously recorded instance. It temporarily changed the shape of the Earth's ionosphere and severely distorted radio signals.

wheee!

The gamma rays originated in a star called SGR 1806-20, located near the center of our galaxy, some 26,000 light years away. In a 10th of a second it released more energy than our Sun produces in 100,000 years.

Scientists speculate that the two events being so close together in time is more than coincidence. Because gamma rays are slowed by passing through electrons and space dust, the gravitational pulse would have hit the Earth at just about the time of the earthquake on December 26.

It is now possible to identify fault lines where earthquakes are likely to occur, but it is still an inexact science to try to predict when they will happen. If their origin is thousands of light years away, we may never know until it is too late.

"If anything, the December 27, 2004 gamma ray burst shows us that we do not live in a peaceful celestial environment... Like the December 26th earthquake and the December 27th gamma ray burst, the next superwave will arrive unexpectedly. It will take us by surprise," says Dr. Paul LaViolette of the Starburst Foundation.

Gravitational pulses don't just come from far away in the galaxy. Early in March 2011, scientists recorded a spectacular X-class solar flare within line of sight of the Earth. The colossal earthquake near Japan, with its resulting tsunami, hit just a matter of a few hours afterward.

Contagion from Space

We are in danger of invasion from space. And the aliens are too tiny to see.

Microbes may travel huge stellar distances attached to comets, scientists now believe, and have almost certainly entered Earth's atmosphere. Because we have evolved without any prior contact with these tiny life forms, we would have no innate resistance to fall back on in the event of infection.

This real-life update of *The Day of the Triffids* enjoys the support of some noted astrobiologists. The recent discovery of microorganisms in the upper reaches of the atmosphere lends further credence to the existence of life from outer space.

In fact, some believe that all life on Earth began when a comet or other astral body deposited microbial life on Earth nearly four billion years ago. This theory, known as panspermia, is defended by well-known scientists such as Professor Chandra Wickramasinghe, Director of the Cardiff Centre for Astrobiology.

Uh oh. A disease from space.

184

It was previously believed that the harsh conditions of space, such as freezing and very high temperatures, lack of oxygen and gravity would make microbial life impossible outside the comfort zone of Earth or an Earthlike planet. But recent discoveries of life in extreme conditions on Earth have given a different picture.

In 1969, NASA recovered streptococcus mitis bacteria from a camera brought back from the moon by astronauts Pete Conrad and Alan L. Bean. The camera had been deposited there 30 months earlier by an unmanned space probe. Because of the rigorous precautions of the space program, it is known that the camera was free of Earth organisms at the time of launch, so the conclusion is clear:

Germs can live on the Moon.

Even more frightening is the discovery that certain bacteria actually grow faster and get stronger in zero gravity. This might mean that the microorganisms that make it through would be even tougher to defeat than the Earth-born ones.

Assuming that antibiotics and antiviral drugs continue to work (see pages 135–134), we can just about manage to avoid mass contagion from germs that share our evolutionary history.

But nobody ever thought that diseases might fall from the sky.

I'm contagious, earthlings.

Earth's Poles Reverse

The world is about to turn upside down.

CLONK

SATELLITE ORBITS ARE DISRUPTED

Scientists predict that a North/South pole reversal occurs every 300,000 years or so. It happens when the strength of the planet's magnetic field diminishes. In such times, what has been the focal point of magnetic compasses gets disordered, finally flipping over, making things work in reverse. Migrating birds get lost. Navigation becomes problematic for everybody, including our satellites, ships and planes.

The present strength of the magnetic field is far lower than in historically verifiable times. Some scientists believe that the "magnetic deficit" accounts for the fact that there are fewer large land animals than in past eras. The dinosaurs thrived during hefty magnetic times.

Our magnetic field is now weak. Very weak. Despite the direst predictions of the lunatic fringe, if the magnetic poles reverse, the Sun

BIRDS FLY UPSIDE DOWN & BACKWARD

will not start rising in the west, and the hot core of the planet is not going to burst its container. At least, most scientists don't think so.

SHIPS GET LOST

But what could actually happen is nearly as bad.

When the Earth's magnetic field gets weak enough to shift poles, the protective envelope that shields us from cosmic rays gets less effective. The atmosphere gets thinner. The planet becomes even more susceptible to the huge emissions of ultraviolet light, X-rays and gamma rays from the Sun. Radiation-generated illnesses such as melanoma increase. Communications systems are disordered, and in a severe enough instance, all digital technology could be rendered ineffective.

As if that wasn't bad enough, our local star flips its magnetic field once every 11 years, and when that happens, huge solar storms increase and produce even more dangerous radiation than usual.

Croydon should be just over the next ridge.

MRS. BELLOW'S SENSE OF DIRECTION LETS HER DOWN

When is the next expected pole reversal for the Sun? 2012.

181

False Vacuum Event

Space is a giant vacuum. One big void, full of absolutely nothing.

False.

Theoretical physicists have uncovered a new and worrying possibility: what if the vacuum we know as space isn't really a vacuum at all, but simply an area of minimum density? And what if the universe, very big indeed if not actually infinite, does contain bona fide vacuums? Some theories suggest that it probably does, give or take a few trillion misbehaving quantum particles.

If such a vacuum got into our cosmic neighborhood, according to physicists like S. Coleman and F. de Luccia, it would arrive at nearly the speed of light and gobble up the solar system instantaneously. There would be no warning, no sirens or flashing red lights, no instructions on building fallout shelters. We would simply disappear as if we had never existed. This is called a "vacuum metastability event," but it's really just another word for curtains.

180

fig b:
THE EDGE OF OUR UNIVERSE
WHOOOOOO...
OUR GALAXY
EARTH
What's that noise?
The end of the universe.
This artist's impression of a false vacuum event is completely inaccurate!
Hmm... Absolute destruction of the whole universe... That's close enough for me.

Imagine that our universe is a bubble of air rising toward the surface throughout the history of the universe. Imagine then what happens when we finally arrive at the surface.

Pop.

BLANK SPACE WHERE
OUR UNIVERSE USED
TO BE

As Coleman and de Luccia say:

. . . after vacuum decay, not only is life as we know it impossible, so is chemistry as we know it. However, one [used to be able to] draw stoic comfort from the possibility that perhaps in the course of time the new vacuum would sustain, if not life as we know it, at least some structures capable of knowing joy. This possibility has now been eliminated.

(*International Journal of Theoretical Physics*, Vol. 45, No. 12)

Solar Storm

By the time you finish reading this page, we could have sunk from Digital Age to Stone Age.

Eight minutes. That's how long it takes light, gamma and X-rays to travel to the Earth from the Sun.

My digital solar flare detector has started counting down to its own destruction.

NEE NAW NEE NAW NEE NAW NEE NAW NEE NAW...

Worried scientists report that the Sun has a regular timetable of intense magnetic disturbances, when huge flares containing light, gamma and X-rays surge outward from the surface. Some of these will reach Earth if we are unlucky enough to be facing the wrong side of the Sun.

During four summer days in 1859, the Sun erupted with huge solar flares. Telegraph lines caught fire and in some cases burned down buildings. Sparks leapt from poles all over the United States and Europe. Some telegraph terminals seemed to go on emitting messages by themselves. The sky was electrified, with an aurora-borealis-style display visible in many parts of the temperate zones. It was so bright that people got up and had breakfast in the middle of the night.

In 2010, solar flares were becoming more active and frequent. In April, a Galaxy 15 satellite was disabled, and has now become an uncommunicative "zombie" orbiting the Earth. In the further flares of August 1, almost the entire Earth-facing side of the Sun erupted. A C3-class solar eruption caused large-scale shaking of the solar corona, radio bursts and a coronal mass ejection.

NASA has warned that a new solar cycle is beginning, and during 2012 will be at its strongest. If the disturbances are severe enough, all electrical grids will be affected, wiping out power networks. Telephones, ATMs and air travel will cease functioning instantly. Computers will be destroyed. Water supplies will be cut off, leaving the populace without any of the life-supporting systems on which they now rely. The situation would last for weeks or months. The possibilities for civil unrest and disease are too dire to consider.

Stone Age people had options to deal with an Earth bare of modern services. We don't.

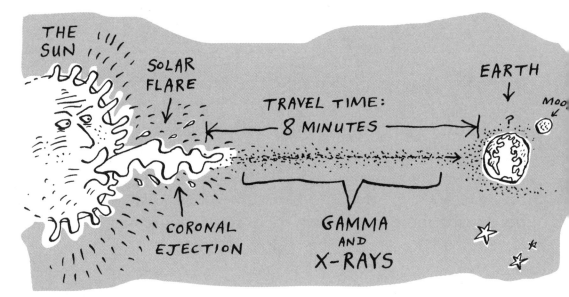

175

Alien Invasion

Ever since the time of H. G. Wells, we've been looking over our shoulders.

Little green men haven't turned up yet, as far as we know, but UFO enthusiasts all over the world would beg to differ. The photographs of the Roswell incident, complete with the supine body of an extraterrestrial visitor, continue to intrigue, despite years of official debunking. It seems that we still expect to meet ET at any moment.

Projections of encounters of the third kind fall into two categories. In the first, the aliens are not just more scientifically advanced—they are better beings than we are. Their purpose is to help, or at least benignly study, earthlings. Some apocalyptic visions include the "rapture" of humanity into spacecraft for a new and better life. One such group, followers of the Hale-Bopp comet sect, were willing to drink cyanide squash in 1997 in order to meet intergalactic saviors of the human race.

The second group is more inclined to believe that any space invaders would do so for selfish reasons, either to occupy or to otherwise exploit Earth's resources. These cosmic bad guys seem to be just ahead in popular films.

Meanwhile, physicists tell us that the whole idea is probably absurd. They point out that the universe is a pretty big place, and that travel between stars—even at or approaching the speed of light—would take too long. Sci-fi writers get around this detail by envisioning "warp drives" and "wormholes" that would make contact easier. But advances in mathematics and astrophysics have offered a new possibility of contact and maybe invasion from somewhere else.

Another dimension.

Ever since Einstein's general theory of relativity turned conventional physics on its axis, there has been the possibility of dimensions beyond the three we are aware of, plus time, a fourth. The more deeply we delve into the

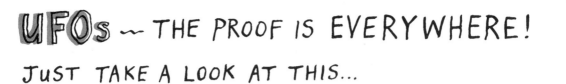

UFOs — THE PROOF IS EVERYWHERE!

JUST TAKE A LOOK AT THIS...

A FLYING SAUCER UTILIZING ITS CLOAKING DEVICE

A FLOTILLA OF FIGHTER ROCKETS USING INVISIBILITY SHIELDS

A VAST SPACESHIP DISGUISED TO LOOK LIKE AN EVERYDAY OBJECT

ALIENS IN LANDING PODS FITTED WITH MIMICRY REFLECTORS

172

OPEN-TOPPED TOURIST
ROCKETS WITH THEIR
TRANSPARENCY FIELDS ON

A SPORTY LITTLE
SHIP EMITTING
THOUGHT-JAMMING
PROJECTIONS

A COLOSSAL AIR-
MINING SPACECRAFT
USING LIGHT-BENDING
TECHNOLOGY TO HIDE
BEHIND A DUCK

171

workings of the universe, the more new dimensions turn up. String theory, which—at least for now—holds the high ground, has come up with eight or nine dimensions that we would not be aware of without mathematics. We would be no more able to see these dimensions than hear a dog whistle, because we don't have the sensory equipment.

Which all means that it's at least theoretically possible that we are sharing space and time with other beings, one of whom might have come up with a way to slip from their dimension into ours. Not intergalactic visitors, then.

Inter-dimensional ones.

Don't stop looking over your shoulder just yet.

A GUIDE TO SOME COMMON CREATURES FROM OTHER DIMENSIONS YOU SHOULD WATCH OUT FOR:

NOTE — THEY CAN REMAIN UTTERLY STILL FOR LONG PERIODS TO LULL YOU INTO A FALSE SENSE OF SECURITY.

RICH TEA

USED → TISSUE

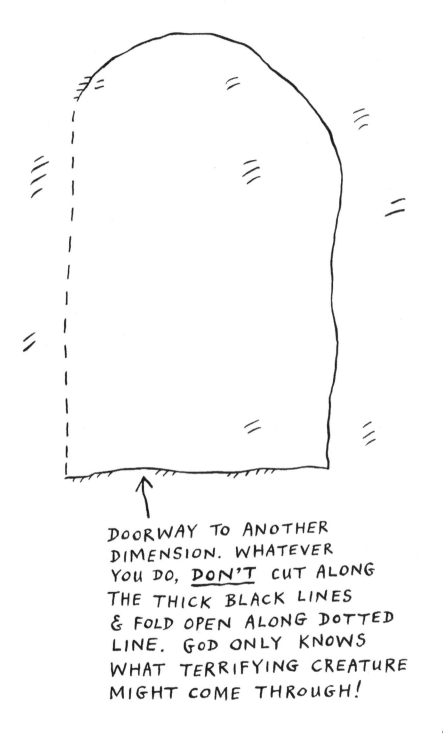

DOORWAY TO ANOTHER
DIMENSION. WHATEVER
YOU DO, <u>DON'T</u> CUT ALONG
THE THICK BLACK LINES
& FOLD OPEN ALONG DOTTED
LINE. GOD ONLY KNOWS
WHAT TERRIFYING CREATURE
MIGHT COME THROUGH!

Death of the Solar System

There are lots of ways the world might end. Some are more likely, others less so. But there is one Doom scenario on the horizon that is certain, total, and will bring about the end of everything we know.

A solar supernova.

Astrophysicists calculate that a star like our own has a life of about 10 billion years. Ours is middle-aged, about halfway there. At some point during the next 5 billion years, in the space of a few seconds, the core of the Sun will collapse in on itself, explode and, for a brief instant, shine at a billion times its present brightness. It will be visible several galaxies away for a short time, then become a neutron star.

As it expands in its initial phase, it will devour Mercury and Venus. We won't mind, of course, because we will long since have vaporized. We won't be aware of being sucked into the black hole the Sun leaves in its wake, and being compressed into an unimaginably small space.

The astrophysicists can only offer us a tiny reassurance. This total end of everything isn't due for quite a while. Even if their theories do change every few years, they know pretty much everything about the universe.

Don't they?

THE **LIFE CYCLE** OF OUR **SUN**

OUR SUN AS A
SKITTISH, YOUNG
STAR. OPTIMISTIC
AND EAGER.

THE TEENAGE SUN.
A BIT BORED AND
KNOW-IT-ALL.

IN ITS "TWENTIES" AND
"THIRTIES" THE SUN
FLARES UP, GETTING
HOTTER WITH FRUSTRATION.

DURING LATER LIFE
IT BECOMES RED-FACED,
SWELLING WITH POMPOUS
FURY.

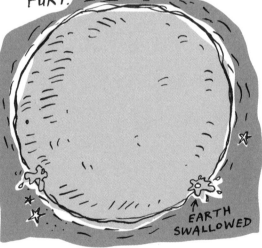

IN OLD AGE IT SHRINKS,
COOLS AND TURNS WHITE.

FINALLY, THE SUN
BECOMES DARK, DEAD
AND COLD FOR ALL
ETERNITY.

Environmental Degradation

It's not just the upper atmosphere we're screwing up. We're making a mess of things down here as well. And some scientists believe that a cumulative disaster could catch us by surprise.

We've got used to the mantra of ecologists by now. We do a bit of recycling, pity the polar bears and put some change in the WWF cup. When we sometimes buy a cheeseburger meal deal and get no fewer than 17 articles of paper and plastic packaging with it, we furtively dump it as soon as possible. We never see the giant panda or the tiger, and the only cod we come across is covered in bread crumbs on a plastic tray.

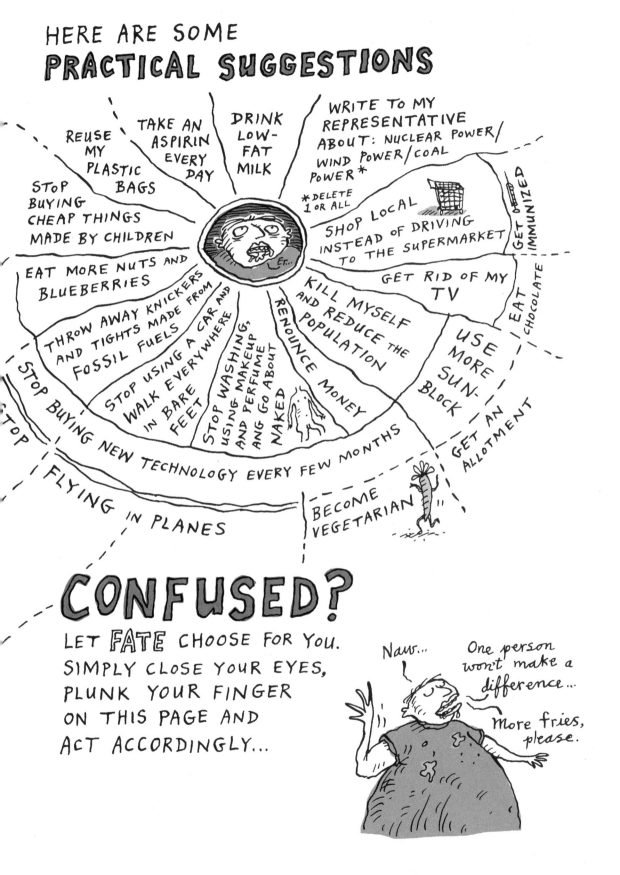

a) Coral Reef Destruction

Coral reefs are beautiful. They draw tourists by the millions and provide income for countries with not much else to offer sightseers. They are a model of biodiversity, with countless species of fish and other sea creatures on which the economies of small fishing communities depend. Called the "rain forests of the sea," they are a rich source of medicines for such maladies as heart disease, leukemia and ulcers. They have been around for millions of years.

And we're killing them off.

Oil spills, waste dumping and other by-products of human activity are causing their destruction, as does acidification of the sea. Recently we have learned that estrogen-like compounds entering the environment are disrupting the reproductive lives of the small marine polyps that form the reefs (see pages 146–144).

We have already lost 10% of the world's coral reefs. In the Philippines, the number is closer to 70%.

Sad, but so what?

Some 25% of the world's fish live near the reefs. In marginal communities that depend upon them, this means famine. Such a loss in numbers would add to the already stressed populations of food fish, and bring the global food crisis one step nearer.

Coral reefs protect coasts from erosion and deterioration

through storm surges. Many places that are now favorite holiday spots would disappear or become useless. This would create more migration, more economic stress and more conflict.

THE LIFE CYCLE OF CORAL

i ~ MALE CORAL

FEMALE CORAL

ii ~ POLLUTION CAUSES MALE CORAL TO TURN FEMALE

iii ~ GAY CORAL PERFECTLY HAPPY BUT NO LONGER PRODUCING BABY CORAL

iv ~ NO CORAL

Even if you live in a landlocked country, never travel and don't eat fish-and-chips, you're helping to wipe out this natural treasure every day. So don't point the finger at the snorkelers.

We're all to blame.

b) Vanishing Fish Stocks

Coral reefs? Big deal. There are plenty more fish in the sea.

MORE!

It's all gone, son.

← GADUS MORHUA

Or are there?

Signs are that we're emptying the seas of fish. According to marine biologists, we have enough fishing capacity to serve four planets the size of Earth. Yet more than 25% of fish stocks are either overexploited or depleted. Despite recent efforts to limit catches and reform bad practices that unnecessarily destroy marine creatures, the trend is worsening.

Some species are so rare that the price has shot up to astronomical levels. A few years ago, a very large bluefin tuna sold at a Tokyo market for almost $400,000. This is a shade higher than what you might expect to pay in your local diner, but it points to the fact that highly desirable fish are, quite simply, running out. Even your favorite, *Gadus morhua*, probably known to you as North Atlantic cod, is at critical levels. Remember when fish-and-chips was a cheap meal?

But the problem affects more than our wallets. Biologists warn that overfishing and species depletion are causing ecological changes to the oceans, which have a fragile balance to maintain in such things as oxygen and sea temperatures.

Sad about the fish, but at least we've saved the whales and dolphins. Haven't we?

More than 20,000 dolphins are killed each year off the coast of Japan. As for whales, pressure by Japan, Iceland and other countries continues on the international community to ease restrictions. "Scientific research" allowances give countries the right to kill up to 1,000 each year.

Bad news for Flipper. Bad news for us, too.

COMMIT THESE FISH TO MEMORY
YOU WON'T GET TO SEE THEM AGAIN

COD & CHIPS

HAKE & CHIPS

SALMON FISHCAKES

PLAICE & CHIPS

TURBOT & MASH

RED SNAPPER & NEW POTATOES

KIPPERS & BREAD & BUTTER

FISH FINGERS & BEANS

FISH-IN-A-BAG & FROZEN PEAS

157

c) Tropical Deforestation

Look! We missed one.

Thank God.

Now we have something to do today.

Anyone for a spot of tree-cutting?

Near the equator, all around the Earth are the areas of greatest biological diversity and productivity. The rain forests of places like Brazil are home to the largest numbers of species known to the planet. We are only beginning to scratch the surface of identifying them. Biologists believe that they probably contain cures for cancer and other diseases, in addition to their many other life-giving properties. They represent the deep end of the earthly gene pool. They help regulate the oxygen levels in our atmosphere, and, according to research by NASA, could make a vital difference in helping to sustain the Earth in the event of a catastrophic "extinction event."

CO_2 IN

OXYGEN OUT

These forests are being cut down at an astonishing rate. If you look at time-lapse satellite photos of the last few years you can see them disappearing like melting snow.

So who's cutting them down? You are. That is, unless you never

156

Nothing to water down there.

Let's move on.

use latex, cork, fruit, nuts, timber, fibers, spices, natural oils and resins or medicines. Not only that, when you buy beef products or grains grown in recently cleared areas of the forests, you might as well have gone out for a day's work with a chain saw.

The people who do the deforestation are not ignorant or heedless. Education programs have been around for years that try to alert the mainly poor exploiters of the forests about the need for sustainability. People need income, because they want to buy some of the things we take for granted. It always just happens one tree at a time.

Something to think about in the cancer ward or when the air gets too thin to breathe. Maybe any one of the problems of deforestation and ocean degradation mentioned above won't be enough to kill us off. But maybe a combination of overexploited resources and ignored scientific warnings will. There are lots of other things we haven't mentioned, all of which add up rapidly.

But you know what they are, don't you?

Ozone Layer Depletion

Did you ever wonder why Australian cricketers still wear that funny white cream on their faces? Wasn't that all about holes in the ozone layer, and haven't we solved that by now?

The white cream is a sunblock. They still wear it because the most optimistic forecast for the restoration of the ozone layer to 1980 levels is 2068. Meanwhile, we are at risk from melanoma, cataracts and crop failure.

The Montreal Protocol of 1989 banned the manufacture and use of CFCs, which were commonly used as propellants in spray cans and as a gas for refrigeration. It has made a remarkable impact on the amounts of new fluorocarbons found in the upper atmosphere, scientists tell us.

But it's still up there.

No one agrees about the long-term effects the polar "ozone holes" will have on Earth life. Where the layer has been all or nearly all depleted, there have been rises in some dread diseases like basal and squamous cell carcinomas.

Oddly, it has been proposed that a depletion in the ozone layer could cause cooling in the stratosphere. By making the Earth cooler, this might possibly offset the rate of global warming. But at the same time, the very gases that wipe out the ozone are "greenhouse gases," so it could go either way.

Keep your sunscreen handy. We'll just have to wait and see.

SPACE

ALIENS

OZONE LAYER

LAYER of FAIRIES

FAIRIES BEING SUCKED OUT INTO SPACE

HOLE

Aaaii!

HELP!

THE ATMOSPHERE

What are you doing with that aerosol?

Spraying a hole in the clouds to let the sunshine through.

PSSST

153

DIAGRAM NOT TO SCALE NOR REMOTELY FACTUALLY CORRECT

Species Extinction

The passenger pigeon, the stegosaurus and the dodo are all kaput. Who's next?

The problem of species extinction isn't a new one. The dinosaurs vanished 65 million years ago after being around for 150 million years. Theories range from an asteroid impact in the Caribbean Sea to an unknown contagious disease. Species disappear when their environmental conditions change, slowly or drastically. This process has always been with us.

But now it's happening faster, and to a lot more animals and plants than we can keep track of. Our grandchildren won't be able to see white rhinos on a vacation safari. Some of those interesting vines that tangle the rain forests might be gone before we ever clock them.

Sad news, but . . . so what?

Ecology is a fledgling science, but we already know how complex it is. Taking just the rain forests, we know that more than 50,000 plant and animal species become extinct every year following deforestation.

Of these, only about 1% have ever been studied. Some scientists believe that the cures for many illnesses, including cancer, may be locked up in the lost flora. Already, 25% of our medicines are based on rain forest plants.

Plants make oxygen. People make CO_2. Assuming that

carbon dioxide is the major culprit in global warming, losing plants means raising temperatures.

Overcultivation of food crops takes us further and further from the original rootstock of plants. When a new disease strikes, such as that affecting the banana, we may have lost the basic genetic material that might save the species.

Every time an insect species disappears, such as the honeybee, it takes along with it part of the vital function of pollination of our food and fiber crops.

We may be on a countdown to our own extinction without knowing it. If a tree falls in the forest and there's no one around to hear it, does it make a sound?

Yes. Ticktock.

Yes, We Have No Bananas

Take the humble banana.

BANANA GRAPH

SHOWING HOW MUCH BANANAS WILL BE MISSED

- - - -LOTS
- - - -A BIT
- - -NOT AT ALL
- - -I NEVER -LIKED THEM ANYWAY
- - -I'M ALLERGIC
- - - -GOOD RIDDANCE
- -YUCK!

Scientists fear that this much-loved breakfast fruit is on its way out, after 15,000 years of human cultivation. Because it has been so intensively grown, it lacks the genetic diversity essential to fight off opportunistic bacterial and fungal infestations.

There has already been one banana apocalypse, when the species of the fruit known as Gros Michel (Big Mike) was wiped out by a fungus related to Dutch elm disease. Big Mike was said to be sweeter and more flavorful than the Cavendish variety we eat nowadays. Now the Panama fungus threatens all remaining versions of the fruit.

INTRODUCING
THE *artificial* BANANA!

MADE FROM SOYBEANS AND SQUASHED INTO A BANANA SHAPE, IT IS DYED YELLOW AND TURNS BLACK JUST LIKE THE REAL THING!

fig a~   fig b~

NB - CAN NO LONGER BE CALLED A FRUIT

The real possibility of Doom is only implied by the banana plague. How many of our over-cultivated and genetically altered crops could fall prey to the same fate? In our successful domination of nature, have we left our genetic flanks fatally exposed?

Bloody things! I thought they were extinct!

Honeybees

No more bee stings? No more weird guys with bee beards? No more honey on our pancakes?

That's the possible future, according to scientists. The humble honeybee is on its way out.

CLICK
WHIRRR
CLICK

This is due to "colony collapse disorder," when bee colonies suddenly lose critical mass in population and spiral toward death. The major culprits are believed to be pesticides and a newly identified viral infection. This organism thrives in the guts of overwintering bees and quickly spreads throughout the hive. More than a third of the North American bee population is likely to disappear over the next year.

And now there's even worse news: you might be killing off bees every time you use your mobile phone.

A recent study at Panjab University in India showed that fixing mobile phones to a hive for two 15-minute periods each day for three months caused bees to stop producing honey, reduced the queen's egg production by half and brought about a drastic reduction in bee numbers. Because bees may rely on magnetic fields for direction, flooding the environment with cell phone signals may make them unable

CLICK
CLICK
CLICK
CLICK...

to find their way back to the hive.

Sad. But can't we live without honey on our pancakes?

Think again. The problem isn't just with the buzzing insects: 90% of food crops rely upon insect pollination, and bees are by far the most effective. If bees were to become extinct, the effect on world food supplies would be catastrophic, and worsen the already declining ability of humans to feed themselves. Subsistence farmers could find themselves plunged into famine in a

WHIRRRRR...

short period of time, and all of us would feel it.

CHUG
CHUG
CHUG
CHUG

Fewer bees means fewer plants means fewer bees means . . .

Fewer of us.

NO BEES? NO PROBLEM!

SCIENTISTS WILL REPLACE ALL THE REAL BEES WITH TINY ROBOT VERSIONS. AS WELL AS POLLINATING FLOWERS, THE ARTIFICIAL BEES WILL BE ABLE TO COLLECT POLLEN, MAKE HONEY, PACK IT IN JARS, STICK ON LABELS AND DELIVER IT TO THE SHOPS.

THEIR STINGS WILL BE INTENSELY PLEASURABLE.

Gender Erosion

Is every creature on Earth becoming female?

Scientists think so. Lately they have discovered alarming levels of estrogen in our rivers and lakes. Estrogen is the cocktail of hormones that make half of the human race female. Everybody has some of it—even men.

Estrogen leaks into the environment through sewage treatment and the coating of aluminium tins. Like many chemical by-products of industry, these substances don't just go away.

Recent studies have identified male fish with female sex organs and anatomically deformed otters, not to mention a dramatic shrinkage of penis size in Florida alligators.

Many scientists believe that human fertility is decreasing through the ingestion of estrogen from public water supplies.

Marine biologists worry that high levels of estrogen will wreck the sex lives of coral reefs, resulting in a shortfall of the world's fish crop of at least a quarter.

No one is sure what to do, but one proposal for removing estrogen from water supplies has come from the University of Ulster, which has ". . . discovered that if you shine an ultraviolet light on titanium dioxide, the titanium becomes activated, and capable of converting the estrogen to CO_2—the harmless everyday gas that puts the bubbles in your fizzy pop."

Carbon dioxide or estrogen: pick your poison.

Global Food Crisis

We thought he was banished forever, but we were wrong. One of the original Four Horsemen of the Apocalypse seems not to have gone away, after all.

Famine.

Our experience with starvation on a large scale has mostly been limited to those terrible television images of Africans during droughts. Emaciated babies, grieving mothers huddled in makeshift shelters, the mass graves. It made us feel so bad that we gave a record amount of money for emergency relief. Pop stars wrote songs and held concerts. Governments made promises. We switched channels.

But the spectre of mass starvation is back. The world is facing fast-approaching scarcities of just about everything necessary to produce enough food for everyone. The lack of fresh water, arable land, nutrients, oil and fats, technology, skills, fish stocks and reliable climates is leading to a famine of hitherto unknown magnitude. And it's projected for sometime this century.

How could this happen?

International organizations monitoring world food supplies warn that a number of interlocking phenomena have created a tangle that we may not be able to escape from. In addition to overpopulation (see pages 65–64), the redistribution of human settlements has caused unpredicted shortages. As more people move into urban conurbations, their use of scarce fresh water increases. As emphasis on a market economy forces the production of cash crops for export, the land becomes degraded through over-cultivation. Fish stocks get depleted, minerals become scarcer in topsoil, erosion turns formerly arable farmland into dust. Increases in meat consumption further aggravate land shortages. And on and on. The pattern is complex, and may seem unbreakable without massive changes in the way we live.

Starvation is not the only way famine turns into Doom. When food gets scarce, prices rise. When high-quality, nutritious food becomes too expensive, people have less of it, become sick, less capable and subject to disease. Mass migration from places of little food to richer sites creates economic and political strife. Ultimately, famine leads to another of the Four Horsemen.

War.

FAMINE, WAR AND THE OTHER 27 HORSEMEN OF THE APOCALYPSE

142

Fossil Fuel Depletion

Oil and gas won't last forever.

That's not news, because we've been hearing it for almost all our lives. If we think about it, we probably just picture windmills humming in some remote future, or hydrogen-fueled limousines zipping healthily down the motorways. But some scientists are warning us that the tipping point for an energy crisis is nearer than we think.

No one knows exactly when the last drop of oil will be pumped out of the ground. Estimates vary from 10 to 65 years. In most scenarios, oil, gas and coal gradually run out, making it cheaper to switch to wind, solar and tidal sources. Helpful industries will find ways to make the transition seamless. We won't even have to give up trips to Machu Picchu and weekends in Las Vegas.

A CLIFF EVENT

But some scientists warn that we're heading for a "cliff event."

This prediction envisions a few sharp shocks as extreme shortages and blackouts multiply and nations begin a policy of energy hoarding with consequent political and military results.

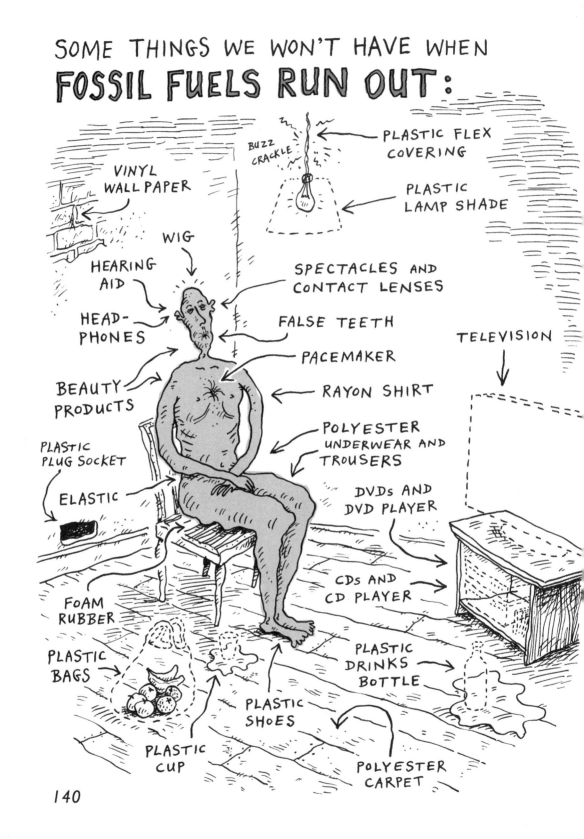

140

We wouldn't have to wait for absolute depletion because disruption in supply would bring on a crisis. The result would be dramatic, not gradual.

Shortages would lead to a scenario that imitates what has happened in famines. Prices would shoot up. The poorest communities would suddenly go from having little energy to having none at all. Widespread chaos would affect the political sphere.

With the loss of inexpensive petroleum products, we would lose more than just fuel for heating and transport. More than 70,000 products we use daily would either disappear or become prohibitively expensive. Things like computer components, mobile phones, eyeglass lenses, common medicines and replacement heart valves would be unaffordable.

Some historians speculate that the entire story of modern civilisation is merely a blip on the long line of preindustrial existence. The discovery of oil made us leap forward technologically, and its disappearance may make us fall back.

Stone axes to satellites, then back to stone axes.

STONE ELECTRIC KETTLE

STONE TV REMOTE

137

Is your neck getting sore from watching the heavens or peering anxiously at the landscape?

Maybe it's time to drop the telescope and grab the microscope.

Clever little beggars...

Microbial War

While we were worried about the superweapons being developed by our enemies in other countries, a much more ancient enemy was developing a sneak attack that is capable of killing people by the million.

Bacteria.  1000s OF BACTERIA CAN FIT ON THE HEAD OF A PIN

Ever since Alexander Fleming discovered penicillin by accident one day in 1928, we have relaxed our fear of these tiny organisms. Diseases that used to kill us were banished with a single jab. Dread sexually transmitted maladies became a thing of the past. It seemed that we had found a magic bullet that would protect us from all those things that plagued our ancestors.

It is true that we heard that strains of bacteria were evolving in ways that foiled treatment with antibiotics, but the clever folk in white lab coats made sure we were ahead of the game by developing new and stronger drugs.

Until now.

When antibiotics were first used, bacteria were hit by threats a million times more potent than anything they had faced before. It should have been game over. But bacteria aren't pushovers. Their response was to evolve a million times faster.

We hit back with newer and stronger formulae. They responded with even trickier moves. In the last 80 years, there has been a seesaw battle going on in arenas too small to see.

As long as we kept ahead of them, we could avoid the possibility of new infections for which we have no inbuilt defenses. But that's all over now.

PLACE YOUR
FINGERTIP   ⟶ ●
ON THIS SPOT

NOW REMOVE IT

YOU HAVE JUST DEPOSITED
A FEW <u>MILLION</u> BACTERIA

NEXT, LICK YOUR FINGERTIP AND
RUB IT ON THE PAGE

YOU HAVE PROBABLY NOW DEPOSITED
CLOSE TO A <u>BILLION</u>*

BETTER BURN THIS BOOK AND BUY
A FRESH, CLEAN COPY. DON'T FORGET
TO READ IT WEARING RUBBER GLOVES

According to an article by Catharine Paddock in *Medical News Today*, the previous rate of new antibiotic products was about 15 per decade. The last 10 years have seen only 6. The reason is that pharmaceutical companies are reluctant to invest in a drug that will only be saleable for 10 years. Meanwhile, the bacteria are getting stronger, mutating happily, gaining ground (see pages 130–129).

It's the longest war humans have ever fought. And the bad guys are winning.

* These figures are disputed by Professor Alan McCarthy, department of microbiology, Liverpool University, who considers them grossly inflated.

SOME SYMPTOMS TO WATCH OUT FOR:

Flu Pandemic

Let's be honest: we're all waiting for the next pandemic.

True, we've had near brushes with swine flu, avian flu and SARS. And not nearly as many people got sick and died as we feared. Scientists are beetling away in labs, tracking the mutations in diseases that begin in ducks and pigs. Provided that they keep on the job, we should be OK, right?

Think again.

Out there in places we've never heard of, viruses are plying their trade of inhabiting warm-blooded hosts. Their lab is the whole muddy world, and ours is just a few clean white buildings. They change and reproduce with such speed that they are becoming impossible to predict or control.

The Spanish flu pandemic of 1918 was so bad that it killed somewhere between 40 and 50 million people, more than the Great War it so closely followed. In the USA alone, 28% of the population was infected and the death rate was so high that life expectancy estimates were down-rated by 10 years. Everyone was fearful. A jump-rope song of the period went like this:

I had a little bird,
Its name was Enza.
I opened the window,
And in-flu-enza.

It was formerly believed that pandemic flu followed the traditional pattern by attacking the weakest members of the population. But strains like the H1N1 variety can occur at any age. Ominously, the virus seems most deadly in young adults, not in the traditional at-risk categories of infancy and the elderly.

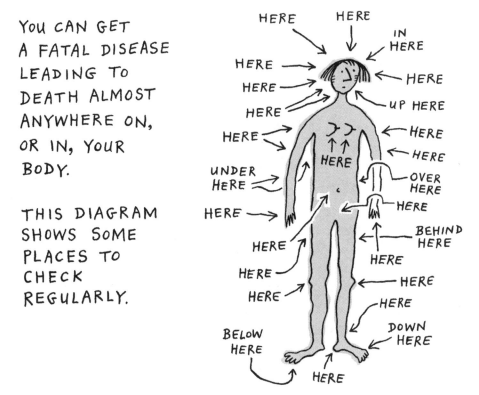

YOU CAN GET A FATAL DISEASE LEADING TO DEATH ALMOST ANYWHERE ON, OR IN, YOUR BODY.

THIS DIAGRAM SHOWS SOME PLACES TO CHECK REGULARLY.

HERE HERE IN HERE
HERE HERE UP HERE
HERE HERE
HERE HERE
UNDER HERE OVER HERE
HERE HERE
BEHIND HERE
HERE HERE
HERE HERE
BELOW HERE DOWN HERE
HERE

Because of the speed and stealth of pandemic contagion, the fear is that a new strain of something like H1N1 will strike before there is any time to prepare, decimating an entire generation, striking those most vital to keeping things running, like hospitals. And ambulances. And flu research labs.

What can we do?

Wash your hands. And don't open the window.

Superbugs

Are miracle drugs past their sell-by date? Could we be returning to a situation like that before the 20th century when we were dropping like flies from simple diseases we have since almost written off? It appears so. A new superbug is threatening to end the life-saving ability of antibiotics—all antibiotics.

And it's all down to promiscuous bacteria.

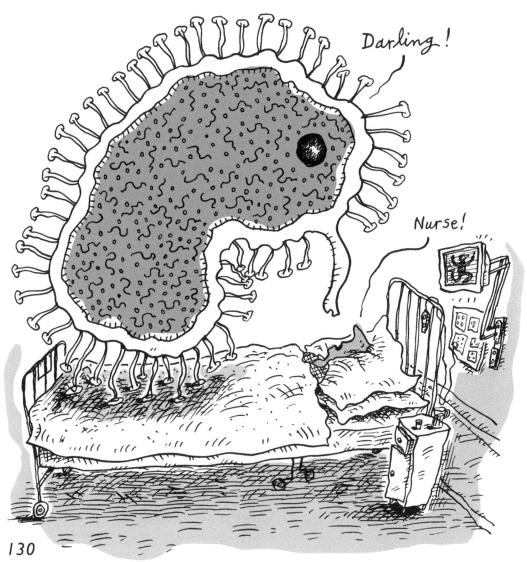

NDM-1 was first seen in India in 2008. It has the ability to produce an enzyme that can make bacteria such as *E. coli* immune to carbapenems, broad-spectrum antibiotics distantly related to penicillin.

According to Hugh Pennington, Emeritus Professor of Bacteriology at the University of Aberdeen, bacteria, though they don't need sex to reproduce, have it anyway. By deliberately jumping onto each other like randy teenagers, they spread the enzyme, making even simple germs able to laugh at drug treatment.

WEAR HAND CONDOMS TO PREVENT BACTERIA HAVING SEX

In an age of "medical tourism," when patients might spend time in different hospitals on separate continents, the bug travels easily. It has recently appeared in hospital wards in rapidly increasing numbers.

At present, the only defense on offer is a renewed appeal for hand washing and hospital sanitation. But success in this area is notoriously difficult to achieve. In places like Scandinavia and Holland, patients transferred from British hospitals are routinely assumed to carry the MRSA bacterium.

As Dr. Pennington said in an article in the *Daily Telegraph*, hoping for new antibiotics to combat the NDM-1 and other micro-villains remains just that.

Hope.

Ebola (Hemorrhagic Fever)

There are just a few diseases that make epidemiologists shudder. One of these is Ebola.

This virus has been found in West and Central Africa, where it has killed a few hundred people in several outbreaks. It is zoonotic (animal-borne), and is often found in primates. It causes high fever and a generalized infection of body organs, which begin to bleed. Recovery rates are low, and anything up to 88% of infected people die from it, usually horribly, in a few weeks.

Scientists believe it is transmitted by the body fluids of an infected animal or person. In some of the largest known epidemics in places like the Republic of the Congo, most victims were either close family or health care workers, who caught it from patients.

THE ETIQUETTE OF SAFE SNEEZING

fig i — Ah ah ah ...

fig ii — ... CHOO!

In laboratory conditions, doctors have found the spores of the virus in droplets in breath. Contagion is not known to have followed as a result of breathing in aerosol particles. But viruses are clever, and have the ability to mutate rapidly.

So far, major outbreaks of the virus have been avoided. Precautions such as surgical gloves and face masks have limited its spread. As with other diseases, such as retroviral ones like HIV AIDS, it is believed you probably can't get it unless you eat dead chimpanzees or come into contact with someone else's bodily secretions.

Moral: Unsafe sex might get a lot unsafer.

SAFE SEX

125

Super Volcano

Just a few miles away from us there's a giant ball of burning rock the size of the Earth. This rock is so hot that it's in liquid form, capable of instantly incinerating everything it touches.

You don't need a telescope to find it. It's just under our feet.

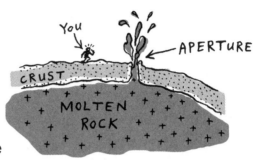

Volcanoes erupt when the pressure caused by massive temperatures forces an aperture in the Earth's crust. As in the Icelandic eruption of 2010, clouds of smoke and dust stream into the atmosphere. This dust can cause disruption to travel and cooling of nearby regions as it blocks sunlight. But these are the small fry of eruptions. There are a few that can alter history and even end it.

Super volcanoes.

This name is given to a class of eruptions that we know about only from geological evidence. We've never witnessed one, because we probably wouldn't still be around if we had. We might have shared the fate of the Neanderthals, who some scientists believe were finished off by the eruption of a south Italian volcano 40,000 years ago.

Take Yellowstone.

This site in Wyoming is the largest super volcano known. If it erupts, some of the effects would be the complete devastation of an area the size of Europe, a coating of ash ranging from six inches to hundreds of feet over thousands of miles, a "winter" caused by clouds of dust and ash that lasts several years, the widespread failure of food crops, probable species extinction and the lowering of global temperatures by up to 20 degrees.

In some ways, volcanoes are predictable. The intervals between eruptions have been noted by geologists and backed up by paleontologists. Yellowstone, for example, has a schedule of eruption activity every 600,000 years or so. The last time it blew up was about 640,000 years ago. Worryingly, geologists have confirmed a recent bulging of the terrain at the site of the volcano, or caldera. This could mean the magma is starting to act.

Of course, it is 40,000 years overdue.

A VOLCANIC EXPERIMENT TO TRY AT HOME

i ~ FILL A BUCKET WITH ASH AND DUST FROM THE VACUUM CLEANER.

ii ~ PRETEND YOU'RE AN EVIL MASTERMIND AND LAUNCH YOUR "MISSILE" TOWARD THE SITTING ROOM CEILING.

Whee!

iii ~ IMAGINE THE SITTING ROOM IS THE WORLD. IMPRESSIVE, HUH?

iv ~ EXPERIMENT OVER. TIME TO GO WATCH TV.

I'm going to KILL you, you... you...

Mega-Tsunami

Earthquakes cause tidal waves. So no earthquake, no tsunami, right?

Wrong, say the scientists.

There's a large chunk of rock teetering on the edge of the Canary Islands that could cause a mega-tsunami of sufficient size to devastate the eastern seaboard of the United States. This is the entire western slope of Cumbre Vieja on the island of La Palma, the site of volcanoes that stretch back to the creation of the island chain itself.

Geologists say that, following an eruption in 1949, a deformity in the rock structure has opened a crack behind a piece of mountain measuring up to 500 cubic kilometers. If you spread that mass out one yard deep, you come up with an area three times the size of Washington, DC. If it falls all at once, it will make a splash like no other in recorded history.

fig i ~

fig ii ~

Ha ha ha!

The worst-case scenario, according to the Benfield Hazard Research Centre at University College, London, is a wall of water the height of a 17-story building that would cross the Atlantic at the speed of a jumbo jet in full flight.

New York City would be entirely flattened, as would the whole of the most populous area of the United States. Large sections of the Caribbean islands would be under water, and some projections say the backwash would severely affect Ireland, France and the western UK.

More recent studies have proposed that this danger has been overstated because the landslide might occur in more gradual stages, with less devastating results. But Bill McGuire, the Benfield director, points to similar events that have occurred within geological history. One example is unexplained large boulders that have been found in the Bahamas 20 meters above sea level, almost certainly carried there by giant waves. On the Canary Island of El Hierro, an escarpment left behind by a previous event contains melted rock, evidence of a dramatic and sudden slippage.

But it's not just the next eruption of Cumbre Vieja which has scientists worried.

The crack in the mountain is gradually being filled with rainwater, which further erodes its stability. When the crack fills up entirely, there will be very little holding the land mass in place.

Recently, rainfall in the Canaries has been at record highs.

DEATH VALLEY SURF SHOP
I always said this was an awful dumb place to put a surf shop, Joe Bob Billy.
Not for much longer, Lurleen.

Clathrate Gun Hypothesis

Maybe global warming is a gradual process. Maybe we will have time to adjust and take measures to keep the Earth habitable.

And maybe we won't.

Trapped beneath the permafrost in the Arctic are huge deposits of a gas called methane clathrate. As long as the polar regions stay comfortably frozen, this gas stays out of the atmosphere. In the event of melting permafrost, however, this gas could explode into the atmosphere with such speed that it has been called a "methane gun."

Methane is a greenhouse gas 60 times more powerful than carbon dioxide. A sudden release of any of the known deposits would trigger a catastrophic heating of the Earth. This may have taken place during the Permo-Triassic extinction event, when the temperature of the globe was raised by six degrees. If it happened again, extinction of most earthly life would almost certainly follow.

Including us.

Most layers of methane clathrate are too deep to surface easily. But in the Siberian Arctic, the deposits are shallowly submerged, with just a layer of permafrost on top. If the climate keeps on heating up, the margins grow thinner and thinner. Any sudden boost in the rate of warming could tip the scales and bring about what has been called "runaway global warming."

It would be sad to see the polar bears losing their habitat if the ice keeps melting. Even worse if the Gulf Stream lost its power to keep us warm. But those aren't the only problems.

If the permafrost disappears, so do we.

SEARCHING FOR SURVIVAL SOLUTIONS, n° 1:

MIKE HAS CONVERTED HIS FRIDGE INTO A HOME

Radon

Just beneath your floor there's a severe threat to your survival. This silent killer is responsible for more than 21,000 deaths per year in the United States. Radon 222. Some areas are more affected, others less so, but no one is totally safe from it without drastic measures being taken to protect their homes.

HOW TO DETECT RADON GAS IN YOUR CELLAR

SNIFF SNIFF

Radon gas is the result of the decay of uranium, which is found in most soils. It is particularly prevalent in mines, but appears in nearly all house basements and under flooring slabs. It has been known about since at least the 16th century, when it was noticed that miners were acquiring a mysterious "wasting disease," but it wasn't until the 1980s that scientists first began to measure its effects on human health. It is now considered the second largest cause of lung cancer.

Around that time people began worrying about what they were inhaling at home. A flock of new preventative techniques surfaced, such as putting ventilation systems beneath basement floors and radiation sheathing under concrete slabs. New construction regulations appeared in the United States, and as recently as 2010, Britain published new safe limits. Test kits are available for home testing, but these have not been widely taken up.

TRYING TO CATCH
RADON AS IT RISES

After the radon mini-panic in the 1980s, it seems we have
become used to the idea that even the air we breathe
holds dire threats to our survival. Just like we did with the flu
pandemics that fizzled out.

Ho-hum. Sssssssss . . .

LETTING THE
RADON ESCAPE
HARMLESSLY

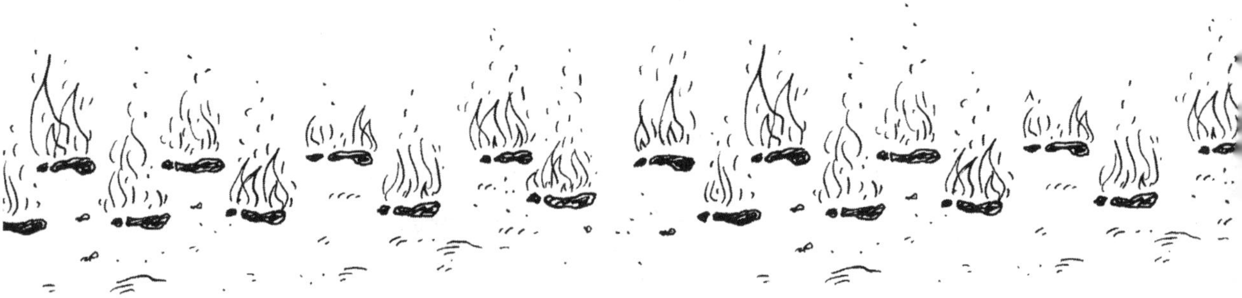

CARBON
FOOTPRINTS

113

Climate Change

We've got big problems with the climate.

You and I, in our heedless consumption of resources and the consequential dumping of carbon atoms into the atmosphere, may have brought about a disastrous future—global warming.

Scientists predict that the climate will heat up by between 1 and 3.5 degrees Celsius during this century. If that doesn't sound like a lot, we are told that the lowering of temperatures by just half a degree following a volcanic eruption in 1816 caused crop failures all over the world. There's not a lot of margin in our ecosystem.

THE WORLD's GOING TO HELL ANYWAY, SO WHY NOT ENJOY FAN HEATER IN-A-CAN™

Spray yourself with aerosol heat WHENEVER and WHEREVER you need it.

Cool! Er, hot.

According to the International Panel on Climate Change, we can expect sea level rises that put more than 100 million people at risk of tidal flooding and lost land. Several Pacific nations will completely disappear. Evaporation rates will rise too, causing deserts to eat away existing farmland. Heat stress will kill many people, as the hot summer of 2003 did to more than 14,000 in France.

Many species will become extinct in even moderate warming.

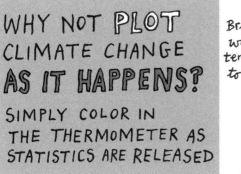

Brilliant! I can't wait for the temperature to go up!

TOAST!

HELP!

AAARGH...

YOU CAN BOIL WATER

I SEE YOU ALREADY HAVE

IT'S HOT ENOUGH TO COOK AN EGG

UNBEARABLE

OOPS. THE AIR CON BROKE DOWN

THANK GOD FOR AIR CON

BLIMEY...

PHEW! IT'S HOT

BETTER SIT IN THE SHADE

WE CAN PUT THE CAR ROOF DOWN

LOVELY WEATHER FOR A PICNIC

VERY NICE

OOH, YES...

PLEASANT

BEARABLE

CHILLY (NOT "CHILI")

BRRR!

JOLLY COLD

FREEZING!

One scientist has said that in order to survive, species will have to migrate away from the equator at the rate of nine meters a day.

Famine from loss of arable land and shrinking of fresh water supplies may strike even the lush farmlands of temperate zones. We can expect massive storms, called "hypercanes," that make Hurricane Katrina look like a summer rain shower. And it's all our fault.

Unless it isn't.

Skeptics abound. The unwillingness to believe that humans are responsible for anything as big as the weather has created a new category of problem people: climate-change deniers.

The best of these difficult types stop short of denying that temperatures are gradually rising. They point to such evidence as the recent discovery of the remains of huge trees in Antarctica to show that the climate is always changing. They invoke solar activity and other natural agents as the source of change in the weather.

A more tenacious group of deniers say that the climate isn't changing at all. They point to some unfortunate recent claims of data fiddling by academics. This empowers them to scoff at the data that hasn't been fudged. Following the lead of some reckless US politicians, their rallying cry has become "Drill, baby, drill!"

But are they the ones who are fiddling, as the world burns?

A TERRIFYING DOOM SCENARIO!

fig 1 ~

I'm BORED of hearing about climate change...

YAWN...

I don't believe it's really happening.

fig 2 ~

Let's go shopping in my new 4×4.

CARBON FOOTPRINTS

GAS
HEATING
BUILD HERE
LOVELY VIEWS
COW CHOW
FEWER TREES SO LESS GREENHOUSE GAS CONVERTED BACK TO OXYGEN
I want... NEW TEETH!
I want CHEAP CLOTHES!
I want CHEAP FOOD!
I want CHEAP HOLIDAYS
I want CHEAP CARS...
I want CHEAP EVERYTHING!
I'll worry about the environment TOMORROW
COVETING
FINALLY, THE ELEPHANT-IN-THE-ROOM TAKES UP AN ENTIRE ROOM
Time to throw away this house and get a bigger one.
THIS DRAWING CONTAINS ONLY TRUE Best Quality TRUTH

a) Vector-Borne Diseases

Warmer temperatures don't sound all that bad, you say. Maybe we won't get as many colds and cases of flu.

Maybe we'll get malaria instead.

The World Health Organization has warned that unchecked warming in northern latitudes could bring back diseases we haven't had to deal with in centuries. Things like malaria, encephalitis and dengue fever. Carried by insects, these ailments already account for more than three-quarters of a million deaths per year, many more than from HIV AIDS.

A warmer climate in the north means longer summers, a wetter atmosphere, and more damp breeding places for mosquitoes and other sources of "vector-borne" diseases.

Where is the damned thing?!
SWIPE! SWAT!

MOSQUITOES WOULD BE SO MUCH EASIER TO FIGHT IF THEY WERE LARGER

Ah ha! There you are!
SPLUT!

The mild increase in temperature we have already experienced—about 0.8 degrees Celsius—has made Azerbaijan, Tajikistan and Turkey danger areas for malaria. Predictions are that the carriers will gradually spread west and north into the temperate zone.

At present, 90% of malaria cases occur in sub-Saharan Africa. The death toll is very high, but probably less than it might be because of gradually acquired resistance to the disease through selection. In northern Europe, we have rarely had to become resistant, so the death toll would probably be much higher.

To add to the threat, ticks and sandflies, carriers of such illnesses as Lyme disease and visceral leishmaniasis, would also find the new, warmer climate agreeable.

So far, no measures beyond computer projections have been taken.

TO COMBAT CLIMATE CHANGE, SIMPLY START USING SOME OF THE EXCITING **NEW** ECO-PRODUCTS BELOW...

REPLACE YOUR TUMBLE DRYER WITH THIS INNOVATIVE SOLAR AND WIND-POWERED DEVICE:

AND HOW ABOUT TRADING IN YOUR CENTRAL HEATING FOR ONE OF THESE CLEVER ITEMS?

b) Killer Bees

Mosquitoes aren't the only flying peril to move north with the
warming climate. A slipup by a replacement beekeeper in
1957 has unleashed a new danger for north-lying countries:
killer bees.

Also called the Africanized honeybee, this species
of insect is much more aggressive than the European
variety and people who accidentally stray into their territory
can be attacked savagely. The venom in the killer bee's sting
isn't more powerful than that of ordinary honeybees. Their
danger lies in the fact that they are more defensive and more
ready to attack as a swarm. They are known to be capable of
killing a grown man.

Formerly bred in the Central American tropics because of their
higher honey productivity, bees from Africa have mated with
native species and created this new and dangerous
hybrid. Because they cannot survive harsh winters, their
spread has been restricted to areas south of Texas. But as the
climate warms, they have begun migrating, and have been
found as far north as Chesapeake Bay, near Washington, DC.

They've got attitude, and they're moving north at the rate of
two kilometers a day.

c) Gulf Stream Disruption

Global warming makes us all get hotter, right?

Wrong.

Geophysicists worry that as the Earth heats up it will melt parts of the polar caps. As the cooler water flows southward from the North Pole, it might deflect the Gulf Stream, plunging Europe and northern parts of America into a new ice age.

The Gulf Stream is a huge conveyor of water from the Caribbean out into the Atlantic. Partway across, it divides and sends warmer seawater north to Canada and eastward to northern Europe. If it were not for this giant convection heater, temperatures would be as much as five degrees lower, making much of the densely populated region all but uninhabitable.

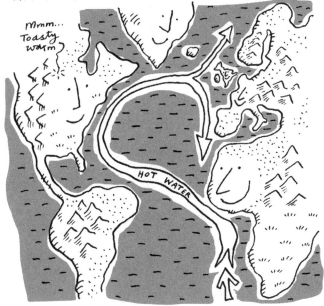

HAPPY MAP of the GULF STREAM

Mmm... Toasty warm

HOT WATER

But the danger doesn't end there. As Bill McGuire, a geophysical hazards professor at University College, London, says, "The possibility exists that a disruption of the Atlantic currents might have implications far beyond a colder northwest Europe, perhaps bringing dramatic climatic changes to the entire planet."

It's all happened before. As recently as 10,000 years ago, during a cold period called the Younger Dryas, the Gulf Stream's force was about two-thirds of current levels, with a corresponding dip in European temperatures of up to 10 degrees. All of which proves how little we know of the effects of climate change.

Turn up the temperature and freeze to death.

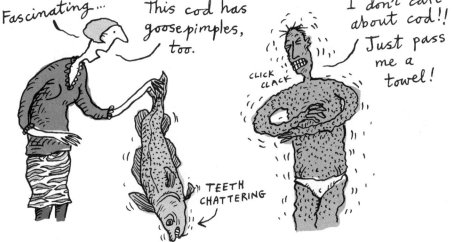

d) Hypercanes

Are super storms on their way?

A theoretical storm called a hypercane would have wind speeds of 500 miles per hour and could cover an area the size of North America. Based on what we know of its smaller cousins like Katrina, present levels of civilization and most of the population would not be able to survive. Luckily, this supersize hurricane is only possible in extreme circumstances.

Like severe global warming.

Scientists calculate that ocean temperatures would have to rise some 15 degrees Celsius in order to produce such an event. That's a lot more than the 3.5 degrees considered possible at present, arising from projections of carbon emissions.

But however fervent a believer in man-made climate change you may be, that's not the only way the Earth gets hotter. Huge underground eruptions, being struck by an asteroid or comet and unusual solar activity could add to our own contributions.

Some meteorologists believe that Katrina was at least partly caused by global warming. They point out that the fuel of giant storms is the water vapor emerging from seas. What began as a category one storm in 2005 became a category five while idling over the warm waters of the Caribbean. By the time it hit the coast of Louisiana and Mississippi it had become the worst weather event in memory.

Some estimates say that the intensity of a hurricane can be predicted by knowing the sea temperature. A rise of 1.5 degrees above average would mean an additional 15–20% in wind speed and size. By that reasoning, a rise of 3.5 degrees would bring us storms of up to 50% more intensity, and they would happen more frequently. Add in some solar flares, an eruption or two and you have a recipe for disaster.

Maybe the storms wouldn't have winds of 500 miles an hour, but 300. And maybe they wouldn't be the size of North America.

Just the size of Texas.

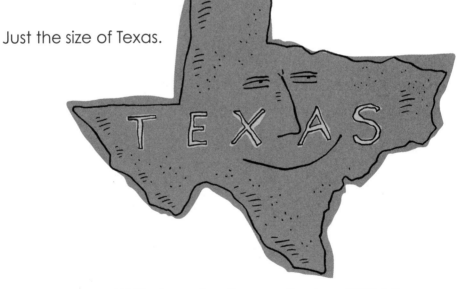

NOT ACTUAL SIZE. REAL TEXAS IS A BIT BIGGER. AND DOESN'T HAVE A FACE.

e) Endless Winter

Never mind global warming. What if summer was canceled?

If something causes a dense enough blanket of smoke and ash to rise into Earth's upper atmosphere, scientists say that what will follow will be a rerun of the "Year Without a Summer" of 1816. Following the eruption of Mount Tambora in Indonesia in 1815, Europe and North America were shrouded in a layer of smoke and ash so thick that temperatures dropped to unheard-of lows.

As far away as China, rice crops froze in the fields and water buffalo died. A dramatic increase in food prices and widespread starvation followed throughout the United States and eastern Canada, and Welsh farmers traveled huge distances begging for food.

WHY NOT TRY THAT VOLCANIC ASH EXPERIMENT AGAIN?

You do, and I'll...

A resulting epidemic of typhus ravaged Ireland, with deaths thought to reach 100,000. There were food riots in Switzerland. Byron wrote his poem "Darkness" during the lost summer of 1816.

There are at least seven known sites of "mega-volcanoes" on Earth, any one of which would eclipse Mount Tambora. The rumblings in Iceland in 2010, which resulted in flight cancellations across a wide area, are thought to be just the beginning of a long series of eruptions of much greater intensity.

But it's not only volcanoes that can cause a drastic global temperature drop.

Nuclear winter is another possibility. For this to happen, it would not be necessary to see an all-out confrontation between the major nuclear powers. A local conflict such as sometimes

A NEW LIFE FORM EVOLVES

seems to threaten between India and Pakistan would do the job. The resulting famine and disruption of the world economy might account for more deaths than the bombs themselves.

Impact winter is the name given to the cloud of debris that would follow a strike by an asteroid or comet anywhere on Earth. The effects would be the same. Those who survived the high winds, tsunamis and blast radius of such an impact would face a lowering of global temperatures of up to 20 degrees. By contrast, the mercury in 1816 fell by less than 1 degree C.

Just when we thought the future was going to be too hot, we hear that we might freeze instead.

95

Robotic Revolt

Revolt of the robots? Artificially created intelligent machines controlling humanity for its own good? Isn't that just science fiction?

Not according to top cyber-scientists, who recently organized a hush-hush conference to discuss the possibilities of artificial intelligence. The conference was the brainchild of Eric Horvitz, principal researcher at Microsoft. Some scientists, like Alan Winfield, professor at the University of the West of England, feel that we are rapidly nearing a point where advances in artificial intelligence should be vetted, as in drug trials, as a protection against harm to humans.

Unmanned predator drones already operate in Afghanistan, programmed to search out and kill humans. Though these are at present controlled by people, they are rapidly moving toward complete autonomy. According to the *Sunday Times*, Samsung has developed

HOW TO ASSEMBLE YOUR OWN PERSONAL ROBOT NANNY

fig 1 ~

fig 2 ~ FIX PART A TO PART B

fig 3 ~ FIX PART C TO PART D

fig 4 ~ FIX PART E TO PART F

fig 5 ~ FIX PART G TO PART H

fig 6 ~ FIX PART I TO PART J

fig 7 ~ FIX ALL THE BITS YOU'VE MADE TOGETHER

fig 8 ~ NOW KEEP GOING WITH ALL THE REST...

fig 9 ~ ...UNTIL YOU'RE DONE! SWITCH IT ON AND VOILA!

autonomous sentry robots, who can be programmed to shoot to kill.

Robots are already available who can learn their owner's behavior, imitate their owner's voice and even recharge themselves when batteries run low. A variety of "virus" robot can be inserted into mobile phones, enabling third parties to masquerade as the owners and penetrate bank accounts.

A new and potentially worrying element of artificial intelligence is known as "swarm robotics," a system linking simple individual machines into a collective intelligence, like that of ants or bees. Linking up would make any cyber revolt ridiculously simple.

INDIVIDUALLY STUPID WASTE-PAPER-BASKET ROBOTS, WHEN LINKED TOGETHER, COMBINE INTO A GROUP INTELLIGENCE.

IF ONE MORE ROBOT JOINS THEY WILL EVOLVE INTO A WARRIOR TROOP.

HERE WE SEE THEM PERFORMING THEIR SINISTER DANCE.

Chillingly, an American firm is developing a "nursebot" to replace or supplement human carers, designed to feign empathy with the patient.

Maybe they'll be smiling as they pull the trigger.

Genetic Engineering

Could we one day split into two separate species?

This idea is one of the scariest that the GM-resisting lobby has come up with. Since the breakthrough that cracked the human genome, it has become clear that it is only a matter of time before genetic engineering reaches into every corner of biological existence. We know of the huge advantages such science will bring: things like curing diabetes, creating high-yielding food crops to cope with the growth in population, and designing laboratory animals that more closely resemble humans for drug trials.

But not everyone is convinced. While America cheerfully produces GM crops for the table, the European Union has held back. They are far from alone. But why?

Among the several nightmare scenarios that haunt the fearful, two stand out. One is that we don't have sufficient knowledge now (or perhaps ever) to know what it is we don't know. In one imagined future, a hardly known disease reappears and attacks an important food crop, such as rice. The original strains of the plant may have had resistance to the virus, but the GM version fails to anticipate this. The only recourse would be to return to the original rootstock, but this will have disappeared under a wave of optimistic genetic meddling.

Result: famine.

Another dire possibility has been proposed by reputable

FEEDING TIME

scientists. It involves the genetic mutation of humans, in order to produce "designer babies." These super-children would have higher intelligence, better looks, longer lives and much more raw talent. Because of the free market system, this "germline" modification would only be affordable to the already rich. The poor would have to reproduce without any assistance, creating babies that in real terms are genetically inferior.

Molecular biologist Lee M. Silver has said that he can foresee a time when the gulf between the modified and "natural" babies becomes so great that humanity actually divides into separate species.

This raises an even more frightening scenario. Our universal injunction against cannibalism applies only to members of the same species. Speaking globally, we don't mind eating cows, whales and even dogs.

Who's next?

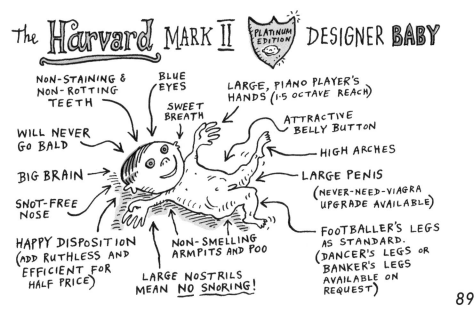

The Harvard MARK II (PLATINUM EDITION) DESIGNER BABY

NON-STAINING & NON-ROTTING TEETH

BLUE EYES

SWEET BREATH

LARGE, PIANO PLAYER'S HANDS (1.5 OCTAVE REACH)

ATTRACTIVE BELLY BUTTON

WILL NEVER GO BALD

HIGH ARCHES

BIG BRAIN

LARGE PENIS (NEVER-NEED-VIAGRA UPGRADE AVAILABLE)

SNOT-FREE NOSE

HAPPY DISPOSITION (ADD RUTHLESS AND EFFICIENT FOR HALF PRICE)

NON-SMELLING ARMPITS AND POO

LARGE NOSTRILS MEAN NO SNORING!

FOOTBALLER'S LEGS AS STANDARD. (DANCER'S LEGS OR BANKER'S LEGS AVAILABLE ON REQUEST)

Backward Evolution

Is the human gene pool getting weaker?

Ever since William Shockley first used the term "dysgenics" and caused dismay in the 1960s by claiming that stupider people had more babies, the notion that we are passing on weaker genes to each succeeding generation has gone underground. Studies have since shown that there is no connection between low IQ scores and number of progeny. The submerged racist nuances angered politicians and affected research grants. Its opposite, eugenics, has remained connected to Nazism and other fascist ideologies.

But since then we have entered an age of genetic science. Now there is a new way for "desirable" and "undesirable" traits to be passed on. Not by what used to be thought of as natural selection, but by manipulation in laboratories.

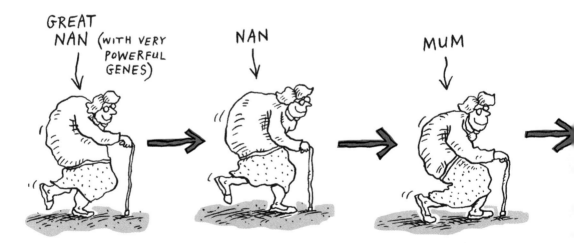

Meanwhile, medicine has developed treatments for diseases that would have been fatal in earlier times. A stroll through the graveyards reveals just how many people didn't survive conditions that are now easily managed.

But this blessing has a dark side. If more people survive who formerly wouldn't have, the diseases and disabilities that might have ended with them get passed on into the future. Scaremongers worry that these conditions may wind up affecting everybody in a few generations.

So it boils down to a race between inherited weaknesses and genetic fixes. A gamble involving "weakness" versus genetically manipulated "strength."

Any takers?

ME (AGE 35)

Thanks to medical science saving her life and preserving her genes, now everyone in the world has my great nan's funny hips, bad back, crazy hair, obsession with Coronation Street and terrible dress sense.

COMPLETE RANDOM STRANGERS

ON AND ON INTO THE FUTURE...

Gray Goo

Self-replicating tiny
machines that eat the
Earth in one weekend.

1950s horror movie?

Not according to certain worried scientists, who foresee the
future risks of nanotechnology. It has long been realized that
one day microscopic robots may be made that can do such
marvellous things as cleaning up oil spills and even removing
carbon atoms from the atmosphere. The technology is still in its
infancy, but signs are that this may become a possibility.

In early conceptions, "nanobots" imitate the biological model.
That is, they are tiny organisms that function in the same way

as microorganisms. Not only would they perform the functions for which they were designed, they would make more and more copies of themselves.

In his 1986 book *Engines of Creation*, Eric Drexler calculated that in just 10 hours an unchecked self-replicating auto-assembler would spawn 68 billion offspring; in less than two days the auto-assemblers would outweigh the Earth. The result would be that the entire planet would be reduced to a kind of "gray goo."

More recent statements from the scientific community have allayed some of these fears. The August 2004 Institute of Physics article by Drexler and Chris Phoenix says: "Nanotechnology-based fabrication can be thoroughly non-biological and inherently safe: such systems need have no ability to move about, use natural resources, or undergo incremental mutation. Moreover, self-replication is unnecessary . . . Accordingly, the construction of anything resembling a dangerous self-replicating nanomachine can and should be prohibited."

That's a relief then. Nothing to worry about. It will be prohibited.

Just like nuclear weapons.

DOOM SCENARIO:
MAD SCIENTIST DOOM

84

Electromagnetic Pollution

Invisible killer rays are all around us.

This sounds like fantasy fiction, but is rapidly becoming science fact. As our electronic gadgets become more and more sophisticated, we may find that we are trading convenience for safety.

Take mobile phones, for instance. The kind of radiation (EMF) found in these handy little wireless devices has long been a suspect in the search for causes of brain and eye cancer. The World Health Organization has concluded that there is no direct causal link between the Big C and mobiles, but recommends limiting their use as a precaution. Others, such as Dr. George Carlo, an epidemiologist, thinks that mobile phone radiation can be very dangerous. And he was heading a study funded by the big cell phone industry itself.

In addition to brain and eye cancer, some of the potential risks include DNA damage, an increase in the female hormone estrogen (see pages 146–144), testicular cancer and loss of fertility, as well as a decrease in the effectiveness of anticancer drugs such as Tamoxifen. Because EMF may disrupt cognitive function, users can become confused while driving. One writer even compares the effects to alcohol intoxication.

Walking into lampposts while talking on your mobile hasn't so far appeared in the research as a potential hazard. Nor has having your private calls and texts hacked into or accidentally found by your partner, but these can also have unpleasant consequences.

Even keeping your mobile away from your head and groin won't offer total protection. We are subjected to something like 100 million times as much EMF as our grandparents. Health therapist Helen Adendorff compares it to being in a room full of heavy smokers, but without being able to leave or open the window.

They used to say that passive smoking was harmless, too.

IF WE COULD SEE
ELECTROMAGNETIC RAYS...

Cyber Warfare

Everyone loves the Internet. It's a great way to buy things, keep in touch with your friends and look at pictures that used to be under the newsagent's counter. But now its ugly face has appeared.

Unknown enemies could use our own computers to destroy us.

ATTENTION!

IF YOU ARE READING THE DIGITAL EDITION OF THIS BOOK, THE AUTHORS ARE LOOKING OUT AT YOU RIGHT <u>NOW</u> FROM YOUR iPAD OR OTHER HANDHELD COMPUTER DEVICE.

BUZZ... CLICK... WHIRR...

IF YOU BOUGHT THE OLD-FASHIONED PAPER VERSION... HELLO! THIS PAGE IS PRINTED IN UP-TO-THE-MINUTE SMART INK™ INCORPORATING NANO CAMERA TECHNOLOGY, AND THE AUTHORS ARE SCRUTINIZING YOU AS YOU READ. NICE SHIRT. PITY ABOUT THE HAIR.

Defense specialists think the threat of cyber attack is real. So much so, in fact, that the British government is now listing it as one of the major threats to national security, alongside terrorist bombs.

As recently as five years ago, the concept of cyber attack hardly existed outside sci-fi novels. It was known that hackers had invaded certain classified websites from time to time, but this was considered to be little more than pranks on the part of teenage computer nerds.

A COMPUTER
HACKER

No more all-night Call of Duty for you, Micron.

Things have changed. A computer virus called Stuxnet recently penetrated the government cyber systems of Iran, Indonesia and India. More than 45,000 computers were infected or destroyed, including those that regulate Iran's burgeoning nuclear industry.

No one knows who the culprits are. The program is too expensive and sophisticated to have been built on a lone malcontent's laptop. It almost certainly has to be the effort of a country. The finger of blame is mostly leveled at Israel, because its relationship with Iran is the most fraught. But specialists think it could be England, Germany or even us.

If it is a national effort, Stuxnet represents the first shot in a war unlike any other in history. The prospect is alarming and government purse strings are being loosened in response.

The fear is that cyber attack can do more than rob information and destroy computers. The sophistication of the new virus has made defense experts realize that enemy hackers could actually disrupt or disable real-world services like water supplies, transport and electricity networks. But freezing in the dark isn't the worst possible nightmare. There's something even worse that could happen.

They could launch our missiles.

Welcome to US military launch station Baco-Z-41. State your name, rank and... BLEEP! Missiles primed...

CLICK

The New Terrorism

I'm a terrorist.

But you look just like me!

Scare them to death.

What's the best way to defeat an enemy of overwhelming size and strength, using secondhand and homemade weapons? The answer is simple.

DANGEROUS JUNK

Terrorists have been around for a long time. Most of them follow a pattern. They feel that the status quo is invalid or illegal. Acts that would seem like despicable crimes in any other context are ennobled by the sense of shared purpose and struggle. It is the very horror of the acts that makes them most effective. Through the continuing fear of what they might do, they weaken and ultimately disable their enemies.

Civil liberties get eroded. Questionable activities such as waterboarding and "extraordinary rendition" follow. Surveillance of citizens increases. And with each new level of suppression, new enemies are created. The spiral continues until the old system becomes brittle and collapses.

The present crop of terrorists follows this familiar pattern. But there are two important differences. One is that the dangerous junk lying around and easily found on the Internet is so much more deadly than in times past. Recipes for poisonous gas and instructions for making explosives are as near as one keyboard click away.

Radioactive materials ranging from spent reactor rods bought on the black market to hospital waste bring the construction of a "dirty bomb" into the reach of amateurs. It is conceivable that crude but effective nuclear devices can be bought or simply assembled. And if a nuclear-armed country such as Pakistan should be taken over by terrorist groups, a full range of Doomsday weapons enter the picture. Even a small nuclear exchange might generate a cloud of dust and debris that would bring on a cataclysmic winter that didn't go away.

The second difference between current and past terrorists is what makes the use of these devices much more possible.

Suicide.

If you believe that dying in the process of blowing up innocents is not just an unfortunate outcome of a necessary act but a divine mission complete with heavenly rewards, you become nearly invincible to ordinary attacks. If dying is a payoff and not a penalty, it's hard to imagine stopping you.

How can we fight the new terrorists when killing them only makes them happy?

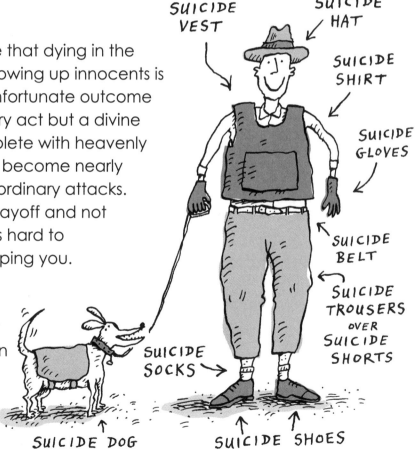

SUICIDE VEST

SUICIDE HAT

SUICIDE SHIRT

SUICIDE GLOVES

SUICIDE BELT

SUICIDE TROUSERS OVER SUICIDE SHORTS

SUICIDE SOCKS

SUICIDE DOG

SUICIDE SHOES

Nuclear War

Remember this one?

Children of the Cold War got used to the idea of living just a button press away from extinction. The Soviet bloc and the West bristled with ICBMs aimed at each other, with enough explosive power to destroy the Earth several times over. Only the fig leaf of Mutually Assured Destruction (MAD) lay between us and lights out. But that's all over now . . . Or is it?

With the collapse of the Soviet Union in the early 1990s the world took a deep breath. Treaties for gradual nuclear disarmament took effect, and lots of nukes were decommissioned with great fanfare. The accidental launch of missiles became less of a possibility. The weapons decreased in number, but they didn't go away.

The unstable new republics of the former USSR held some of the nuclear weapons within their territories. Rumors began to emerge of black market sales of radioactive materials and software. Western intelligence agencies had their hands full with tracking down missiles and warheads through the murky waters of new states we had never heard of.

Meanwhile, the proliferation of nuclear arms continued. India, Pakistan, China, Israel, North Korea—even South Africa, until they renounced them after the end of apartheid. Rumors surfaced that Saddam Hussein was close to developing an A-bomb. Now we know that Iran is bent on the rapid development of nuclear missiles. Some comfort is being taken from the fact that most of these states haven't yet produced a missile that can reach our shores. The numbers of nukes aren't that great yet, either. That means that any nuclear skirmish would be "local" and over very quickly.

But the chilling truth is that any nuclear war anywhere would be capable of wiping us all out. If some suicidal fanatics take over the government of Pakistan, for instance, and launch a missile at Israel, they might as well draw a bead on London or New York. What would follow such an attack is the massive disruption of the global economy, freezing the exchange of food and energy, a storm of radioactive fallout that would encircle the globe, and a dense blanket of atmospheric dust that could cut out the Sun's light for years.

If the blast doesn't get you, the endless winter will.

MAD US
PRESIDENT
DOOM

Economic Meltdown

You can't do a lot about natural disasters, except try to cope. If an asteroid has our name on it, that's outside our control. If an unknown virus that lives in a species of bats in a Madagascan cave suddenly mutates into a global pandemic, all we can do is work to save ourselves with science. But there's one looming Doomsday scenario that we can foresee, but not prevent. Something we're doing ourselves.

Global economic collapse.

Depressions come and go like shuttle buses. They ebb and flow within the limits of a worldwide economic system that contains boom and bust years. They seem to average out, and after a time of hardship, rejoin the orderly queue of a system that is constantly growing and improving. Sooner or later, everyone benefits.

Or so we believe.

Where have all the trees gone?

To be pulped and made into banknotes.

72

But now some mainstream economists are joining the ranks of loony survivalists and Internet paranoids who predict the total collapse of the world economy. Ask any two of them how this might happen and you will get three answers. Some of the warning signs are things like China's metastasizing economy, the rapid depletion of fossil fuels and scarcity of food crops, the sheer enormity of world debt and the spectre of runaway inflation.

A PIE CHART SHOWING THINGS TO SPEND MONEY ON

You can look at the current global economy as a chain letter. As long as you can sell stakes in some future payoff to those below you on the chain, you'll do just fine. Maybe the chain grows at 3% per year, like the ideal national economy. But at some point the scheme reaches a point of saturation. People refuse to buy into what seems a rickety, top-heavy structure. The network of promises seem less and less likely.

HOW A CAPITALIST ECONOMY WORKS

One significant default by a major economy is like pulling one card from a card house.

What frustrates the idealists of the international marketplace is that economic boom and bust is down to a single, stubbornly resistant element: confidence. If the mood of the players is optimistic, things go humming along nicely. When things are overpriced and overleveraged, that's fine, as long as nobody spots the emperor's nonexistent clothes.

But in a year when solar flares, shifting magnetic fields and unusual seismic activity have already made us uneasy, confidence starts to drain away. Instead of buying, people begin to save and hoard. As this activity deserts the market, things get worse. People lose their jobs. Countries erect trade barriers for self-protection, creating tension and skirmishing. As a currency wobbles, runs begin on banks. People store up foodstuffs and even ammunition in some places, and look suspiciously at their neighbors. In a full-blown financial panic, rioting, looting and civil collapse beckon.

Chaos.

But surely this couldn't happen here, you might think. Not in a civilized country with a long tradition of democratic stability. There must be laws in place. There must be some reasonable people in charge who know what to do. There are right-thinking, benevolent experts who know how to manage it all, aren't there?

Of course there are. The bankers.

Obesity Epidemic

Are you sitting comfortably while reading this book? Neither too hot nor too cold? Not feeling hungry?

The world's ending, I'll eat as much as I like!

You're killing yourself.

Being comfortable is making us some of the world's fattest and least healthy people. If we're not a bit cold or too hot because we rely on central heating and air conditioning we're not burning enough calories to stay fit, medics tell us. In 2010, more than 10,000 British people needed urgent hospitalization because they were so fat that their lives were in immediate danger. And it's not just adults at risk; nearly a third of our kids are overweight or obese. Doctors aren't mincing words: this is an epidemic.

It seems that if we live what we now think of as a "normal" life, we're becoming prey to a whole catalogue of ailments, including diabetes, heart disease and some types of cancer. Everything we've ever achieved in terms of creature comforts has become a threat to our continued existence.

The labor-saving meals that line the supermarket shelves are laden with calories, fats and salt we cannot properly use. The machines that we longed for in the mid-20th century have begun to weaken and sicken us. The computer games and the fizzy drinks our children consume may well make their life spans briefer than our own.

HOW TO HOLD AN END OF THE WORLD PARTY!

PANIC BUY LOTS OF DRINK, NIBBLES, CAKE, CHOCOLATE & SUGARY FOOD.

LOOT PAPER CUPS, STREAMERS, NAPKINS AND HATS.

HAVE A DRINK AND STUFF YOURSELF.

NO ELECTRICITY, SO MAKE YOUR OWN ENTERTAINMENT. SING SONGS WHILE PLAYING UKULELES.

If you don't SHUT UP I'm going to KILL you!!

PLOING PLUNK PLINK PLONK PLINKA PLUNK PLOINK... PLUNKY

HAVE ANOTHER DRINK, MORE FOOD, THEN SOME MORE FOOD.

DRINK UNTIL YOU CAN'T REMEMBER WHY YOU'RE PARTYING.

Whose... birthday is it?

I... LOVE you, man...

BELCH!

CRACK!

HOW To HAVE AN END OF THE WORLD PARTY IF YOU'RE THIN

Wahoo.

EAT AND DRINK
IMAGINARY FOOD

Paradoxically, the overfed live alongside the hungry. Obesity has recently become a problem even in so-called underdeveloped countries. As wealth improves, health risks multiply. Because fat and fashion don't mix, our young people are increasingly prone to malnutrition and severe eating disorders such as bulimia and anorexia nervosa.

With few exceptions, if you want to live a long and healthy life, you have to return to the modern equivalent of heavy toil and effort. That's why the gyms as well as the hospital wards are filling fast.

It's as if all the things we thought would make life easier and more enjoyable have conspired to finish us off. We're victims of our own success.

Be careful what you wish for.

Overpopulation

Do we need a second planet to survive?

Some scientists have warned that, at the current rate of population expansion, we will need a second planet by the middle of this century.

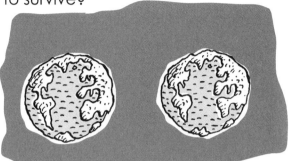

Until the beginning of the Industrial Revolution, Earth's population was fairly stable at about 250 million. We hadn't lost ground since the Black Death. But around the beginning of the 19th century, we started rapidly adding numbers, breaking the billion mark for the first time. By 1960 we had hit three billion, and in the next four decades we doubled that to six billion. We're now weighing in at 6.7 billion and counting. Even though the rate of increase has tailed off recently, most theorists believe that we will be living alongside 10 to 11 billion others by 2050.

Estimates of maximum sustainable population vary, but some scientists are warning that we have already exceeded the level at which the planet can keep us all fed and watered. If the current population of the world ever manages to consume at the levels now enjoyed by Europe, we would need three times the available resources. Although most scientists agree that advances in technology may be able to keep abreast of the need for food, there are risks involved in turning the Earth into a "giant human feedlot." Species extinctions and environmental damage would be the certain consequences.

If we can't stop making new people, what can we do?

Cynics snarl that we needn't worry, because overpopulation will trigger wars, pandemics and famines and the planet will simply shrug off its excess inhabitants.

Optimists toil away in the laboratories for the perfect contraceptive. Some visionaries are actually working out ways to locate an empty planet somewhere in our galaxy and tow it into the solar system.

Maybe we could try cold showers?

THE PERFECT CONTRACEPTIVE —
A PORTABLE COLD SHOWER

Health & Safety

Imagine a world in which nothing bad could possibly happen to you. Where there was no danger of falling, being electrocuted, ingesting something fatal, being too hot or too cold or being infected by germs from someone else. Imagine a safer, kinder world, where gentle global rangers wearing Prozac smiles ensure that nothing we might ever do or ever wish to do could possibly bring harm or distress to ourselves or others.

Wouldn't that be wonderful?

The more advanced our civilization becomes, the easier it is to predict and prevent danger. Comedy workmen used to fall from ladders or routinely smack each other's heads while carrying planks over their shoulders. Now hard hats make those routines impossible. It's safer, but a lot less funny. And new laws to protect us are being ground out in ever-increasing numbers.

Legislators, doctors, social workers and psychologists are working overtime to ensure that nothing bad can happen to you. Ever.

Doesn't that make you want to throw in the towel?

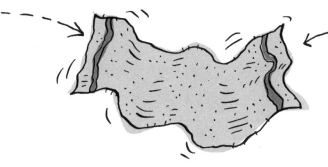

UTTERLY
HARMLESS,
ANTIBACTERIAL
FAIR TRADE
SAFETY TOWEL

61

Religious Doom

When it comes to foretelling Doom, no one can compete with the world's religions.

The sheer variety of coming destruction in the holy books would make the most pessimistic of scientific doomsayers tremble. But, ominously, many of these Doom scenarios closely resemble the current worst-case speculations of the scientists.

In Islam, the world is hit by such huge earthquakes that the "body of the Earth is broken." One in the east, one in the west and one in what must seem like the center of the world, the Arabian Peninsula. The sun will rise in the west, too, which sounds like a complete polar reversal. All the nonbelievers will die before winding up in hell, but the righteous will just get head colds.

The Christian version is best represented by some lines in the Book of Matthew, who says that the end will be a "great tribulation, such as was not [seen] since the beginning of the world." It will happen so suddenly that anyone who happens to be standing on his roof is warned not to go downstairs to get his things. He says those who are pregnant or breastfeeding will have it the worst, which suggests the possibility of nuclear fallout. He also tells us we should hope our flight from danger is not on the Sabbath, when you're not meant to do anything much.

Matthew even tells us how to recognize when the time is getting near. He says "nation shall rise against nation, and there shall be famines and pestilences and earthquakes" in many places. That sounds a lot like where we are now, doesn't it?

But things get even worse. Immediately "after the tribulation of those days shall the sun be darkened, and the moon shall not give her light, and the stars shall fall from heaven, and the powers of the heavens shall be shaken."

In all the "Abrahamic" faiths, the believers—also known as the "righteous"—get saved. The Muslims get taken to heaven by Allah. The Christian "elect" survive the cataclysm and, similarly to the Jews, are escorted by a Messiah to a new version of the Earth.

Everyone else is toast.

And that means YOU, reader.

59

ATHEISTS AND RELIGIOUS ZEALOTS CLASH OVER PARKING SPACES IN HELL

Even the mild-mannered Buddhists weigh in with a nightmarish prediction of the Earth heating up, going dry and finally exploding. As far back as 500 BC, global warming was an issue. The Buddha apparently thought this was a good idea, as it helped his followers see the world as something to be transcended.

So who's right?

Since the holy books agree that the faithful are saved and everyone else is condemned or destroyed, that means hell is going to be crowded.

If you take just the Mediterranean, for example, you've got hundreds of millions of people who are nominally Christian on one side, and hundreds of millions more on the other who are mostly Muslims. If either of their holy books is accurate, the better part of the population of the other side is in big—call it eternal—trouble.

Take your pick.

Holy War

There's another possibility for Doom that arises not from external sources, but from religion itself.

Every once in a while, human beings get all worked up about religious ideas. At present, we've got the brand of Islam known as Wahhabism, a fundamentalist version of the Sunni branch. This was the root of Osama bin Laden's holy war against virtually everyone who didn't agree with him.

But he's not alone. There are groups who define themselves as Christians who are infected with the same malady of absolutism, and who aren't above blowing up abortion clinics and shooting medics. Some of these True Believers are known to be awaiting the great war on the Plain of Armageddon, when the troops of the Antichrist (Muslims, Jews, Catholics, atheists—everyone except your own lot) are finally defeated.

If you too closely identify with what you consider the only truth, you begin to despise people who don't agree with you. This can bring about things like the Orthodox versus Roman Catholic split in the Balkans, the slaughter in Sri Lanka, and—oh yes—don't forget Northern Ireland.

When cultural change happens too rapidly, when economies get depressed, when confusion seems to be the state of just about everybody, that's when you start looking around for a new saviour. There often seems to be one handy. Then you're just one step away from guns and sexy uniforms. And Holy War.

Yippee!

WHICH RELIGION WILL REWARD YOU WITH EVERLASTING LIFE FOR ALL ETERNITY IF YOU TAKE THEIR SIDE FOR ARMAGEDDON?

BE SURE TO CHOOSE CORRECTLY...

WRONG

WRONG

WRONG

WRONG

53

Philosophical Doom

It is clear from reading the great philosophers that your existence isn't just nasty, brutish and short—it's an illusion.

You don't exist.

To prove it, try answering this little philosophical riddle:

> *If a tree falls in the forest, and*
> *there is no one to hear it,*
> *does it make a sound?*

That question was first posed in the 18th century by George Berkeley, and it's been a big hole in the socks of philosophers ever since. Berkeley was a "subjective idealist," meaning that in order for something to have an existence, it must be seen and noted by someone. His words, in Latin, naturally, were *"Esse est percipi"* or "To be is to be perceived."

You can't disprove that argument. You can just take it or leave it. The noise a falling tree makes needs an ear to hear it before it can come into existence.

If Berkeley was right, then we are not "discovering" new galaxies with our telescopes, we are creating them. Without an observer, they wouldn't exist at all. If you're born, live and die without anyone ever seeing you, you've never existed.

Berkeley's day job was being a bishop, so he found a way around all this. He said that the noise made by the falling tree did exist, because God heard it. Of course, proving the existence of God is a lot more complicated than looking around in the woods for missing decibels.

So what does this have to do with Doom?

Doomsday might be next week or not, but everyone agrees on one thing: sometime in the next five billion years, our Sun will become a supernova, instantly eradicating us, our descendants, and any trace that we ever existed. Nothing will remain. No record, no monuments, no memories, no witnesses.

It will be as if we never were.

In fact, according to Berkeley's logic, it *will* be that we never were.

49

Sometimes Doom can come to an individual without the need for earthquakes, pandemics or gamma rays. Victims can be seen cowering in the background in our cities and towns, avoiding daylight and flinching from all human contact. These unfortunates are living, but utterly without hope.

This is **Personal Doom**, which can strike without warning and leave you wishing for something as relatively mild as global destruction.

Read on, if you dare.

No one has phoned me, e-mailed or sent me a text message ALL DAY.

SILENT

47

Sexual Ruin

Sex is liberating!

Sex must be constrained!

Sex is for continuing the human race.

CONFUSING, ISN'T IT?

Of course you're safe from sexually transmitted diseases. Like all sensible people, you rely upon monogamy, or at least take precautions.

But the bugs are getting cleverer.

NEW SEXUAL DISEASE BACILLI

Ha ha ha ha...

He he he he he...

A plague that begins as a malaise of green monkeys in Africa can pop up in singles' bars in San Francisco. The epidemic of syphilis that shook Europe in the16th century was probably imported from the Americas by a few randy seamen, and nobody saw it coming.

Viruses, bacteria, fungi and parasites keep changing shape. They might well be evolving in ways the laboratories can't foresee. The bugs aren't in a hurry. They have lots of time.

Do we?

46

THIS NEW SEXUAL DISEASE BACILLUS CAN CHEW THROUGH CONDOMS

AND HERE'S ANOTHER WHICH CAN BE TRANSMITTED BY KISSING OR EVEN JUST TOUCHING A BREAST

THIS ONE IS CONTRACTED BY MERELY _THINKING_ ABOUT SEX

BELCH!

BUBBLE OF COMPLACENCY

These new STDs are alarming...

But we're ok, aren't we, darling, being married and monogamous and so on.

Of course we are, darling.

BEEP BEEP BEEP

A TEXT MESSAGE ARRIVES FROM HIS LOVER

Cooee!

BRIAN
DAVE
SID
SUE
FRANK
EZRA
HELEN
CHRISTOPH

WOMAN
DRIVEN BY THE INSTINCTS TO REPRODUCE AND CUDDLE.

MAN
DRIVEN BY THE INSTINCTS TO SPREAD HIS SEED, HAVE FUN DOING IT, PLUS TEMPTATION FROM THE DEVIL.

P.T.O.

REAL WORLD

SOME MORE PERSONAL DOOM MOMENTS

42

41

ADD SOME OF <u>YOUR OWN</u> PERSONAL DOOMS HERE:

- - - - - - - - - - -
- - - - - - - - - - -
- - - - - - - - - -

- - - - - - - - - - -
- - - - - - - - - - -
- - - - - - - - - -

- - - - - - - - - - -
- - - - - - - - - - -
- - - - - - - - - -

- - - - - - - - - - - -
- - - - - - - - - - -
- - - - - - - - - - -

- - - - - - - - - - -
- - - - - - - - - - -
- - - - - - - - - -

HERE'S A PERSONAL DOOM THAT WILL BE FAMILIAR TO MANY

ONE FORM OF PERSONAL DOOM IS REALIZING THAT...

I may play only a tiny role in the global network of living creatures, but at least I PLAY a role by helping to balance the ecology of the planet.

You, on the other hand, merely mess the planet up!

SQUISH! STAMP!

Ha. Who's the more significant one now?

INADEQUATE CHILDREN DOOM

METAPHORICAL DOOM

Getting a spot on my wedding day would be the end of the world!

LITERAL DOOM

Do We Love Doom?

The unmistakable lure of Doom raises all sorts of questions about us. Surely we can't enjoy contemplating a terrible end to ourselves and all we cherish.

Can we?

You might as well suppose that we don't love horror movies or being tossed about by scary rides at theme parks. That we avoid the gory details of crimes in thrillers. Or that we scrupulously stay away from any risks to our safety, such as hang-gliding or rock climbing.

After all, what we really want is to be safe, secure and happy.

Isn't it?

Let's imagine that in the future our descendants have perfected a way of completely separating their lives into relentlessly happy and consistently unhappy compartments.

They do this by separating each individual—at birth—into two clones.

These identical people go through life side by side, one person experiencing only the comfortable, happy and pleasurable things in his—or her—life, the other living only the anxious, unpleasant and painful moments.

Meet David Jones and David Jones.

The Joneses are a successful man with a good income, a lovely home and a beautiful wife, Jane.

JANE JONES

David Jones—let's call him Jones 1 and Jones 2—has had his fair share of good and bad experiences.

Jones 1 had a completely happy childhood.

Jones 2 had a miserable one.

Jones 1 was applauded at school and did well.

Jones 2 struggled and was bullied.

Jones 1 cuddles and coos with his lovely wife...

...while Jones 2 argues, slams doors and smashes things.

32

One morning the police are called to the Jones home, where they find that David Jones has hanged himself in the garage.

David Jones stands silently nearby.

The mystery the police must solve is this:

Which David Jones couldn't take it any longer and killed himself?

Someday you're going to die. Whether it's in a comfy bed, surrounded by grieving relatives, or under the wheels of a number 11 bus, the result is the same. One day it will be all over.

So why is Doom any different? If you die alone or with 6.2 billion other people, isn't the result identical?

DOOM vs DEATH

ONE OF THESE TWO PEOPLE HAS JUST BEEN TOLD THEY ARE ABOUT TO DIE. THE OTHER HAS LEARNED THAT THE WORLD IS COMING TO AN END. CAN **YOU** TELL WHICH IS WHICH?

Aaargh!!

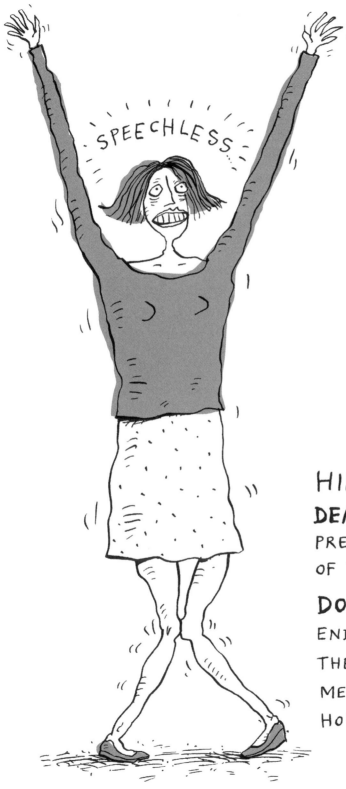

HINT~

DEATH IS THE PREDICTABLE END OF YOURSELF.

DOOM IS THE END OF HISTORY, THE FUTURE, MEMORY AND HOPE.

29

A Glimmer of Hope

Some Certain Dooms That Haven't Happened (so far)

BONK BONK BONK BONK BONK BONK BONK

FALSE ALARM CLOCK

a) Man-made Black Holes

Before the Large Hadron Collider at the European Organization for Nuclear Research (CERN) started shooting protons around its 17-mile tunnel in 2008, panicky stories began to appear in the press. While earnest scientists looked for a theoretical quantum particle called the Higgs boson, laymen braced themselves for the emergence of small black holes that would metastasize and gobble up the Earth.

Black holes are mass compressed into such a small space that they swallow up everything they touch, including light. Around these is an area called the "event horizon," which is the point of no return for anything unlucky enough to come into a black hole's powerful gravitational field. It has been compared to canoeing upstream away from a waterfall. At some point, you take the fall.

It made a perfect scenario for both pseudoscientific cyber geeks and for religious doomsayers. The science buffs had the theoretical possibility of black holes, while the prophets of apocalypse were animated by the Higgs boson's nickname.

The God particle.

They're still firing subatomic particles under a Swiss mountain,

THE INSIDE OF A TENNIS BALL

A CIRCLE FILLED IN WITH BLACK PEN

THE ENTRANCE TO A DARK TUNNEL

FALLING INTO A BOTTOMLESS PIT

A BLACK HOLE

AN EMOTIONAL BLACK HOLE

Darling...

I love you!

I'm going to suck you in and destroy you.

EVENT HORIZON

but so far we haven't been attacked by black holes. Meanwhile, some Chinese physicists have built a "black-hole generator" out of copper wire in a disk that seems to suck up all known radiation, including light. It has several possible applications for industry. It will collect solar heat better than anything we now have, which is good news for our alternative energy plans.

It may also defeat radar screens, making it possible to fly warplanes into someone else's airspace undetected.

Which is bad news for all of us.

b) The Millennium Bug

The coming of the Third Millennium threw up a predictable number of end-of-the-world scares, but one in particular seized the imagination of scientists, politicians and business leaders. This was called the Y2K Problem or the Millennium Bug.

Because most computers used only the last two digits of a date in their calculations, it was widely feared that the machines that run our civilization would either stop working altogether or else chuck us all backward to 1900.

Anticipating disaster, big corporations spent millions on technicians to fiddle with their digital equipment. Some banks suspended the operation of swipe cards three days before the new year actually came in. Horror scenarios abounded: looting, air crashes, economic collapse and the unintentional launch of nuclear missiles.

SOME DATES TO WORRY ABOUT:

No 1 ~ TOMORROW

A Horseman of the Apocalypse! RUN!!

Calm down, Stewart. It's only little Judy practicing for the gymkhana.

YOWL!

YIP!

24

When the day actually came, nothing much happened.

In the United States, a hundred slot machines at several race tracks in Delaware stopped working. Bus ticket machines backed up in two Australian states. A French meteorological channel showed a nonsense date on one of its weather maps.

The computers, it seemed, were either too smart to be fooled or too dumb to notice.

That should sort things out for the next century or so, you might think. Unfortunately, many computer specialists predict it might happen again in 2038. That's because the original Unix time stamp stores a date and time as a 32-bit integer, counting the number of seconds since January 1, 1970. After 2038, this number will be too large to be contained in 32 bits. Some computer applications are already switching to 64-bit systems to head this off.

But if any of the other things in this book come to pass, we probably won't have to worry about 2038 anyway.

SOME THINGS THAT WILL BE GONE FOREVER

The sparkle of sunlight on water.

Children's voices in the bright air.

SCREECH! SCREAM! WAIL!

The smell of cut grass on a summer's day.

Summer.

Also autumn, winter and spring.

Woodsmoke curling up into a still evening.

The scratchy feeling of wool on bare skin.

The anticipation of a good meal.

The smell of freshly brewed coffee.

The sun rising over the sea.

The splash of a fish in a limpid pool.

The cries of lovers.

Aah! Aah! Aah! Aah!

22

Frost on a car windscreen.

Car windscreens.

Cars.

Afternoon tea and hot buttered crumpets.

The warm breath of a dog.

The honk of a vast juggernaut.

TOOT!

The taste of fried food.

The smell of a fresh baby.

SNIFF

Waking in a warm bed and drifting off to sleep again.

Mmm...

Snowballs.

The ideas contained in books.

REMEMBRANCE OF ER... SOMETHING OR OTHER... M. Proust

Books ~ like this one.

Phew. Thank goodness this book will be gone. It's making me feel rather low.

DWELLING ON DOOM <u>CAN</u> BECOME A BIT DEPRESSING, SO WHY NOT DISTRACT YOURSELF BY MAKING THIS ATTRACTIVE

STRAW TO CLING ON TO?

SIMPLY:

i ~ CUT ALONG THE SOLID LINES.

ii ~ ROLL STRAW AROUND A PENCIL.

iii ~ APPLY GLUE TO TAB A.

iv ~ PRESS TAB A TO TAB B UNTIL SET.

v ~ CLUTCH FINISHED STRAW TIGHTLY UNTIL DOOM TAKES PLACE.

That's much better...

NOT <u>TOO</u> TIGHTLY! BE CAREFUL NOT TO CRUSH IT.

TAB B UNDER HERE

TAB A — COVER WITH GLUE

ROLL

SEARCHING FOR A LOOPHOLE*

*Unlike a BLACK HOLE, a LOOPHOLE is not recognised as a true scientific term. A LOOPHOLE is merely a legal, political or economic term.

HOW WORRIED ARE YOU?

Scientists tell us that, whatever happens, the Earth is going to end when the Sun becomes a supernova in about five billion years. So why aren't we bothered?

At what point do you start getting worried? Put a tick next to the first date when things will begin to alarm you.

ZZZZZZZZZ Z...

☐ 1 BILLION YEARS

☐ 1 MILLION YEARS   YAWN...

☐ 1 THOUSAND YEARS   Doesn't affect me.

☐ 100 YEARS   Relax. You'll be 105.

☐ 10 YEARS   Better get on with having some fun.   Honey, cancel our retirement policy!

☐ 1 YEAR   This is getting SERIOUS!

☐ NEXT WEEK   I wonder what life is really all about?   And who would have won the Super Bowl?

AAAAAARGH...

☐ NOW!

WHAT TO TELL YOUR CHILDREN
SOME USEFUL & EMPTY DENIALS & REASSURANCES

I'll protect you, darling.

Nothing bad will happen while I'm here.

The scientists will come up with something.

Don't believe everything you see on TV.

They invent new medicines every day.

It'll be all right in the morning.

Everything is going to be ok...

17

HOW DOOM MIGHT HAPPEN...

i – INSTANTLY AND WITHOUT WARNING.

It might happen before I reach the end of this sentence...

Or me this one...

ii – QUICKLY, BUT AFTER A LONG BUILDUP.

Plenty of time to chat while we're waiting.

I'll get my novel finished, too.

iii – SLOWLY, OVER MONTHS AND YEARS.

I've run out of things to say.

Thank God.

iv – ANTICLIMACTICALLY.

Aw... I thought it would be a HUGE bang.

It's more of a fizzle...

PSSST...

PSSSST...

PSSST...

16

v – INSIDIOUSLY.

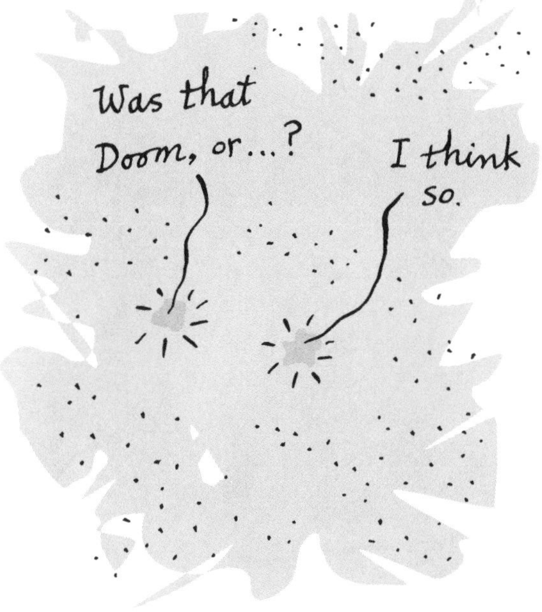

vi – RELIGIOUSLY.

vii – WITH IRRITATINGLY BAD TIMING.

viii – SURPRISINGLY.

Doom is a great time to discover your deep beliefs. Here are some sample responses by people with different points of view. Which one matches yours?

The Stoic: "Well, what did you expect?"

The Born Again: "Rapture should be along any minute now."

The New Ager: "We're just moving to a higher level of vibration."

The Meditator: "OM."

The Holy Book Thumper: "You were warned."

The Optimist: "Maybe this is a fresh start."

The Mystic: "Those gamma rays are really the wings of the Spirit."

The Hedonist: "Let's get naked."

The Pew Sitter: "Quick, someone play 'Abide with Me.'"

The Scientologist: "If only I'd paid enough to get to the next level."

The Agnostic: "Will somebody please explain what's happening?"

The Atheist: "Bugger . . ."

POSITIVE DOOM THERAPY

COMPARED TO IMPENDING GLOBAL DOOM, ALL YOUR PERSONAL PROBLEMS WILL MELT INTO INSIGNIFICANCE.

I'll never have to go to work ever again!

I won't be lonely in my old age!

Worrying about the pointlessness of life now seems pointless...

I don't have to worry about having no pension. Or paying the bills.

I don't have to watch any more reality TV. Or read a newspaper.

My oedipal issues concerning my father are gone! ←TRANSVESTITE

No need to give up smoking — or go to the gym.

I can stop worrying about money.

All in all, DOOM's the therapy for me! CHEERS!

I can continue to ignore all the unresolved issues concerning my sexuality.

I don't have to mend the fence or decorate the kitchen.

THE ETIQUETTE OF DOOM

SHOULD YOU RUSH ABOUT PUSHING AND SHOVING AND SCREAMING, OR WAIT PATIENTLY IN AN ORDERLY QUEUE FOR DOOM TO HAPPEN? ISN'T THE ANSWER OBVIOUS?

BE DIGNIFIED

REMEMBER TO SHAVE

BRUSH YOUR HAIR & TRIM YOUR EYEBROWS

KEEP YOUR UPPER LIP STIFF

DON'T FORGET DEODORANT AT THIS SWEATY TIME...

AND CLEAN UNDERWEAR

IF THERE'S TIME, GET YOUR SUIT CLEANED

POLISH YOUR SHOES

SMILE STOICALLY

DON'T FORGET SOME TASTEFUL MAKEUP

PLAY SOMETHING JOLLY ON YOUR INSTRUMENT

AND IF YOU DON'T PLAY AN INSTRUMENT START TAKING LESSONS

WEAR NICE CLOTHES. DON'T LET YOURSELF GO. REMEMBER TO IRON EVERYTHING ~ IT'S IMPORTANT TO KEEP UP APPEARANCES AT A TIME LIKE THIS.

WAX YOUR LEGS!

REMEMBER
ALWAYS SAY "PLEASE" AND "THANK YOU" AND TREAT OTHERS AS YOU WOULD LIKE TO BE TREATED. GOOD MANNERS COST NOTHING, EVEN WHEN THE WORLD IS ENDING.

12

WHAT TO WEAR

SOMETHING SMART AND DRESSY...

...OR JUST SOME OLD, COMFORTABLE THINGS YOU DON'T MIND GETTING RUINED?

A PRACTICAL COLOR WHICH WON'T SHOW MARKS AND STAINS WOULD BE SENSIBLE.

IDEALLY YOU WANT TO LOOK ATTRACTIVELY CRUMPLED WHILE STILL APPEARING EFFORTLESSLY IN CONTROL.

11

Disaster Grab Kit

Lots of people are assembling little bags called Grab Kits, 72-hour kits and GOOD (Get Out of Dodge) bags. You can even buy these from online shops specializing in survivalist supplies for anything up to a few hundred pounds. The deluxe models contain things like food and water for three days, light-weight tents and emergency blankets—even portable toilets.

When Doom strikes, if it is one of the slower models, you might wish to survive for a few days while it really gets going. So, what to pack?

HERE'S BEAUJOLAIS BROWN, 16:

whatever.

SPOT CREAM

MAKE-UP

CONDOMS

MOBILE

SHADES

TIGHTS

iPOD

BREATH MINTS

SHOES

HARIBO

LIPSTICK

CIGARETTES

VEST

WARM COAT

No way. Mum!

CHEWING GUM

DEPILATORY CREAM

AND HERE'S CYRIL BROWN, BEAUJOLAIS' DAD:

STOUT WOOLLEN SOCKS

DENTAL FLOSS

HIKING BOOTS

WELLIES

EXTRA SOFT LOO PAPER

CREDIT CARDS (JUST IN CASE)

BRITISH BIRDS

BINOCULARS

ALL BRAN

HI-VIZ VEST

POCKET GUIDE TO WATCHING BIRDS

REGULAR CEREAL

SAT NAV

"Turn right... Turn right.... At the next crater..."

BREATH MINTS

FISHING TACKLE

SPARE READING GLASSES

NOSE HAIR CLIPPERS

SWISS ARMY KNIFE

EAR PLUGS

COMPASS

18-YEAR-OLD SINGLE MALT

WINDUP FLASHLIGHT

SOAPY KLEEN

WASHING-UP LIQUID

DOG WHISTLE

DEODORANT

HEMORRHOID CREAM

A WARM COAT AND VEST FOR BEAUJOLAIS

Your Own Grab Kit

Use this page to make a list of all the essentials you will need to survive out in the open, fight off cannibals and make that last, desperate trek to a high, defensible place with a clean water supply. We've filled in the first few to get you started.

1 Bag – to put it all in.

2 Sledge (in case of endless winter)

3 _ _ _ _ _ _ _ _ _ _ _

4 _ _ _ _ _ _ _ _ _ _

5 _ _ _ _ _ _ _ _ _ _

6 _ _ _ _ _ _ _ _ _ _

7 _ _ _ _ _ _ _ _ _ _

8 _ _ _ _ _ _ _ _ _ _

9 _ _ _ _ _ _ _ _ _ _

10 _ _ _ _ _ _ _ _ _ _

12 _ _ _ _ _ _ _ _ _ _

13 _ _ _ _ _ _ _ _ _ _

14 _ _ _ _ _ _ _ _ _ _

15 _ _ _ _ _ _ _ _ _ _

16 _ _ _ _ _ _ _ _ _ _

17 _ _ _ _ _ _ _ _ _ _

18 _ _ _ _ _ _ _ _ _ _

19 _ _ _ _ _ _ _ _ _ _

20 _ _ _ _ _ _ _ _ _ _

21 _ _ _ _ _ _ _ _ _ _

22 _ _ _ _ _ _ _ _ _ _

23 _ _ _ _ _ _ _ _ _ _

24 _ _ _ _ _ _ _ _ _ _

In case all else fails –

25 _ _ Rope. _ _ _ _ _

Topicality Disclaimer

The authors realize that since this book went to press there will undoubtedly have been many new and terrifying Doom scenarios. In order to keep the book up-to-date, please list them below.

1 _ _ _ _ _ _ _ _ _ _ _ _ _ _ _ _ _

2 _ _ _ _ _ _ _ _ _ _ _ _ _ _ _ _ _

3 _ _ _ _ _ _ _ _ _ _ _ _ _ _ _ _ _

4 _ _ _ _ _ _ _ _ _ _ _ _ _ _ _ _ _

5 _ _ _ _ _ _ _ _ _ _ _ _ _ _ _ _ _

6 _ _ _ _ _ _ _ _ _ _ _ _ _ _ _ _ _

7 _ _ _ _ _ _ _ _ _ _ _ _ _ _ _ _ _

8 _ _ _ _ _ _ _ _ _ _ _ _ _ _ _ _ _

9 _ _ _ _ _ _ _ _ _ _ _ _ _ _ _ _ _

10 _ _ _ _ _ _ _ _ _ _ _ _ _ _ _ _ _

11 _ _ _ _ _ _ _ _ _ _ _ _ _ _ _ _ _

Continue on a separate sheet if necessary.

The Meaning of Doom

Everybody seems to be
thinking about the end of
the world these days.
So much so that the prestigious
journal *Scientific American* devoted a special issue to it
in September 2010 called "The End."

It's not just the rash of Hollywood disaster-film producers and
pulp-fiction writers who exploit a widespread and growing
anxiety about Doomsday. Nor is it only the usual Internet
alarmists who feed upon a mélange of prophecies and
astrological signs and portents.

It's all of us.

Doomsday has been predicted dozens of times in our
written and oral history. So far, every one of these predictions
has turned out to be a false alarm. As the 20th century came
to an end, the scientists and politicians became convinced
that adding two zeros to the date would send computers into
freefall and bring about the total collapse of civilization. The
"Y2K" phenomenon provided short-term employment to a few
nerdy scientists, but January 1, 2000, came and went without
a single crash.

This should have been at least somewhat reassuring. Dismissed
as millenarian hysteria and consigned to history. But instead
we began to hear new voices crying, "The sky is falling!" These
voices are from the scientific community itself. Even such
illustrious sources as Sir Martin Rees, Astronomer Royal, add to

the anxiety. According to *Scientific American*, he has offered a standing bet that up to one million people will die as the result of a biological catastrophe before 2020. The fact that earlier predictions such as that of the economist Thomas Malthus (1766–1834), who foresaw that population growth would inevitably be checked by mass starvation, and later the seeming certainty of destruction offered by the nuclear arms race, haven't brought about the apocalypse doesn't make any difference. We know Doom is approaching. Don't we?

① IMAGINE THIS BUTTON WILL DESTROY THE WORLD. ② PRESS IT.

③ FEELS GOOD, DOESN'T IT? ④ PRESS IT AGAIN.

As soon as one Doom scenario passes harmlessly by, we select another. If an asteroid misses us by a cosmological country mile, we begin to fret about solar flares. If swine flu turns out to be less than a biblical plague, we turn our attention to diseases like Ebola.

We seem to need Doom. But why?

No one is sure, but theories float to the surface. One easy answer is that worrying about the end of civilization is somehow more comforting than facing the fact of our own personal Doom awaiting us in some distant hospital bed or roadside. It's exciting, where death is simply depressing. According to this theory, it's almost like the displacement of anger, as when being criticized by your boss makes you kick your dog.

Another theory is that it makes us feel important. The idea that we are living in exceptional times makes things less pedestrian. When we go to disaster movies and watch giant waves devouring cities, or super viruses laying waste to whole countries, we do so with relish. Being in, as Rees put it, "our final century," adds glamour to a world made dull with taxes and telemarketing calls.

But there's a third possibility.

As *Scientific American* points out, we are creatures of the savanna, programmed over thousands of years to see patterns and trends in a multitude of events. As sociologist John R. Hall has said, "If the world appears to be going to hell . . . maybe that's just what is happening." As part of our basic survival equipment, we may be gifted with a kind of intuition that looks at things as they happen and makes predictions based on the emerging pattern. In other words, we may be right.

Dogs bark before earthquakes, don't they?

WHAT CAN WE DO
TO PREVENT IT?

TURN THE PAGE TO FIND OUT...

1

Touchscreen Interactive Index

Use your eyes to scan this page until you locate a subject that interests you. Next, touch the subject with your fingertip to be transported instantly to the page you require.

Alternatively, if you are using the old-fashioned, economy, paper edition, select a subject using your eyes as described above, then memorize the page number. Next, insert your finger between two pages and manually lift and turn. Repeat until correct page is reached.

The  END